Southern Exposures

Locations and Relocations
of Italian Culture

Edited by
Alan J. Gravano & Ilaria Serra

ITALIAN AMERICAN STUDIES ASSOCIATION
Volume 42 • 2013

Library of Congress Cataloguing in Publication Data
available upon request

Printed in the United States.

Published by
ITALIAN AMERICAN STUDIES ASSOCIATION
John D. Calandra Italian American Institute
25 West 43rd Street, 17th Floor
New York, NY 10036

Volume 42
ISBN 978-0-934675-63-5

TABLE OF CONTENTS

ACKNOWLEDGMENTS (v)

INTRODUCTION (1)

Michael Dell'Aquila
"Long Ways to Go": Sterling A. Brown, Diane Di Prima, and the Specters of Their Southern Roads (5)

Angela Oberdan
Celebrating the Poetry of Leo Luke Marcello: Italian American Themes and Southern Subtleties in Marcello's Reckoning of Life as an Italian American Southerner (26)

Alison Bertolini
Based on Actual Events: The Lynching of Italian American Immigrants in Tallulah, Louisiana, as depicted by Donna Jo Napoli in Alligator Bayou (46)

Stefano Luconi
The Lynching of Italian Americans: A Reassessment (58)

Maria Lizzi
In Brooklyn, They Love the Guv'ner? Italian Americans for George Wallace (79)

Karen Williams
Saint Expedito's Role in the Italian American: Community of Independence, Louisiana (96)

Elisabetta Violi LeJeune
From Cucina *to* Kitchen: *Italian Cooking vs. Italian-American Cooking in Tangipahoa Parish* (107)

William Boelhower
"Dearer to me than any other": New Orleans, the Massacre of 1891, and the Arrival of Sister Frances Xavier Cabrini (123)

John Lowe
    Tutto è burla: *Humor and Identity in Italian American Culture* (164)

John Paul Russo
    Italia Sacra*: San Severino Marche, Orvieto, Bevagna* (200)

INDEX (245)

ACKNOWLEDGEMENTS

We wish to express our thanks to Louisiana State University, which made it possible to host the 42nd annual conference of the Italian American Studies Association (formerly, the American Italian Historical Association). More particularly, we would like to extend our gratitude to the Louisiana State University Foundation and the Greater Baton Rouge American Italian Association, as well as to John Lowe, William Boelhower, and especially to Joseph V. Ricapito and Josephine Gattuso Hendin.

In the end, we thank the participants. Without each of you, no conference can take place. Without the contribution of the individuals in this Selected Essays, the discourse on Italian-American themes could not be continued.

Each individual, whether student or academic, organizer or participant, behind-the-scenes or in-front, each individual earns our special thanks.

INTRODUCTION

The selected essays gathered in these pages are inspired by the range and depth of the forty-second annual conference of the American Italian Historical Association, held October 29-31, 2009, in Baton Rouge, Louisiana. The general title of the conference, *Southern Exposures: Locations and Relocations of Italian Culture*, focuses attention on the themes of Italian immigration and ethnicity in the American South. The large response to the theme of Southern Exposures in the many panels was a welcome surprise; so too were both the variety of thematic approaches to the topic and the numerous research styles and methods. This diversity is further proof of the liveliness of Italian American studies in the United States.

The papers selected in this volume orient themselves around three main themes: Southern Italian-American literature, political history, and cultural studies. Michael Dell'Aquila draws a challenging parallel between the Italian-American poet Diane DiPrima with her Southern Italian roots and Sterling Brown with his origin in the American South. After asserting that both poets use rhetoric and irony to gain respectability for their oppressed Southern communities, Dell'Aquila ends with a critique of their poems, characterized by similar multifaceted language.

Angelina Oberdan comments on Italian American themes and Southern subtleties in Leo Luke Marcello's poetry. He was born in Louisiana from a Sicilian family and died at the age of sixty in 2005. In this poet, Oberdan sees a reconciliation of what she finds is the discordant identity of the Southern-Italian-American, not really Italian American—because not from New York or New Jersey—nor really Southern—because not Anglo-Saxon or French.

Alison Bertolini considers the historical fiction in Donna Jo Napoli's *Alligator Bayou* (2009). The novel, geared at young adult readers, focuses on a true historical fact, the lynching of five Sicilian grocers in Tallulah, Louisiana in 1899, through the eyes of a boy, Calogero, who serves as a link between old Italian life and new alligator hunts in Louisiana.

The sombre theme of lynching is touched by Stefano Luconi's article, which calls for a "reassessment" of the causes that led to the lynching of some thirty-four Italian immigrants and Italian Americans, in the United States, especially in Southern regions, between the mid-1880s and the early 1910s. Luconi challenges the conventional wisdom stressing that Italian Americans were victimized since they were not regarded as being fully white, and argues that it was instead a consequence of economic, political, and labor rivalries that exploited the newcomers' dubious racial status.

Maria Lizzi takes a close look at the support Italian Americans gave George Corley Wallace as third-party candidate in the 1968 presidential election. In her essay, she tries to explain a surprising fact: Why did the governor of Alabama, previously known for his racist attitude, gain a strong support among many working-class white ethnic voters, including Italian Americans—the same people he had once referred to as "lesser breeds?"

Two charming essays explore the Italian American religious and culinary folklore of the South. Karen Williams traces the interesting story of Saint Expedito, lesser-known in the wide world, but particularly meaningful for the small community of Independence, Louisiana. The mysterious

2

origin of this saint and his miraculous appearance in the small town is linked with his present value, as the spiritual overseer of the Italian flood relief that helps hurricane victims.

Elisabetta Violi LeJeune's essay looks for the fleeting meeting between Italian and Southern flavors in the kitchens of Tangipahoa Parish, a county running along Highway 51, in Louisiana. She explains the composition of new dishes, among which is the Muffuletta sandwich, invention of the Lupo family, owners of the Italian grocery store that opened in 1906 in New Orleans' French Quarter.

Highlighting both the lows of Louisiana history, the lynching of Italians, and the highs, food and saints, our next contributor who was also involved in the organizing of the conference in Baton Rouge, brings together these seemingly disparate histories. William Boelhower in "'Dearer to me than any other': New Orleans, the Massacre of 1891, and the Arrival of Sister Frances Xavier Cabrini" begins with what at first appears to have no connection at all to Cabrini, the shooting of nine Italians and the lynching of two others in Congo Square in connection with New Orleans Police Superintendent David Hennessy's murder. However, Boelhower fuses the racial violence perpetrated on the Italian community with the charitable life of Sister Cabrini. The essay is a tour de force on the life of Sister Frances Xavier Cabrini and her contributions to the city of New Orleans.

Two essays depart from the Southern theme of the conference. John Lowe's "*Tutto è burla:* Humor and Identity in Italian American Culture" and John Paul Russo's "Italia Sacra: San Severino Marche, Orvieto, Bevagna." The first—John Lowe's key-note address—treats the theme of humor on and of Italian Americans. From the Italian American characters of the New York comedies by Edward Harrigan

3

at the turn of the century, to the vignettes drawn in the novels by Jerre Mangione, Pietro Di Donato, and Mario Puzo, Lowe follows the trajectory of Italian American humor and its Bakhtinian aspects. Passing by the "humorless" women authors and characters, he concludes his essay with the consideration of a novel of the new Italian American Renaissance, Mark Binelli's *Sacco and Vanzetti Must Die!*, "a raucous, postmodern comedy."

John Paul Russo's creative non-fiction essay is a "sentimental guide" to Italy, to use poet Diego Valeri's expression. This excerpt from a larger work-in-progress is a beautifully-written travelogue of a lesser-known itinerary in the Italian central regions. It blends travel reminiscences, historical information, art criticism, religious devotion, myths, and symbols that yield a new brand of scholarly impressionism, where erudition and art meet.

The publication of these selected essays is a collective enterprise, and it is a pleasure to record our many debts of gratitude. In particular, we would like to thank the Conference Chair: Joseph V. Ricapito; additional Program Committee members Anthony Tamburri and the John D. Calandra Italian American Institute. We would also like to thank the LSU Foundation, the Greater Baton Rouge American Italian Association, and Bobby Lonero and his band.

Alan J. Gravano
Ilaria Serra

"Long Ways to Go"
Sterling A. Brown, Diane Di Prima
and the Specters of Their Southern Roads[1]

MICHAEL DELL'AQUILA
Freelance Writer

INTRODUCTION

Long after the abolishment of plantation slavery in the American South, the issue of racial inequality continues to haunt the United States. Because of the nation's ignominious past, the disparities between social classes were historically viewed as being ethnic problems and, in the nineteenth century, many people reduced the issue to a black-white divide. More often than not, Northern progressives attacked the attitudes of their Southern counterparts and located the genesis of these cultural tensions in the states below the Mason-Dixon Line. Racist institutions are an in-

---

[1] The lives of Sterling A. Brown and Diane Di Prima run parallel in a number of ways, as this paper aims to illuminate, but they also overlap at some surprising intersections as well. Perhaps most significant to either poet's life is the status of being a generation removed from the traumatic events that influence their work. Being the son of a former slave, the reality of southern horrors could never be very far from Brown's mind and as a voice of that community, the shadows of that past darken many of the poetic and critical works that he produced over the course of his life. Likewise, Di Prima felt a strong connection to both her immigrant family and the anarchist society that her grandfather belonged to. While her career did not always seem to overtly reflect the influence of her ethnic background, the glimpses into the Italian American world from which she sprung offer a glimpse of a significant influence on her revolutionary spirit. Where these two poets' lives curiously intersect is with the life and work of a third poet Amiri Baraka (LeRoi Jones). Baraka was a student of Brown's at Howard, and his work builds on the traditions of one of his mentors, but the fact that he was both a professional collaborator with and husband to Diane Di Prima also unites the two poets under discussion in this paper. In this way, the bifurcated themes of social revolution and ethnic reclamation are not simply coincidentally evident in the poetry of Brown and Di Prima but one could also see how Brown is actually an indirect influence of the younger poet's work.

escapable part of the country's history and, as such, the looming specter of the American South overshadows what is actually a more complicated struggle for upward mobility. While there is no denying that skin color was once the quickest and easiest bellwether for determining class position, such a reductionist point of view does not account for the rise of individuals or even entire ethnic groups into the dominant culture of mainstream America. One's race then, is, only one brick in the wall dividing the empowered from the subordinate.

As whiteness became harder to define and delineate in the late nineteenth century, skin color and ethnic background alone could no longer be an indicator of someone's rank in society. The acquisition of cultural and economic capital by former slaves and ethnic immigrants exposed the artifice of "the old pseudoscientific and class-informed racialisms whose dynamic we are more used to deciphering" and began to build a platform upon which the disenfranchised could develop a culture in opposition to the dominant mainstream (Morrison 318). Among the most crucial pieces of acquired cultural capital is the appropriation of language and literacy. In its most successful applications, the eloquence and sophistication of ethnic writers complicate or challenge outright the stereotypical roles to which they are often assigned. Whether rhetorical or poetic, philosophical or political, the empowering ability for a subordinated community to produce a literature of their own is a crucial step in lifting its position up from the lowest rungs of society.

While the importance of literacy itself cannot be overstated, it is not simply the ability to read, write, or speak alone that confers a new social agency upon an upwardly mobile group. In fact, literacy without shrewd social awareness can sometimes do no more than reinforce the expectations of the dominant culture. To spur social progress through a minority literature, then, an ethnic writer must address both the inherent prejudices of the dominant culture without ignoring or misrepresenting the diversity that exists within their own communities. Striking the right balance between formal eloquence and proletarian realism becomes the necessary goal if one is to create literature that is equally aesthetic and political. Finding that middle ground is no small feat, but poets like Sterling A. Brown and Diane Di Prima do not only prove that such a stance can be achieved, but also create poetry that demonstrates an ability to revise and reform the conventions of their respective ethnic identities. Together, these two poets use their linguistic acumen and shrewd political insight to extend the boundaries of ethnic literature and explore new possibilities for a hyphenated identity in the United States.

To fully understand both the skill these poets possess and the reasons why their work has had a lasting impact on the production of ethnic American literature, one must revisit the cultures that produced them in the late nineteenth and early twentieth century. After establishing the importance of acquired cultural capital—specifically language and literature—a close analysis of each poet's most successful ethnic projects will help illuminate the ways in which these writers broke new ground and resisted the urge to recreate the prejudicial conventions of the dominant culture.

SOUTHERN ROAD(S)

The upward rise of some of America's poorest classes, whether geographic or metaphoric, begins along southern roads in both the states below the Mason-Dixon Line and also in the regions of southern Italy known as the *mezzogior-no*.[2] These southern cultures complement each other in interesting and even surprising ways. Plantation slavery in the American South became an economic boon to the British Empire and later to the United States because of free labor exacted from enslaved Africans and the relationship between labor and exploitation also defines the historical background for the Italian American community.

The brutal treatment of African slaves along the Middle Passage combined with the tyrannical system of chattel slavery in the American South are together damaging enough to the generations that bore the brunt of mistreatment along with their progeny, but the full oppression of British and American slavery was not simply physical in nature. The heavy-handed applications of cultural hegemony not only established a racial hierarchy, but it also oversimplified the subaltern community. Although the majority of slaves were from the Western parts of Africa, they were hardly a single, homogenous community. The tribal affiliations, marked by language and custom were both stripped upon captivity as these individuals were reprogrammed in an English-speaking society. This hegemonic ordeal did more than simply rob the newly arrived slaves of their cultural backgrounds, it also fused together, by cruel and unusual forces, a new class of human property: the blanket term "negro," of course, reduces these individuals to a single race that is at once bound to one another and to physical service solely because of their shared blackness.

The formation of an Italian American community, such as one exists, begins in the southern regions of the Old World

---

[2] This is thee region of the Italian South stretching from the provinces below Rome to Sicily. During the Great Migration, the greatest numbers of peasants fled from these various regions.

and results from a different sort of tyranny. Throughout the Bourbon-controlled *mezzogiorno*, peasants were prohibited from traveling beyond the edges of the Kingdom of Two Sicilies in order to insulate them "from developments outside the boundaries of their circumscribed world that might inspire them to disturb the status quo" (Mangione and Morreale 46). So instead of being forced into labor on foreign soil, these southern Italian peasants were instead left with few economic options besides an agrarian lifestyle that was strikingly similar to the Reconstruction-era system of sharecropping. Trapped, subordinated, and exploited by the dominant foreign power, these disenfranchised *paesani* were not only relegated to the lowest social positions, but they were incapable of developing strategies for advancement—save for outright liberation from Bourbon control.

The case for African slaves and Italian peasants was so grave and deep-seeded that neither of the two great liberal causes of the nineteenth century—the *Risorgimento*[3] and the US Civil War—did much to significantly transform their lives. In both instances, the economic conditions in the unified Kingdom of Italy and the United States became worse than they had been before their respective "liberations." While the foreign rulers had been expelled from the *mezzogiorno* and the slave owners no longer maintained explicit ownership of their former slaves, there was very little done in the way of institutional support to replace the tyrannical social systems with improved options for both survival and economic advancement. This struggle was especially evident in the American South, where masters no longer felt the need to provide their slaves with the bare necessities for living and working in the fields. It would be up to the

---

[3] The period of the nineteenth century marked by the political and military actions leading to the unification of an Italian kingdom.

freedmen to forge their own way in the world, and while this newfound freedom did grant more control over their lives, they were also responsible for paying for goods that had once been provided for them and fighting for compensation that could be considered commensurate with their new social status. As the American historian Claude H. Nolen points out,

> Of great immediate importance was the freedmen's need for economic opportunities in place of the forced labor of slavery. As slaves, they had been paid with very little more than coarse clothing, corn meal, bacon, molasses and crude shelter. As freedmen, they expected fair return for their labor.... Then they could escape the vestiges of slavery and enjoy the fruits of their labor. (178)

As previously mentioned, the sharecropping system replacing plantation slavery in the American south bears much in common with the feudal farming communities found in the *mezzogiorno*. In both societies, the subordinated citizens labor endlessly without the compensation that ought to be rewarded for their amount of work. While the economic disparity in southern Italy might not appear to be as outwardly racist in origin as the Southern Reconstruction was in America, the new conditions in the young Italian kingdom were undeniably similar:

> Despite the best intentions of the new rulers to provide liberal reforms that would ameliorate the conditions of the poor, their situation became worse than it had been under the Bourbons. At least then, in the tradition of the Feudal Era, the ruling elite had treated them with a certain degree of paternalism. (Mangione and Morreale 63)

The cultural tensions discussed in this passage persist in the present day. Although the word *Italian* conjures up a homogenous culture for most Americans, the divisions between Northern and Southern regions have been tangible and intact for centuries. Although the Northern power and influence after the unification of Italy was unimpeachable, the southern peasants' inability to advance economically and culturally is ultimately what uproots these rural laborers more so than any cultural conflicts. Once again, the historical parallels resurface: although the supposed economic freedoms conferred upon former slaves in the United States and newly minted Italians failed to deliver on its lofty goals, it did provide them with new chances for migration and seek a better life elsewhere.

What both those transient groups discovered, however, was that social progress was not just a matter of geographic relocation. Crossing the Atlantic, the Mason-Dixon, or just the divide between rural enclaves and cosmopolitan cities did not immediately correct the economic and cultural disadvantages of these poor laborers, nor did it provide them with notably better opportunities. Where there had been country shacks there were now tenements; sparse farm work was traded for industrial labor. As a result, quality of life did not significantly improve. Many who were freed from the bondage of plantation slavery or escaped tyrannical economic systems in their homeland spent the rest of their lives laboring without significantly shifting their position in society.

Education became the aim for advancement when the hard-work ethic perpetuated by self-help Progressives failed. The education gap for freedmen was much more significant than simply a lack of formal schooling. More often than not, these men and women were completely illiterate, but to say they received no education at all is to ignore the way that slaves were programmed in accordance with the dominant culture of the American south. As Nolen asserts, "Slavery was not maintained by the violence of the lash alone.... It was supported also by the education of slaves in a sense of inferiority" (56). One can only combat such racist thinking through exposure to alternative ideas, and while the Northerners prided themselves as more socially progressive and humane, the acquisition of literacy was what provided the families of former slaves with an opportunity to distance themselves from savage stereotypes and to create a dialogue for advancement more than simply fleeing the racist institutions of the south.

Not surprisingly, the peasant communities throughout the *mezzogiorno* were also controlled by systematic (mis)education. Just as plantation slavery controlled the flow of ideas and information to slaves, the Bourbons' feudal arrangements also withheld a proper education from their subjects as another tactic of control. However, this situation still did not improve after the creation of a united Kingdom of Italy. While Agostino De Pretis, the nation's first prime minister, made a nominal attempt to improve the harsh conditions in the south by creating a law that made public education available and required for children, that law "was sabotaged in many sections of the *mezzogiorno* by local authorities, who saw no advantage in educating the children of the poor" (Mangione and Morreale 77).[4] If educa-

---

[4] The lasting effects of this problem in American society can still be felt. While many individual members of the Italian American community have gone on to lead prosperous lives in a variety of industries, the unavoidable stereotype of the illiterate, dumb street kids remains an unfortunate caricature against which the upwardly mobile constantly fight. While those upper and upper middle class individuals may often avoid confronting the shameful stereotypes, an inquiry into their historical genesis not only points to the fact that the problem of widespread illiteracy was social in nature, but it also deconstructs the stereotype by proving that this specific lack of education was enforced and not inborn.

tion, coupled with new economic opportunities, was the key to social advancement, then the post-Risorgimento Italian kingdom left their poorest subjects with no choice but to seek a better life beyond the borders of their homeland.

Because the acquisition of proper English is a crucial step along the path of assimilation into the mainstream, the language itself becomes both a cultural asset as well as an aesthetic tool for the ethnic writer. While many second-generation authors trade their newly acquired cultural capital for a higher class position, neither Sterling A. Brown nor Diane Di Prima is satisfied with simply *passing* for authentic American writers. This is not to suggest that they lack the knowledge or ability to write themselves into the middle classes—at different turns they both display the talent required to make such a jump. Instead, these poets approach literature as a tool for social progress and consciously position themselves outside of the mainstream.

SING IT, SLIM

A generation removed from slavery and Southern Reconstruction, Sterling A. Brown was not only aware of the new opportunities that were made available to African Americans, he was also aware of the negative bi-products of social progress. Brown "feared that [African Americans] would passively consume bigoted popular culture or... be co-opted into producing art that pandered to the economic demands and stereotypes of the dominant culture" (Anderson 1023). This fear manifests itself in most of Brown's poetry; preserving an authentic African American voice becomes an immediate challenge.

The question of cultural authenticity is, of course, a difficult puzzle to solve. Not only does an individual bear some responsibility to preserve or promote the agreed-upon traits

13

of the community at large, but he or she must also revisit the static group narrative in order to discover ways in which it could be improved. For most black writers, the dilemma can be sufficiently explained through the tensions resulting from speaking the language of the dominant culture versus retreating toward a racialized caricature. Finding a middle ground that can preserve a specific cultural voice without projecting minstrel show approximations is especially difficult but unavoidable. In terms of a poem like "Southern Road," Brown uses a version of broken English easily found throughout the American South but he is also carefully to avoid projecting the implicit degradations found in more inauthentic representations of black culture during this period of time:

> Swing that hammer—hunh—
> Steady, bo';
> Swing that hammer—hunh—
> Steady, bo';
> Ain't no rush, bebby,
> Long ways to go.
>
> Burner tore his—hunh—
> Black heart away
> Burner tore his—hunh—
> Black heart away
> Got me life, bebby,
> An' a day. (52)

As any reader can see, the spelling, cadence, and lexicon of this poem are undeniably black and, although these first two stanzas may at first appear to be guilty of the cultural pandering Brown sought to resist, the use of broken English and phonetic spelling aim to do more than create a black-faced literary minstrel show.

"Southern Road" employs two different linguistic strategies with its structure and narrative voice. First, the poem's rhythm and repetition both artfully capture the meter of a chain gang chorus so well that the printed words on the page jump out as being inescapably musical. There is also a connection with the field songs of earlier generations: one can see how the meter and language are both faithfully preserved. The poem's second strategy calls immediate attention to itself: the guttural "hunh," surrounded by dashes, transforms the swinging hammers from a purely physical realm into a poetic act unto itself. To Brown, there is no distance between the laborer and the poet, one works for advancement through the acquisition of economic capital, while the other strives for progress of a different sort.

The cultural and aesthetic achievement of "Southern Road" may not seem so impressive to the modern reader, which may actually bear some testament to the success of Sterling Brown's poetic project. In a post-Civil Rights setting, most American readers have no doubt normalized the act of lifting racial and ethnic *others* out of the dregs of society and thrusting them into the terrain of serious literature, but the Whitmanesque poetic agenda was at one point a radical proposition. The musicality and colloquial language both resonate with readers because of their authentic portraits, but one should not lose a perspective that accounts for the cultural risk implicit in an educated and accomplished poet like Brown as he retreats toward his ancestral Southern roads rather than simply moving into the acceptable roles for African Americans during his own era.

While "Southern Road" attempts to elevate the field songs and spirituals into the sphere of highbrow art, this poem is in no way an exhaustive representation of Brown's entire body of work. Although many of the works in his eponymous first collection share a similar aesthetic strategy, it is important to remember that as Brown developed a "culturally functional alternative to the established but inadequate academic form of ethnographic reportage" he simultaneously "created a multi-voiced, polyphonic, self-reflexive, diversely genred oeuvre" (Skinner 418). This ethnic project is apparent in a poem like "Southern Cop":

Let us forgive Ty Kendricks.
The place was Darktown. He was young.
His nerves were jittery. The day was hot.
The negro ran out of the alley.
And so he shot.

Let us understand Ty Kendricks.
The negro must have been dangerous
Because he ran
And here was a rookie with a chance
To prove himself a man.

Let us condone Ty Kendricks
If we cannot decorate
When he found what the Negro was running for,
It was too late;
And all we can say for the Negro is
It was unfortunate.

Let us pity Ty Kendricks
He has been through enough
Standing there, his big gun smoking,
Rabbit-scared, alone,

16

Having to hear the wenches wail
And the dying man moan. (458)

Brown's narrative voice is not the only difference between this poem and "Southern Road." Instead of the familiar singular first-person narrator, "Southern Cop" uses a pluralized voice to serve as a sort-of Greek chorus linking Ty Kendricks with the murdered "negro." More significant than the plurality of the narrative voice, the words, spelling, and sentence structure are all stripped of the lower class and ethnic identifiers found in the previous poem. Without relying on an overtly "black" voice, Brown adds an ethnic shadow to this poem through the use of irony rather than simply replicating the speech patterns of lower class African Americans. Instead of sympathizing with the murdered black man, the narrator seeks to "forgive," "understand," "condone," and "pity" Ty Kendricks. By its understanding of the murder of an innocent and nameless "negro" and ironically positioning the Southern Cop as the character deserving of the reader's pity, Brown's poem does not simply bear the mark of shrewd, class-conscious writing, it also demonstrates the possibility of ethnic American writing without relying on linguistic caricatures. "Southern Cop" still addresses the racial inequalities found throughout the United States, but it does so in a way that limits the importance of the writer's race and class position without abandoning the perspective of the subordinate.

While these poems represent only a small sample of Brown's body of work, they are nevertheless emblematic of the two main options presented to the African American writer. However, Brown's lasting influence may not stem from the ostensible aesthetic decisions as much as his ability to complicate both the minstrel caricature and standardized English and to add both a subtlety and complexity found in few of his southern predecessors.[5] So whether subsequent generations sought to protect a serious portrait of dialect-speaking subalterns or undertake the ironic, signifying[6] practices of a poem like "Southern Cop," Brown's early poetry advanced the cause of minority literature in both subtle and overt ways.

LOVE SPELLED BACKWARDS

Just as Sterling A. Brown's polyphonic poetic project attempts to broaden rather than narrow the scope of African American literature, so too must an Italian American poet adopt a multi-faceted linguistic strategy. In both cases, the forced removal of native languages[7] requires the respective literary communities to develop approximations for the absent *lingua materna*. To this end, the amalgamated language of a second-generation writer is "a confusing array of dialects and 'grammars'" and in order to use this complicated linguistic foundation effectively, a poet must "seek deliberately to devise a rhetoric that can employ the vernacular as a tool of self-conscious literary art" (Viscusi 39).

---

[5] There are a few African American writers who predate Sterling A. Brown and can be described with such ability. One of the best examples of the short story writer and novelist Charles W. Chesnutt. In Chesnutt's fiction, there are ample examples of the dialect-heavy trickster tales which complicate the once-popular genre through surprising depictions of atrocities and the more overt racial inequalities that extended long after the emancipation of black slaves. In other works, the narrative voice rarely departs from standardized English and instead advances a critical discussion through irony and more sophisticated applications of literary language.

[6] I am referring here to the type of black Signifyin' that Henry Louis Gates Jr. deconstructs in his landmark critical work *The Signifying Monkey*. For a complete explanation, read the Introduction and first chapter.

[7] I have previously discussed why and how the native languages were taken away from African slaves. For the Italian Americans, the catalyst for the eradication of their language in the United States takes place one day after Benito Mussolini declared war on the Allied forces on December 8, 1941.

This rhetoric is not and probably should not be a cartoonish voice that simply adds a vowel at the end of every Anglophonic word nor should it require a writer to insert Italian words (whether national or regional dialects) simply for the sake of adding Italian flavor to an American poem.

The linguistic struggle for authenticity can often reveal a lot about the cultural insecurities Diane Di Prima faces. In much of her poetry, we see both the "historical episodes of conflict between margin and mainstream" along with "the lasting impact of immigration on individuals who may be second or third generation" (Hendin 13). Di Prima couples the ethnic conflicts in question with broader political rhetoric. Unlike many Italian American poets whose work attempts to elegize or revive inherited *italianità*, her work avoids simplistic and predictable settings or ethnic signs. In fact, while the ethnic difference in her writing stems from her Italian background, the revolutionary lens through which she spies on the world is hardly ever narrow enough to focus only on what is or is not part of her individual identity. The result is the development of a literature that is inclusive enough to envelop all the counter-cultures developing in the mid-twentieth century without losing a sharp, revolutionary focus.

What Diane Di Prima's poetry may sometimes lack in subtlety, she more than makes up for it with clear, precise attacks against the dominant culture. Like Brown, the act of writing for her is both a political and revolutionary act, but instead of Brown's poetic sidearm, Di Prima's language bears more in common with a landmine—after detonation, the landscape must be changed as a result and the difference must be noticeable. Di Prima's poem "Rant" not only demonstrates her ability to speak directly to a reader instead of hiding behind heavily coded ethnic signs but also addresses directly the belief that language is inherently democratic and literature inescapably ideological:

> There is no way out of the spiritual battle
> There is no way you can avoid taking sides
> There is no way you can *not* have a poetics
> No matter what you do: plumber, baker, teacher. (143)

In the wake of the counter-cultural revolution and ethnic revivals of the 1970s, it may seem commonplace to assert that even the working classes can create a poetic, but previous to the democratization of American literature, the acts of writing and reading were reserved for the ruling classes. With clear, concise language, Di Prima both validates herself as a credible poetic voice and also argues for an expansion of what constitutes American poetry.

While there should be no doubt as to the authenticity of Di Prima's ethnic identity, it may still be worthwhile to consider the political implications behind her celebration of otherness. The emotional and thematic terrain of an Italian American lifestyle not only provides a colorful cultural backdrop, but it also becomes a platform with which Di Prima can both distance herself from the dominant culture and simultaneously indict the mainstream. This distinction should not be confused with a cynical aversion to ethnic reclamation; instead it brings the political implications of such an assertion to the fore. The transcendental strategy of writing from outside society—or, at the very least, from its fringes—can be seen in many different subcultures and minority literatures, but the significance of Di Prima's broader message and expansive scope lies in the fact that cultural plurality becomes the method through which the mainstream loses hegemonic control. In other words, Di

Prima believes that it is only through the unification of various powerless minorities that the masses can gain social agency and, in turn, create a multicultural space running counter to the dominant society.

Where "Rant" is global in scope, we find a more intimate source of this revolutionary spirit in "April Fool Birthday Poem for Grandpa." At first glance, this poem may seem to be nothing more than the Italian American literary habit of using immigrant figures to construct "narrative myths of origin," but the poem quickly changes from a tribute to a symbolic and actual patriarch into a call to action for all counter cultures (Gardaphé 129). At the same time that most of the members of her second generation Italian American cohort are satisfied with a quick and quiet assimilation into the mainstream, Di Prima revisits and resurrects the revolutionary lessons of her anarchist grandfather in order to resist absorption into the dominant class.

Di Prima not only connects the Civil Rights movement and the counter-cultural revolution with the anarchist movements created within the immigrant communities half a century earlier, she underscores the inescapable role that the acquisition and application of language and literature play in those struggles. Not surprisingly, the literary traditions carried over from Italy informed the old anarchists and inspire Di Prima herself to strike her revolutionary chords. "You would love us all," Di Prima writes to her grandfather, "would thunder your anarchist wisdom / at us, would thunder Dante and Giordano Bruno" (140). Dante, like Shakespeare, represents many things to many people and, as such, it is important to know why such a revered figure shows up in this work. Instead of using the premier Italian poet as a legitimizing figure, Di Prima alludes to the political agency found in his work. The Dante of her grandfather is not the imperial, canonized Titan championed by T.S. Eliot and the literary elite; he is the exiled Tuscan poet who exacts his revenge against Florentine rivals throughout the course of *The Inferno.*

"April Fool Birthday Poem for Grandpa," then, draws a straight line of lineage from this revolutionary incarnation of Dante to the Italian American anarchist-writers whose merits Di Prima hopes to emulate. "Well I want you to know," she writes that "we do it for you, and your ilk, for Carlo Tresca / For Sacco and Vanzetti, without knowing / it, or thinking about it" (140). Instead of the expected shame of such an un-American heritage, there is only a sense of pride in these infamous figures. She draws inspiration from both their actions and their writings, enamored with the ways they were "talking love, talking revolution" (140). In the end, Di Prima does more than simply anticipate the ethnic revivals of the 1970s and their celebrations of hyphenate identities; she instead serves as a literary catalyst for such a point of view. Unlike a poet such as John Ciardi, Di Prima's strategy draws on an Italian difference that is inherently incompatible with the mainstream, and while a figure like Dante provides a curious connection between these two writers,[8] there is no question that this poem attempts to reclaim an ethnic difference instead of synthesizing two different cultures.

At the end of "April Fool Birthday Poem for Grandpa," Di Prima expands the confines of this anarchist tradition from being simply Italian or Italian American. The movement she attaches herself to is a much more global spirit of revolution, one that is not necessarily violent, but a political and

---

[8] I am alluding to Ciardi's massively successful translation of Dante Alighieri's *Commedia* into English, which solidified his position as a leading poetic voice and, more importantly, leveraged his ancestral background into granting him entrée into the literary elite.

artistic position that can claim a moral high ground because of its position outside the imperialistic and exploitative mainstream:

We do it for
The stars over the Bronx
That they may look on Earth
And not be ashamed. (140)

The collective *we* explicitly refers to all the revolutionary figures she names throughout the poem, but it could also include a poet like Sterling A. Brown, a subaltern figure who uses the power of language to spur social change. What ethnic and minority poetry should aspire to, from Di Prima's perspective, is to step out of the shadows cast by the specters found along their interconnected southern roads to create a new and inclusive dialogue and to fulfill the goals of their ethnic and literary forebears.

Although this paper has primarily categorized Diane Di Prima as an Italian American poet, part of the complexity of her writing stems from the fact that she often permeates the traditional boundaries of rote topographies. The rebellious streak that defines much of her oeuvre not only satisfies the Italian American revivalist, but it also fits into the programs of feminist, counter-culture, and Beat Generation writers. While the advocates for various group narratives have just cause to celebrate Di Prima's poetry as a premier example of their literary achievements, the fierce individualism combined with an unwavering commitment to speak for all disenfranchised members of society avoid the chauvinistic trappings traditionally associated with self-applied hyphenate identities.

CONCLUSION

Despite the impact of the Civil War, the Great Migration, the Civil Rights Movement, and the counter-cultural revolution, the specter of the American South still looms large in both an historical perspective and also the United States' lingering racial problems. The conflicts between classes and ethnic minorities continue though the groups and contact zones sometimes shift. Those changes in society at large can sometimes overshadow or at least obscure the uniqueness and the relevance of writers like Sterling A. Brown and Diane Di Prima. As each camp collects its literary forebears, there is a danger in over-simplifying the work of these poets when they are read exclusively for endemic ethnic traits.

While it can be said that both poets may have anticipated or envisioned an America that embraced ethnic diversity instead of enforcing assimilation into the dominant culture, the lasting ethnographic importance of their works stem from the exploration around the margins of the lines dividing white from black, mainstream from subculture. By challenging the conventions of both Middle America and their own ethnic communities, these poets found new ways into a routine conversation and fought against the endless binaries that divided the culture into contrived segments. Because the task of social evolution is filled with all sorts of socioeconomic variables, Brown and Di Prima must both be read as being a part of a much larger movement toward multiculturalism and cultural pluralism. However, their work continues to warrant re-examination not simply because racial prejudices linger in society, but also because their work encapsulates the moments when they and their peers acquired language and literacy and learned to push back against the boundaries of prescribed social positions.

WORKS CITED

Anderson, David. "Sterling Brown's Southern Strategy: Poetry as Cultural Evolution in Southern Road." *Callaloo* 21.4 (Autumn, 1998): 1023-1037.

Brown, Sterling A. *Southern Road.* New York: Harcourt, 1932.

_____. "Southern Cop." *The Oxford Book of American Poetry.* ed. David Lehman. New York: Oxford UP, 2006.

Di Prima, Diane. "April Fool Birthday Poem for Grandpa." *From the Margin: Writings in Italian Americana.* eds. Gardaphé, Fred, Paolo Giordano, and Anthony Julian Tamburri. West Lafayette: Purdue UP, 2000.

_____. "Rant." *From the Margin: Writings in Italian Americana.* eds. Gardaphé, Fred, Paolo Giordano, and Anthony Julian Tamburri. West Lafayette: Purdue UP, 2000.

Gardaphé, Fred. *Italian Signs, American Streets.* Durham: Duke UP, 1996.

Hendin, Josephine Gattuso. "Italian American Writing as Ethnic Art." *MELUS.* 28.3 (Autumn, 2003): 13-39.

Mangione, Jerre and Morreale, Ben. *La Storia: Five Generations of the Italian American Experience.* New York: Harper Perennial, 1993.

Morrison, Toni. "Black Matter(s)." *Falling into Theory.* ed. David H. Richter. Boston: Bedford/St. Martin's, 2000.

Nolen, Claude H. *African American Southerners in Slavery, Civil War and Reconstruction.* Jefferson: McFarland & Co., Inc., 2001.

Skinner, Beverly Lanier. "Sterling Brown: An Ethnographic Perspective." *African American Review.* 31.3 (Autumn, 1997): 417-422.

Viscusi, Robert. *Buried Caesars and Other Secrets of Italian American Writing.* Albany: State U of New York P, 2006.

Celebrating the Poetry of Leo Luke Marcello
Italian American Themes and Southern Subtleties in Marcello's Reckoning of Life as an Italian American Southerner

ANGELINA OBERDAN
Clemson University

In many ways, Italian American Southerners feel very con-nected, but we also feel very separate because we aren't really considered Italian American—because we're not from New York or New Jersey—nor are we really considered Southern—because we're not Anglo-Saxon or French. But in Marcello's poetry, this discordant sense of self is portrayed beautifully. And somehow, in the depiction of all the con-trasting motives and melodies of an Italian American Southerner, there is an aria. Leo Luke Marcello is able to reckon the divisions of his identity—Italian American, Southerner—and to exemplify the delightfulness of life as such by writing poetry that is composed of Italian American themes and Southern subtleties.

Marcello recollected in Sonny Marks's article, "Poet's Book Focuses on Immigrant Experience" published in the *American Press*, that he was always fascinated by his herit-age. He said, "I realize that some people just sort of took something for granted about who they were and where they came from. But I knew there was something very rich and different in my background" (qtd. by Marks D4). And Mar-cello's collection, *Nothing Grows in One Place Forever: Poems of a Sicilian American*, reflects his delicate memories of his

26

immigrant grandparents as well as his insights into being Italian American from a Southern perspective.

Within this collection of his poetry, *Nothing Grows in One Place Forever,* we see the themes of Italian American literature and Southern nuances working in accord with each other. Robert Viscusi writes in his book titled *Buried Caesars and Other Secrets of Italian American Writing* that "reading Italian American writing well means understanding its secret themes, where they come from, how they work, and what they accomplish" (6). Because Marcello has been thoroughly recognized as a Southerner writer,[1] it is necessary to examine his poetry from an Italian American critical standpoint and to point out some of its Southern niceties.

One of the most prominent themes of Italian American literature that reflects the Italian American experience is that its literature inherently contains mixed feeling in regard to Italy. Viscusi writes in the introduction that "[i]n Italian American writing, *Italy* is a word [and a concept] that means both 'homeland of desire' and 'the empire that failed'" (xii). And these conflicting sentiments can be found throughout Marcello's work.

Italy—as an "empire that failed," as a place left behind—is portrayed in the poem titled "Frayed Papers":

Months after the funeral, she found
stacked in cardboard boxes
the yellowed immigration papers.
The facts uncurled with the flowery script:

---

[1] Not only did Marcello win the Deep South Award for Poetry, but the reading series in his honor, at McNeese State in Lake Charles, Louisiana, features Southern writers.

her father's name, his father's name, and
her father's father's and her father's mother's
and her father's widowed sister's and the orphans'
and the dates of the departure.

The sixth of January, a likely feast,
another Epiphany, unlikely.

The tickets have grown thin,
limp as a wet leaf, but dry,
tiny fragile slips of paper,
senseless, really, how such fragments
could portend so much—the dreams,
the new beginning. Did they really
look out across that gray ocean
and believe the future more
than cardboard boxes? (lines 1-19)

Marcello conveys in the last stanza that while the speaker is doubtful that the immigrant's future seemed more promising than what they had—even if all they had fit in worthless cardboard boxes—he understands that his Italian ancestors felt obliged to leave their homeland because they thought the future of Italy was so bleak that they had no alternative. Interestingly, the lists of names is important to the immigrants for purposes of remembering their families, but conveyed in a list of relationships, as Marcello writes it, is subtly Southern because it imparts an understanding of the speaker's place within these familial relationships.

The variety of feelings about Italy fills Marcello's work. If "Frayed Papers" is discontented with Italy, love for Italy, the "homeland of desire," can be seen in Marcello's poem, "Kissing My Hand" (28). The poem is in the voice of an immigrant and begins

My great-great-granddaughter brags.
Her little classmates hiss.
Not royalty, they cannot comprehend
but fear the regal blood that connects
this child to me, her great-great-
grandmother. (lines 1-6)

This poem reflects the sense of Italian nationalism that many Italian Americans still harbor, and later the speaker defends Italy: "Do not even dare think it. / Ours was not an evil rule" (lines 13-14). "Kissing My Hand" also illustrates that in the South, a region wrought with aristocratic mentalities and traditions, second- and third-generation Italian Americans do feel some measure of privilege to be of Italian descent in a way that separates them from their neighbors; while hissed at, regal Italian American blood is also revered. Perhaps not included in the hierarchy of Southern-aristocracy, Italian American Southerners do not feel strictly segregated but regal in their own right.

Discordant feelings about Italy are coupled in Italian American literature with American and immigrant ideologies. Marcello's poem "Parking Lot" exemplifies both the mindset of the Italian immigrant and the Italian American. The premise for this poem is that his *nonna's* house is going to become the parking lot of a Pentecostal church. In his previously mentioned interview with Marks, Marcello says, "I can still see the house in my memory. It was a great big house with a big, beautiful yard and hydrangeas, fig trees, and all kinds of life around it. We'd play on the porch, we'd play upstairs, we'd climb out on the roof" (D4); his poem makes the house come alive for the reader:

In the big two-storied house
with the swing on the front porch,
horseshoe over the back door,
yard full of trees and hedges,
pecan, hydrangeas, orange, fig,
chicken coop and pen in the rear,
quiet streets along the side and front,
people used to come from all over the state,
sometimes at dinner twenty-five around the table,
laughing, feasting on pasta or homemade sausage,
singing Old Country songs, drinking to the future. (lines 1-11)

The exterior of this house appears Southern with its foliage and chicken coop, while the interior of the house is essentially Italian with its table packed with loud and jovial company. And yet, the fact that the house and land are easily sold—and just as easily turned into a parking lot—reflects the immigrant sentiment, "This land is not *really* our land."

The story of Marcello's Italian immigrant family letting go of the house and the land shows that while his *nonna* and his Aunt Bennie filled the space with what they loved—family and figs—it wasn't a place they felt connected to. He writes in the third stanza of the poem:

In the Old Country the Cappuccini monks
used to hang the dead in hallways of the convent,
propping them against the walls or laying them on tables.
The living visited the dead, changing the burial clothes,
discussing family troubles until the sight was unbearable,
death-smiles peeling away with the skin, bones protruding,
until it became easier to talk at home, in a street, in a garden.
But this is not the Old Country, and no one hangs in hallways.
(lines 27-34)

30

If they had a connection to a physical place, it was to the soil of Sicily where they felt close to deceased family members (whom they could talk to "at home, in a street, in a garden")—not the ground of Louisiana.

And yet, this moving day happens too quietly for the speaker of the poem; the poem ends with an image of police cars warning passers-by "who might be going too fast" (line 54). The hesitation, or perhaps fear, of the young Marcello, who is presumably the speaker, as the poem closes exemplifies that while his Italian immigrant forbearers—his *nonna* and Aunt Bennie—didn't feel connected to the Louisiana land, he (a second generation Italian American Southerner) does. Marcello is well aware of discord between the immigrant sense that "this land is not *really* our land" and connection between Southerners and their land that is as deep as Cyprus roots and makes them return to the land they own even after their homes have been destroyed by hurricanes. In this way, we can comprehend both the attitudes of the Italian immigrant and those of the Italian American in regard to the land.

The emotions of the speaker in "The Parking Lot" shows that Marcello is trying to create his own land—and sense of place—through these poems. Viscusi includes in his themes of Italian American literature the repetition of stories about home and place because by telling stories about a place, we make it our own, which is exactly what Marcello does. This theme has a basis in Etruscan and Roman tradition, and it dates back to—at least—Virgil's description of Aeneas founding Latium.

While Marcello wants to create his own land, he is able to empathize with his grandmother. His poem titled "The Will" ends

Within these layered envelopes,
I keep this ancient Sicilian will.

They are all dead, the land all gone.
There is a slight smudge across the paper,
a wet spot, as if the ink had smeared
with a stray drop of rain or been
smudged by a damp finger. (lines 19-27)

In this poem, it is evident that if in "Parking Lot," Marcello feels a stronger affinity to the soil of Louisiana than his Italian immigrant grandmother did, he also understands how the loss of the Old Country makes her feel that she is of no land.

By incorporating Italian language into his poems, Marcello makes the South more Italian. Viscusi believes Italian American writers are able to celebrate Italy and America by incorporating both languages in their poetry, and Marcello does this—includes Italian words and phrases—throughout his poetry, especially when he discusses foods. For example, in his description of a Saint Joseph's Day celebration in "Good Wine Wasted and A Place to Rest" (62), Marcello writes that

Every March 19, white-robed children approached
the candlelit saint standing on the table
surrounded by flowers and the rare breads,
the sugary *sfingi*, the fig cakes, the clustered *pignolata,*
or clove-scented, teeth-breaking Dead Men's Bones. (lines 20-5)

Leslie A. Wade explains in "The Performance Ritual of Saint Joseph's Day: A Stranger at the Door" that the celebration of St. Joseph's Day and the creation of bountiful altars comes was introduced by Sicilan's in the late 19th century. She states that

> The holiday, celebrated on March 19th, is perhaps most widely known for its elaborate altar displays, where a bounty of breads, fruit, and pasta dishes are presented in honor of the saint. The event commemorates the fatherly example of Saint Joseph and gives occasion for celebrating the bonds of the family. The event also calls for performances of thankfulness for blessings bestowed over the course of the year. Celebrants exhibit their appreciation through an act of culinary charity; the bounty of the altar is shared not only with friends and family, but with the needy, and with visitors who may arrive as complete strangers.

Just as this tradition of celebrating St. Joseph's Day is incorporated into the culture of Louisiana, the Italian language is incorporated into Marcello's poem. The bits of Italian Marcello incorporates do not seem forced, but natural movements from one language to another, even with their explanatory modifiers.

Marcello was not fluent in Italian although he undoubtedly knew and understood many phrases. In his poem "Hydrangea," Marcello ruminates about the languages of Italian and American English:

> We dangled legs from the high porch.
> My cousins used words I didn't comprehend.
> Inside, Nonna continued to die.
> She'd been dying all my life,
> confined to bed.
> I did not even know why
> my cousins laughed at me.
> I jumped from the porch

into the flowers, picked up
a crushed blue hydrangea blossom
and held it gently in my lap.

Then I raised it high into the air
above my head, and like the priest
with the white host at Mass, I sang,
"Hocus pocus, God is here."
They said I'd go to hell.
I ran inside
and placed it in her
thin, white hands.

She blessed me
in the language
I understood.

Even if, for Marcello, Italian isn't a language of shame (as it was for many other second generation Italian Americans), it wasn't a language that he learned. Although his cousins laughed at him for only being able to speak English, this poem shows that Marcello learned to communicate with his Italian family, despite any language barriers, "in the language / I understood," the language of familial love.

Joanna Clapps Herman, an editor of *Wild Dreams: The Best of Italian Americana,* writes in the introduction to that collection that the use of language in Italian American poetry has an "*alto basso*" quality, or, in other words, it simultaneously expresses the high (the cultured, the sacred) and the low (the common, the local, the profane). She notes "Italian Americans lay claim to this high aesthetic *and* to the archetypal ordinary," and in his poem "Resurrection

Scherzo,"[2] Marcello combines the *alto* and *basso* immaculately. In this poem, he reflects on "the percussion of our streets" (line 42) by combining higher truth, symphonic jargon, and everyday images; he relates the death of a common man, a professor, a friend—who was hit by a car while crossing a street—which is a seemingly accidental moment in a world we like to believe is well planned. The general trend of the poem begins with the day-to-day and finds a more profound meaning in it.

In the first stanza of "Resurrection Scherzo," Marcello writes that

Three cars struck.
He must have bounced back and up
like a pinball on that street he'd walked
for twenty years in broken shoes
the headlights cracking in the dark. (lines 1-5)

The reader sees this ordinary man dying accidently, quickly, a death that has no reason or explanation. And Marcello describes how this friend died as though explaining it to his next-door-neighbor; the phrase "like a pinball" makes the scene less solemn and more humorous; the event becomes almost a joke, a scherzo. The described incident seems so unreal that even the news camera, in the last lines of this stanza, cannot understand this random moment; it "avoided / the body but lingered on the isolated / doubly crushed shoe" (lines 6-8). Like us, the news camera—in this case not even a person—can deal with the material object, the

---

[2] In English, "scherzo" refers to a light musical piece (sometimes in the third movement of a symphony), which has a quick, rapid rhythm. In Italian, "scherzo" means "a joke" or "a jest."

broken shoe, more easily than it can deal with a lost life, something comparatively incomprehensible.

In the second stanza, the classical music in the background begins to interlace itself with the ordinary and to bring some meaning to this seemingly purposeless end of a life. In the speaker's memory, the moment he hears of his friend's death is associated with eating crawfish (such standard Louisiana fare), listening to a scherzo playing in the background, and drinking white wine (as opposed to listening to zydeco and chugging beer). By incorporating those "frenetic violins," Marcello again adds a light-heartedness to the subject matter, and he begins the climb from the everyday to higher ground, as Herman discusses, by his allusion to the classical piece.

The speaker then tries to empathize with the man who died, but can only think of him as "going home hungry" and "empty" (lines 16-7). However, in the fourth stanza, the speaker is able to relate to his departed friend by—as in the previously mentioned news camera—understanding the material/physical leftovers of the man's life that seem strange without the man: his empty office on campus, the "neat stacks of final essays" (lines 20-1). But the things seem too neat—"files cleaner than in the past"—and too life-less, which is "unusual except as casual other facts / of the day's official resignation" (lines 22-4). In other words, these artifacts would be abnormal because of their lack of viabil-ity and their tidiness if the man was still alive, but because he is not, they signal the end of his life.

Indeed, in the fourth stanza, the speaker parses through the specific material/physical leftovers of death whereas in the fifth stanza, the speaker begins to find deeper meaning in a death so sudden. Marcello constructs a somber tone:

Over the coffin the priest denied
coincidence, praised the blessing
of being struck down when
there's nowhere else to go.
Even those not crying knew
Monsignor was right.
We get what we need. (lines 26-32)

In this stanza, which describes the funeral of a friend, the speaker begins to comprehend this death as something more than an insignificant accident or a joke. This change in understanding signals the turn between this stanza and the next.

To be sure, there is a turn between the fifth and the sixth stanzas, and the poem becomes reflective. The sixth stanza reads as follows:

Christ, the violence of a scherzo
recognized months later, Beethoven,
the movements of such last music
we live and die in—Christ,
how we want to rise out of it
in new shoes and straightened backs. (lines 33-8)

The scherzo, one of Beethoven's that was playing in the background when the speaker heard the news, is a surprising piece as is his friend's death. "The movements of such last music"—the violence and the vigor and, even, the playful brevity—lead to the dual meaning of the next line: "we live and die in—Christ," which is a statement and an exclamation. We will die in the previously mentioned violence and playful brevity of our quotidian lives, the profane, but we also—in accordance with Marcello's Catholicism—live and die in Christ, the sacred. The *alto*, the enlightened moments

of our lives contrast with the *basso,* the random, the profane, and it reminds us "how we want to rise out of it / in
new shoes and straightened backs."

After the scherzo in a symphony, the harmonies are resolved as they are in the final stanzas of "Resurrection
Scherzo." Through the juxtaposition of the daily (the eating,
drinking, and grading papers), the unexplained and sudden
death of a friend, the light-hearted scherzo, and the larger
truth, the speaker and the reader are resurrected:

> We step, breathing out our blood
> scherzo, relieved by what cannot be
> accident, but stuck by the familiar
> percussion of the streets.

We are resurrected in the belief that there is a meaning to
our mundane days, to the "percussion of the streets." There
is a greater truth, a greater hope, because the particular
harmonies are resolved. In this way, Marcello's poem quilts
the *alto* (the high, the cultured, the sacred) and the *basso*
(the common, the quotidian, the secular) together as seam-
lessly as they are combined in much of Italian American literature. If the combination of the high and the low is inherent in Italian American poetry, then the low or the local
makes this pieces particularly Southern.

Marcello combines the *alto* and the *basso,* and he also
blends images of his Catholic faith into much of his poetry.
In fact, his collection, *Blackrobe's Love Letters* (Xavier UP
1996; Cramers Press 2000), is about the life and work of
Saint Katharine Drexel, and was produced in collaboration
with his brother, Christopher Marcello, a visual artist. Additionally, Marcello wrote and published *15 Days of Prayer
with Katharine Drexel* (Liguori Publications 2002).

In an article in the *National Catholic Reporter*, Pamela Schaffer writes, "Leo Luke Marcello, professor and poet, can't remember precisely when or how St. Katharine Drexel won him over, but win him over she did." Indeed, later in the interview, Schaffer writes, "Marcello said, he thinks it was Drexel's connection to black Americans, so many years before the civil rights movement that inspired him." Drexel worked against prejudice and hatred to help a displaced people, and perhaps, because Marcello understands what it is to never quite assimilate, he felt that she could have helped him. Marcello describes her as being "destined to be a Philadelphia debutant," but the life she led was completely unexpected. And leading an unexpected life is another aspect of her that Marcello was able to relate to because he thought of his life as unexpected. Unfortunately, the only example of how Marcello's life was unexpected given in the article is that Leo Luke Marcello didn't expect to be close to Chris, his brother, because of their sixteen-year age difference. One can only presume what else Marcello thought unexpected, but it is impractical to draw any conclusions. Although both Leo Luke and Chris Marcello's works related to their Sicilian heritage are mentioned in Schaffer's article about *Black Robe's Love Letters*, probably Marcello found someone to look up to in St. Katharine Drexel because her unexpected life was one lived in spite of opposition—from her wealthy family in the North and the Ku Klux Klan (who called her order of nuns, "the n----- nuns") in the South—as can be seen in his poem "The Loneliness of the World":

Honored dear Miss Katie,
We go to sleep dressed, prepared
for fire, prepared for what to save.
The morning light may find our mission
a spot of ruins and ashes.

Fortunately, the nuns who worked with St. Katharine Drexel encouraged and sustained her with their devotion to their mission and their readiness. And while Marcello had his Italian parents and grandparents (especially his father who was a doctor) to look up to, he didn't have many heroic Americans he could relate to so he found a muse within his Catholic faith: the American Saint Katharine Ann Drexel.

In Schaffer's article about how the Marcello brothers were inspired by Saint Katharine Ann Drexel, Schaffer briefly mentions that Marcello's poem "The Fig Tree," from the previously mentioned collection titled *Nothing Grows in One Place Forever: Poems of a Sicilian American,* "was incorporated into a sculpture on display at Ellis Island last November [in 2000]" (15).

About Old World customs and heritage, "The Fig Tree," a meditative narrative, is also about the similarities and the dissimilarities of the New World and is optimistic about its freedoms. The first stanza of "The Fig Tree" establishes the situation:

> I've planted a tree for you,
> a cutting from a city where
> neither of us has lived except
> in old immigrants' afternoon dreams. (lines 1-4)

In other words, an uncle planted a fig tree for his nephew; in Sicilian tradition, a father plants a tree, usually a fig or an olive tree, to celebrate his son's birth and to symbolically show that the earth has much to offer his new child. This poem varies slightly from the tradition because the speaker of the poem, possibly Marcello himself, plants the tree for his nephew, not his son. As the speaker notes, this cutting that was planted for the nephew was originally from a tree in Sicily where neither the nephew nor the uncle ever lived but where their ancestors did. And because of this, the newly planted cutting is much like the nephew; his lineage is Italian, but he will grow up in the American South.

The second stanza contrasts the differences in thought between the second-generation uncle and his third-generation nephew who know little of his ancestors:

> You never heard their broken voices.
> You do not know what their sleep retrieves.
> You find Spiderman easier to believe in
> than my stories of their bravery, legends to you.
> They wait at a safe distance, ghosts,
> not touching you except through their names,
> Old Country flowers, almost wilted, and
> in our bodies, the New World fruits of theirs,
> transplanted into the newest season. (lines 3-13)

Whether or not the boy understands the ghosts of his ancestors or how they affect him, they "wait at a safe distance." The speaker points out that both the uncle and the nephew have the Old Country in them ("Old Country flowers, almost wilted....") and that they are the "New World fruits" of their ancestors, only "transplanted into the newest season."

The cyclical nature of both the fig tree and even familial ties is discussed in the third stanza.

> You aren't yet awake to this dying,
> the passing away of delicious fruit,
> bees humming in our hair. You sit,
> as I did, daydreaming, a child until
> one of the old people surprises you by
> running a piece of straw along your chin
> and wakes you, laughing or crying. (lines 14-20)

In this first three lines of this stanza, the uncle reasons that the young boy doesn't yet understand the seasons and how the figs will die and how the tree will be pollinated again by the "bees humming in our hair." In the second half of this stanza, Marcello connects the nephew's lack of understanding of the seasons to his ignorance about his Italian heritage. However, when the child daydreams, the "old people"—or possibly the ghosts in a surreal sense—will wake him up as his uncle was awakened. In other words, one day the boy will become aware of the seasons of the fig tree just as he will become aware of his heritage.

The fourth and last stanza of "A Fig Tree" is about the New World more so than are the previous stanzas.

> If this tree lives and you like purple figs,
> plant your own cutting wherever you want,
> because I may be neither here nor there,
> and anyway, nothing grows in one place forever.

The speaker becomes hesitant in this stanza; in the previous stanza, he was confident that his nephew would be awakened by the old people (even if he might wake "laughing or crying"), but this stanza begins with the phrase "If this tree lives and you like purple figs" as though the uncle worried that the Italian traditions of their family won't continue and that if the traditions do live on, his nephew will disparage them. While the speaker is more dubious about his nephew's appreciation for the fig tree (and for his heritage), the uncle is hopeful that the boy will replant a cutting from the tree wherever he goes because the boy has the freedom to go wherever he wants and because "nothing grows in one place forever"—not fig trees or traditions or people. Like the cutting from the fig tree, parts of traditions can move with their people, and this is what the speaker is hopeful that his nephew will take some part of their Italian heritage and traditions with him.

Undeniably, Marcello has infused his poetry with his Italian heritage (as he recommends his nephew should in "The Fig Tree") and included Southern subtleties. Through his poetry, which is a well-orchestrated composite of Italian American themes and Southern nuances, Leo Luke Marcello is able to reckon the divisions of his identity—Italian American, Southerner. In the poem titled "Frayed Papers," Marcello writes about Italy as a failed empire and reflects the Southern emphasis on relationships within families and communities. In contrast, "Kissing My Hand" connotes a love for Italy despite the feeling that Italian Americans can't be assimilated into Southern aristocracy. Marcello depicts a Southern home filled this Italian and Italian Americans in his poem "Parking Lot," but this is a home that is easily sold to become a parking lot because his relatives feel little or no connection to the land. Marcello sympathizes with this sentiment in "The Will," but, in a sense, his poems claim the South as his own. The poem "Good Wine Wasted and a Place to Rest" is about the Italian American celebration of St. Joseph's Day in Louisiana, and, just as this tradition is incorporated in to the culture, the Italian language is integrated into Marcello's poem. While he can intertwine some Italian words or phrases into his parlance and his poems, Marcello was not fluent in Italian, and this is described in "Hydrangea." "Resurrection Scherzo" is a complex, multi-layered poem in which the Italian American combination of the *alto* and the *basso* (in this case, the Southern emphasis on the local is the *basso*) is evident. In his poems about Saint Katharine Ann Drexel, it is evident that Marcello found an American muse in addition to being inspired by his Sicilian roots. In "The Fig Tree," Marcello reminds us to keep something of the Old World with us in the New World—whether it be an understanding of our heritage or a cutting from a fig tree—because as he says, "nothing grows in one place forever."

In Marcello's poetry, there is a reflection of Italian American Southerners that is greater than Marcello's carefully chosen words and fastidiously composed lines. Despite whatever disconnection Italian Americans in the South may feel, here in Leo Luke Marcello's poetry, there is vivid expression of what it is to be an Italian American Southerner.

WORKS CITED

Gardaphe, Fred L. Introduction. *Leaving Little Italy: Essaying Italian American Culture.* SUNY Ser. in Italian/American Culture. Albany: State U of New York P, 2004. xi-xix.

_____. "Mythologies of Italian America: From Little Italys to the Suburbs." *Leaving Little Italy: Essaying Italian American Culture.* SUNY Ser. in Italian/American Culture. Albany: State U of New York P, 2004. 37-50.

Gioia, Dana. "What is Italian American Poetry?" *Beyond the Godfather: Italian American Writers on the Real Italian American Experience.* Eds. A. Kenneth Ciongoli and Jay Parini. Hanover: UP of New England, 1997. 167-189.

Herman, Joanna Clapps. "Poetry—The Aesthetic of *Alto Basso*." *Wild Dreams: The Best of Italian Americana.* Eds. Carol Bonomo Albright and Joanna Clapps Herman. New York: Fordham UP, 2008. 5-7.

Marcello, Leo Luke. *Nothing Grows in One Place Forever: Poems of a Sicilian Amercan.* Time Being Books, 1998.

_____. *Silent Film.* Edwin Mellen Press, 1997.

Marks, Sonny. "Poet's Book Focuses on Immigrant Experience." *American Press.* 30 Oct. 1998: D4.

Schaffer, Pamela. "Inspired by a Saint." *National Catholic Reporter.* 6 Apr. 2001: 14-5.

Tamburri, Anthony Julian. "Beyond 'Pizza' and 'Nonna!' Or, What's Bad about Italian/American Criticism?: Further Directions for Italian/American Cultural Studies." *MELUS* 28.3 (2003): 149-74.

Viscusi, Robert. *Buried Caesars and Other Secrets of Italian American Writing.* SUNY Ser. in Italian/American Culture. Albany: State U of New York P, 2006.

Wade, Leslie. "The Performance Ritual of Saint Joseph's Day: A Stranger at the Door." *LouisianaFolklife.org.* Louisiana Division of the Arts. 2000.

Based on Actual Events
The Lynching of Italian American Immigrants in Tallulah, Louisiana, as Depicted by Donna Jo Napoli in *Alligator Bayou*

ALISON GRAHAM-BERTOLINI
Louisiana State University

Donna Jo Napoli's[1] *Alligator Bayou* is an historical fiction based on the lynching of five Sicilian grocers in Tallulah, Louisiana in 1899. The text, published in 2009, and winner of the Parents' Choice Gold Book Award for Historical Fiction, is written for young adults for the purpose, writes Napoli, of sharing an aspect of immigration with which her readership is likely unfamiliar, the story of a people who looked "evil in the face and still kept their dignity" (Forward 1). Napoli's story reconstructs the events that led to the Tallulah lynchings, including a fictional version of the altercation between the Sicilian grocers and the town's doctor. Her story raises questions about the insidious nature of racism and the alienation that inevitably follows in its wake.

Newspaper reports from the 1890s document six incidents of mob violence directed toward Italian Americans, three of which occurred in Louisiana. Edward F. Haas, author of "Guns, Goats, and Italians: The Tallulah Lynching of 1899," writes that the most famous case involved the shooting of a police superintendent in New Orleans who reportedly whispered "The dagoes did it," before his death. As a

---

[1] Donna Jo Napoli is the author of several books for children and young adults, including the award winning *Stones in Water* (1997) and *Breath* (2005). She grew up in an Italian American family in Miami, Florida, and attended Harvard University as an undergraduate and graduate student. She is currently a Professor of Linguistics at Swarthmore College, in Pennsylvania (*Encyclopedia World Bio* 1).

result of this comment, approximately twenty Italian men were arrested and jailed. On March 14, 1891 a mob of angry citizens stormed the jail and "systematically shot or clubbed to death, eleven of the Italian prisoners." A later investigation excused the mob's actions (1). The second lynching incident occurred five years later in St. Charles Parish. A mob of about fifty men stormed the local jail, seized six Italians, and hung three of them (1). The final incident took place in Tallulah. According to reports, "five men comprised the Italian community of the town. On July 20, 1899, a fierce mob brutally lynched all five and forced two other Italians who lived in nearby Milliken's Bend to flee" (1).

Napoli chose to convert the third of these news items into a historical fiction because, she writes,

> Documentation of the investigation that came afterward allowed me to see details of what happened on the day leading up to the murders. Also, because this case became a cause célèbre in Italy, I could read quite a lot from the Italian perspective, which was markedly different from that in the American press. The Italians saw the case as an economic question from the get go. (Forward 1)

Napoli was inspired to write *Alligator Bayou* after discovering an old news article about five Sicilian grocers in Tallulah, Louisiana, in 1899, who reportedly served a black customer before serving a white one, and were lynched as a result (Afterword 273). Although historian Clive Webb does not mention the specific incident to which Napoli refers, he does state that "The Sicilian merchants lynched in Tallulah ... had aroused the ire of the local community since they traded freely with African Americans and associated with them nearly on terms of equality" (57). He notes that the specific incident leading to the Tallulah lynchings concerned "the attempted murder of a local physician" (53). Edward Haas supplies further details, citing newspaper reports claiming that the violence in Tallulah began with "an altercation between Frank Defatta [one of the Italian grocers] and Will Rogers, son of a leading citizen" (1). Although the initial argument between Frank Defatta and Will Rogers was quelled, it led to tension between the Italians and Dr. J. Ford Hodge, the town's doctor and coroner. Dr. J. Ford Hodge was bothered by "a number of goats that Frank Defatta allowed to roam freely near his shop" (1). The goats tramped about on the doctor's front porch at night, disrupting the doctor's sleep (1). The doctor reportedly shot one of the goats, which led to violence between the two men, and to the lynching of all five of the Italian men living in Tallulah (1).

Alligator Bayou candidly depicts the discrimination experienced by Italian immigrants during the late nineteenth century, while simultaneously demonstrating how Italian immigrants negotiated the divide between their Italian identity and their Italian American identity. The novel is a work of fiction, but as Napoli attests, she built the characters for the book around actual people; people who "testified or were talked about in the testaments taken after the Tallulah lynching" (Afterword 273). Moreover, Napoli notes that although there is some disagreement in the historical documents regarding the names and ages of the lynched men, there is consensus regarding the following facts: Dr. Hodge was shot but recovered completely. Giuseppe Difatta (age 36, Italian citizen) and Carlo Difatta (age 54) were both hanged in the town's slaughterhouse on July 20, 1899. Francesco Difatta (age 30), Rosario Fiducia (age 37) "and a third person whose name might have been Cerami or Cerone Fiducia or Giovanni Cirano or Cerano ... were dragged from the jailhouse and hanged from a cottonwood tree outside the courthouse" also on July 20, 1899. Napoli writes that "All the bodies were so riddled with bullets that they were disfigured almost beyond recognition" (Afterword 275).

In the late nineteenth century Tallulah Louisiana was an insular community that did not adapt well to the influx of new people, ideas, and cultures. In *Alligator Bayou* Napoli filters the historical prejudices of the region through the eyes of recently emigrated Calogero, a fourteen-year-old boy who lives and works with his uncles and young cousin. Throughout the story, he struggles to understand why local whites discredit and demean his family based solely on their ethnicity. As Webb attests, "Although Southerners did not regard Sicilians as 'black,' they nonetheless sought to prescribe their place in the social hierarchy on the basis of skin color. The Sicilians therefore occupied an anomalous position within the southern racial order which undermined the white/black binary" (48). Calogero and his uncles are hard working and industrious, and contribute to both the local economy and the well being of the town. The resistance to their presence in the community thus makes little sense. Yet, because the white townspeople mistrust those whom they do not understand, Calogero must forge a new and autonomous identity for himself to navigate the divide between the false definitions of "Italian" and "Sicilian" put forth by his white neighbors, and his lived experience. As Webb writes "during the late nineteenth and early twentieth centuries, Sicilians were portrayed in the pages of both the popular press and supposedly scientific journals as a treacherous and bloodthirsty people with a natural propensity toward crime" (51). Webb further notes that "mob violence against Sicilians was legitimated by constructions of them principally as murderers" (48). The novel thus models for young readers the potential power that an image possesses to influence, incite, and spark emotion, and demonstrates the importance of seeing past the false and damaging messages of those who appeal to fears, anger, biases, and prejudices rather than to facts and reason.

The whites of Tallulah tolerate the Italian grocers and purchase their "superior produce" but are simultaneously threatened because the family refuses to conform to their hierarchical system of racial superiority. Cirone, Calogero's uncle, makes clear the absurdity of the white townspeople's attitude toward them when he comments, "I don't get why people here don't like Sicilian. Our family supplies this town, Tallulah, with the best fruits and vegetables. You'd think the sound of Sicilian would make their mouths water. Instead, we hold our tongues—or speak English if we can— in the presence of townspeople" (Napoli 2). Cirone pinpoints both the absurdity of the racial bias experienced by the grocers, as well as the need for the Sicilian family to conform to the expectations of their host community.

The white townspeople fear the economic encroachment of the hard-working Sicilians on the produce market. Napoli writes, "We like to imagine that evil is like a disease—it strikes at random and for no good reason. But the evil behind the lynchings in the American Reconstruction period was often based on people trying to maintain their wealth and power. That's far worse than a disease—that's a calculated decision. That's chosen evil" (Afterword 275). The hatred and mistrust between races is often motivated by economic factors; those with financial power wish to maintain that power, and will often go to extremes to do so. As noted by Webb,

Starting out as lowly street peddlers selling their own garden produce, Sicilian immigrants had by the late nineteenth century secured a monopoly over the importation, distribution, and sale of fresh foods throughout Louisiana ... Resentment at the economic prosperity of Sicilians resulted in accusations that it had been attained through corrupt and brutal business practices. (60)

The Sicilian grocers of Tallulah were seen as a threat to the white economic dominance of the region, and were targeted as a result.

A good example of an economic division driving racial tension occurs early in *Alligator Bayou*, when Calogero's uncle Carlo upsets one of his white customers by serving a black customer inside the store. The white customer, Willie Rogers, takes offense, and concludes that the store is "dirty" (Napoli 10). In fact, he may be threatened by the expanding customer base that the Italians are cultivating. Carlo reacts in anger to Willie's insults, miffed that anyone would be so bold as to tell him how to run his business. Calogero's family understands the Jim Crow laws, which state that black and white customers cannot be served food in the same room at the same time—but because the law does not specify a procedure regarding the selling of groceries to different races, they see no reason not to serve their black customers just as they serve the whites. They believe this is a matter of respect, of human dignity, to treat all customers as they would expect to be treated. This makes good economic sense, because black customers continue to frequent their establishment.

Because the Sicilians adhere strictly to the laws, they believe they are in the right. Accusing the Italian family of being dirty and breaking the law violates the code of honor to which the family adheres. When Willie Rogers calls the grocers "criminals," Francesco, Calogero's youngest uncle and "leader" of their family, responds, "If he calls us criminals in front of people, he'll dishonor us" (11). Francesco fears that their honor has been besmirched and must be defended. It is this code of honor that prompts Carlo to wait with a shotgun for Willie, to confront him for the slur. It is Calogero who must warn Willie not to take his usual route to work (16). Calogero then, functions as the intermediary between the old and new worlds. In Italy feuds were settled independently, without the involvement of the law. In the U.S., such behavior would land Carlo in jail, or worse, and would confirm the suspicions that he is a criminal.

The economic threat posed by the Sicilian grocers is compounded by a series of cultural misunderstandings, such as the dichotomy between the old world code of honor and the new world adherence to the law, that takes place between the Sicilians and the local whites. While such occurrences certainly appear to amplify the townspeople's mistrust of the Sicilians, they additionally are used as excuses to ensure that hatred of the "foreigners" is maintained. For example, Calogero's uncle lets his goats run free, instead of confining them to his own property. When the townspeople complain, he responds, "Goat go where goat go. Is nature. Is how God want. Who can prevent?" (38). He cannot fathom the penning of the goats, as all his life he has been taught that goats roam free. On the other hand, the goats are an affront to the local doctor when they repeatedly run across his front porch, scuffing and dirtying it. The doctor complains to Calogero's family, but when the goats return, he overreacts by slaughtering the family's favorite goat, Bedda. When Carlo confronts the doctor, the doctor reacts with fear, certain that Carlo means to retaliate with violence. The Sicilians are called "cold-blooded murderers" (251), "monkeys" and "a scourge" (251), "dagoes" and "worse than trash" (224), labels that circulate on the basis of fragmentation and misunderstanding as opposed to reflection, understanding, and identification.

Soon after Carlo questions the doctor about the slaughtered goat, the doctor rallies a mob to lynch the grocers. He fears, mostly because of rumors circulating about the violent tendencies of all Sicilians, that if he does not harm Carlo, then Carlo will harm him. From this example the reader is made privy to how different traditions, although seemingly minor, can provide the impetus for violence, and how labels and hearsay, terms such as "mafia" and "criminal," can wield power that escalates beyond reason.

The damage rendered by derogatory names and images is also evident in the newspaper articles that Calogero collects from around the United States that identify Sicilians as murderers (224). Such representations again fragment the truth via omission, leading to further misunderstanding between the whites and the Italian Americans. Yet such images are deemed factual by the white populous, which struggles to maintain an economic (and thus social) advantage. The white community is reluctant to relinquish their dominance, and fears the appropriation of their power by the freed blacks and the hard-working Italians. The grocers understand and resent the hierarchy in Tallulah. Francesco says to a black field hand, "Willy Rogers, he want see you and me we no get nothing for our work, no money, no matter how hard we work. He want see us poor, like dirt, and never change. Everybody like you, you father, you grandfather, they slave before the war. Everybody like me, from other country. He want us to go to him for help. Like children" (39).

The Italian family's refusal to adhere to a caste system is frowned upon, and their position in the community is complicated further when Calogero meets Patricia, a smart and sassy black girl his own age. Calogero's crush soon becomes evident to the reader—yet his feelings for Patricia and the growing friendship between them must be kept secret from the community, which frowns on interracial socializing, and would never allow interracial marriage. Although it is never stated, the broader impetus for the segregation imposed by the townspeople is to prevent underprivileged factions of society from coming together for the purpose of eliminating oppression.

Calogero's character is key to the narrative, because he communicates a first-hand account of his old way of life in Italy, as well as a taste of life in Louisiana, complete with alligator hunts and sweet potato roasts. Calogero is schooled in English and the ways of his new nation by a sympathetic tutor. His ability to speak and write English is important because it allows him to personally counter notions of Sicilian criminality by not only behaving in opposition to such labels, but by voicing his frustration that such labels exist in the first place.

In this story words hold power. It is thus ironic when Carlo states that "We run a legitimate business. Everybody knows. Words don't change the facts" (9), because in this case, words do change the facts. In truth, words provoke the lynching of the grocers. The words used by the larger populace in reference to the grocers, words such as "mafia" and "violent" and "murderers," convince the white community of Tallulah that the grocers will retaliate for the slaying of their goat, so the whites slay the grocers instead. Words are used by the whites in this novel to falsely define not only the Italians, but also blacks and Native Americans. Napoli does an excellent job of demonstrating how such insidious representations are believed and perpetuated despite evidence to the contrary, and how such false representations can do harm.

The intersection of false images with the lived experience of ethnic peoples leads Calogero to new ways of understanding difference. This is most evident in his encounter with the Native American, Joseph, from the Tunica Tribe. Joseph provides Calogero with additional insight into how the dominant members of society divide and conquer the lower echelons to maintain their power; for example, how American Indians were told that Sicilians brought yellow fever to the U.S., a disease that virtually destroyed the Indian nations. Such false information drove a wedge between the two peoples, preventing them from working together to counter their mutual oppression. Joseph reflects, "If you don't want people to like someone, just call him disease infected" (70). In this way Calogero's instinctual identification with the marginalized black community and the Native American character, who literally lives on the edges of society, is fostered. Calogero has been instructed to treat white people better than the blacks; however, personal experience shows him that the blacks possess a basic human decency that makes them equal in every way to their white counterparts.

Finally, the untamed wilderness in this novel is representative of the unrestricted and unlawful behavior of the local whites, who feel justified in attacking the Sicilians based on nothing but hearsay. The local whites are linked symbolically with two animal predators, the alligator and the panther. The alligator is a dangerous creature that lives within the swamp, an area of ground difficult for outsiders to navigate (just as the cultural norms in Southern Louisiana are difficult for the Sicilians to navigate). Similarly, the panther is a dangerous predator that prowls the wilderness. Calogero observes, "Panthers. If you run, they chase. I have to run" (261). The image of the panther chasing its prey forecasts the hunt for Calogero that takes place after the whites of Tallulah realize that Calogero has fled. The irony is that those doing the chasing are supposedly civilized members of an advanced society, not uncultivated savage beasts.

Despite the bleak events upon which the novel is based, the text ends with Calogero's escape, and with his escape comes the potential to continue changing hearts and minds with his actions and words. As Joseph from the Tunica tribe tells him, "You are free. You can choose. You can become what you choose" (270), in other words, you are now free to define yourself, to make of yourself what you will. The ending of *Alligator Bayou* is thus a hopeful one. Yet, we must ask ourselves, as the novel suggests, what did it mean for the Italian American community to integrate the traumatic experience of immigration into their national identity? What does it mean to the continuing Italian American narrative of identity? The novel leaves this question unanswered, however Calogero's final words, "I'll be back... I will be back" (272) suggest a determination and drive on the part of the oppressed Sicilians to overcome stultifying forces such as racism and miscegenation that impeded their human rights and dignity.

WORKS CITED

Encyclopedia of World Biography: Donna Jo Napoli Biography. Accessed June 28, 2011. Updated 2011.
<http://www.notablebiographies.com/news/Li-Ou/Napoli-Donna-Jo.html>.

Haas, Edward F. "Guns, Goats, and Italians: The Tallulah Lynching of 1899." North Louisiana Historical Association 13 (Summer 1982). <http://www.rootsweb. ancestry.com/~lamadiso/articles/lynchings.htm>.

Napoli, Donna Jo. *Alligator Bayou*. New York: Wendy Lamb Books, 2009.

Webb, Clive. "The Lynching of Sicilian Immigrants in the American South, 1886-1910." *American Nineteenth Century History*, 3,1. (Spring 2002).

The Lynching of Italian Americans
A Reassessment

STEFANO LUCONI
University of Padua, Italy

The issue of lynching in the United States has recently elicited new interest among historians, who have produced a few overviews of such a phenomenon and its implications. These studies, however, have tended either to pay only cursory attention to the casualties of Italian origin or even to neglect them completely.[1] Against such a backdrop, the purpose of this essay is to re-examine the case of the victims of mob violence from Italian background and to reconsider the prevailing interpretation for their killings in episodes of summary justice before World War I, namely during the period that witnessed the great bulk of these crimes against people of Italian descent. Contrary to conventional wisdom stressing that Italian Americans were victimized since they were not regarded as being fully white,[2] this chapter argues that they were lynched not only because their membership in the white race was usually challenged at that time, but also as a consequence of economic, political, and labor rivalries that exploited the newcomers' dubious racial status.

---

[1] For the former approach, see Michael J. Pfeifer, *Rough Justice: Lynching and the American Society, 1847-1947* (Urbana: U of Illinois P, 2004) 22-24, 74, 203; Manfred Berg, *Popular Justice: A History of Lynching in America* (Chicago: Ivan R. Dee, 2011) 127-31; for the latter, Amy Louise Wood, *Lynching and Spectacle: Witnessing Racial Violence in America, 1890-1940* (Chapel Hill: U of North Carolina P, 2009).
[2] This view has been lately restated by Peter Vellon, "'Between White Men and Negroes': The Perception of Southern Italian Immigrants through the Lens of Italian Lynchings," *Anti-Italianism: Essays on a Prejudice*, ed. William J. Connell and Fred Gardaphé (New York: Palgrave Macmillan, 2010) 23-32.

According to an estimate by historian Patrizia Salvetti, at least thirty-four Italian immigrants and Italian Americans were lynched in the United States, especially in southern regions, between the mid 1880s and the early 1910s.[3] The most infamous and notorious of such hideous crimes occurred in New Orleans in 1891. Here a blood-thirsty mob killed eleven defendants of Sicilian extraction who had just been acquitted of the murder of the local police superintendent, David C. Hennessey.[4] According to Salvetti's account, the last instance of summary justice against people of Italian origin took place in Tampa, Florida, in 1910. There, on September 20, law enforcement officers arrested two Sicilian newcomers, Angelo Albano and Castenge (alias Castenzio and Costanzo) Ficarotta, on charges of complicity in what ultimately turned out to be the fatal shooting of J. Frank Esterling, an accountant for the Bustillo Brothers and Diaz Cigar Company, a large cigar manufacture in West Tampa. While Albano and Ficarotta were being taken to the county jail, at the time Esterling was still alive though hospitalized in critical conditions, a crowd of twenty-five to thirty people stopped the horse-drawn hack by which the two suspects

---

[3] Patrizia Salvetti, *Corda e sapone: Storie di linciaggi degli italiani negli Stati Uniti* (Rome: Donzelli, 2003).
[4] Herbert Asbury, *The French Quarter: An Informal History of the New Orleans Underworld* (New York: Knopf, 1936) 403-16; John N. Coxe, "The New Orleans Mafia Incident," *Louisiana Historical Quarterly* 20 (1937): 1067-1110; Frank Shay, *Judge Lynch, His First Hundred Years* (New York: Washburn, 1938) 161-68; John S. Kendall, "Who Killa De Chief?," *Louisiana Historical Quarterly* 22 (1939): 492-530; Richard Gambino, *Vendetta: The True Story of the Largest Lynching in US History* (Garden City, NY: Doubleday, 1977); Liborio Casilli, "Un drammatico episodio dell'emigrazione italiana: Il linciaggio di New Orleans del 14 marzo 1891," *Studi Storici Meridionali* 11 (1991): 125-39; Jerre Mangione and Ben Morreale, *La Storia: Five Centuries of the Italian-American Experience* (New York: HarperCollins, 1992) 202-13; Giose Rimanelli, "The 1891 New Orleans Lynching: Southern Politics, Mafia, Immigration, and the American Press," *The 1891 Lynching and US-Italian Relations: A Look Back*, ed. Marco Rimanelli and Sheryl Lynn Postman (New York: Peter Lang, 1992) 53-105; Teresa Fava Thomas, "Arresting the *Padroni* Problem and Rescuing the White Slaves in America: Italian Diplomats, Immigration Restrictionists, & the Italian Bureau, 1881-1901," *Altreitalie* 40 (2010): 61-62.

were being moved, seized the two prisoners from the policemen's hands, went to a nearby grove, and hanged them.[5]

Commenting on this latter event and its implications for the plight of Italians in their adoptive land, the New York City-based daily *Il Progresso Italo-Americano*—the most influential Italian-language newspaper in the United States—elaborated a theory of its own about summary justice. Specifically, it pointed out that

> those who know statistics about lynching are aware that the victims are Black people. Europeans have not been lynched except for Italians only. In fact, a white person—probably a Bulgarian—was lynched in Baton Rouge in 1907. Yet it was a misunderstanding. The thugs there attacked a group of workers from Macedonia. But they actually intended to give chase to Italian laborers living nearby.[6]

This statement was incorrect. Between 1880 and 1930, 723 whites—who belonged to disparate ethnic and religious minorities, ranging from Norwegian and German to Jewish and Syrian, and included Anglos as well—were lynched in the United States.[7] Salvetti, who draw her data exclusively

---

[5] "Two Men Taken from Officers and Hanged," *Tampa Morning Tribune*, 21 September 1910: 10; Laura Pilotti, "La serie 'Z-Contenzioso' dell'Archivio Storico-diplomatico del Ministero degli Affari Esteri," *Il Veltro: Rivista della Civiltà Italiana* 34 (1990): 104-8.

[6] "All'indomani dell'eccidio di Tampa," *Il Progresso Italo-Americano* 25 September 1910: 1. For *Il Progresso Italo-Americano* and its owner, Carlo Barsotti, see Samuel L. Baily, *Immigrants in the Lands of Promise: Italians in Buenos Aires and New York City, 1870-1914* (Ithaca, NY: Cornell UP, 1999) 182-84, 205-6.

[7] William Fitzhugh Brundage, *Lynching in the New South: Georgia and Virginia, 1880-1930* (Urbana: U of Illinois P, 1993) 259. For the 1889 lynching of a Norwegian immigrant, Hans Jacob Olson, in Preston, Wisconsin, see Jane M. Pederson, "Gender, Justice, and a Wisconsian Lynching," *Agricultural History* 67 (1993): 65-82. For the 1918 case of German newcomer Robert Prager in Collinsville, Illinois, see E. A. Schwartz, "The Lynching of Robert Prager, the United Mine Workers, and the Problems of Patriotism in 1918," *Journal of the Illinois State Historical Society* 95 (2002): 414-37. For an account of the notorious 1915 lynching of Jewish-American businessperson Leo Frank in Marietta, Georgia, see Steve Oney, *And the Dead Shall Rise: The Murder of Mary Phagan and the Lynching of Leo Frank* (New

upon research into the records of Italy's Ministry of Foreign Affairs and did not use US sources, is likely to have underestimated the real figure of the Italian-American victims. Italian diplomats may have overlooked those immigrants who had become US citizens as well as the US-born children of the newcomers because the Italian government had no jurisdiction over these people.[8] In addition, it is possible that killings in small centers without Italian consular agents sometimes went unreported and left no evidence in the archives of the Ministry of Foreign Affairs. An article by Clive Webb, who relied on unspecified sources in the records of the Tuskegee Institute and the National Association for the Advancement of Colored People, mentions additional lynchings of Sicilian immigrants in Shelby Depot, Mississippi, in 1887, in Marion, North Carolina, in 1906, and in Chathamville, Louisiana, in 1907.[9] Moreover neither Salvetti's study nor Webb's essay include the cases of Joseph Speranza, alias Sparanzo, and Louis Carrari. A posse of a few hundred people hanged the former, a Sicilian miner, in Johnston City, Illinois, in 1915 following innuendos that he had shot a farmer and wounded his daughter.[10] The latter was killed in the mining village of West Frankfort, Illinois, in 1920 while he was trying to protect his house from looters in the wake of an outburst of anti-Italian hysteria arising from the murder of two young boys, who had been allegedly kidnapped

---

York: Pantheon, 2003). For the 1929 collective killing of Nicholas Romey, an immigrant from Syria, in Lake City, Florida, see Sarah Gualtieri, "Strange Fruit? Syrian Immigrants, Extralegal Violence, and Racial Formation in the Jim Crow South," *Arab Studies Quarterly* 26 (2004): 63-85. As many as thirty-nine Anglos were lynched in Texas only. See David L. Chapman, "Lynching in Texas," M.A. thesis, Texas Tech U, 1973, 94-95.

[8] Salvetti ix.

[9] Clive Webb, "The Lynching of Sicilian Immigrants in the American South, 1886-1910," *American Nineteenth Century History* 3 (2002): 45-76.

[10] Dominic Pulera, *Sharing the Dream: White Male in Multicultural America* (New York: Continuum, 2004) 21-23.

by an Italian-American crime organization. Following a murderous ritual, as happened to many African-American victims of lynching, Carrari was also horribly mutilated.[11]

Even assuming that Salvetti's list is shorter than the casualties' actual number;[12] Italian Americans were only a very small minority among the whites who were lynched. In any case, the mistake that *Il Progresso Italo-Americano* made to account for the alleged Italian monopoly of the white targets of mob violence and summary justice is revealing of Italian Americans' insecurity as for their racial standing in their adoptive land. While attempting to give reason for the allegedly "systematic lynching" of Italian newcomers, the daily pointed out that "only racial hatred can explain it."[13] It is unclear why *Il Progresso Italo-Americano* overlooked the other-than-Italian white victims of lynchings. But it might be plausibly suggested that the daily intended to overemphasize anti-Italian prejudice in the United States in order to make its own appeals to Italian Americans to join forces against discrimination more compelling.[14] At any rate, at that time the word "race" was a rather ambiguous term in the Italian-language press in the United States. Many newspapers used it as a synonym for what today could be more

---

[11] "Riots Are Renewed at West Frankfort," *New York Times* 7 August 1920: 11; "Mob Kills Italian Renewing Race War," ibid. 8 August 1920: 8.

[12] Strictly speaking, the last lynching of an Italian occurred at Fort Lewis, Washington, in August 1944. However, the victim was not an immigrant, but a prisoner of war. In this case, the killers were five black US soldiers who resented the fact that former enemies allegedly enjoyed better treatment than African-American troops. See Stanley Sandler, *Segregated Skies: All-Black Combat Squadrons of WWII* (Washington, DC: Smithsonian Institution P, 1998) 73.

[13] "All'indomani dell'eccidio di Tampa."

[14] The protection of Italian immigrants had been a priority for *Il Progresso Italo-Americano* since the daily was established in 1880. Actually, Carlo Barsotti created *Il Progresso Italo-Americano* because, in his opinion, the only Italian-language newspaper published in New York City at that time, *L'Eco d'Italia*, failed to defend with sufficient energy an Italian newcomer who had been sentenced to death, allegedly on the grounds of ethnic biases. See Adolfo Rossi, *Un italiano in America* (Treviso: Buffetti, 1907) 177-78.

aptly called "ethnicity."[15] In the instance of the article in *Il Progresso Italo-Americano*, however, we can reasonably take the meaning of such expression at face value. After all, reporting Carrari's lynching, the *New York Times* called his murder the result of a "race war."[16]

Indeed, at the turn of the twentieth century, Italian immigrants—especially those from the southern regions of their motherland such as Sicilians like Albano and Ficarotta themselves or the New Orleans victims—occupied an "inbetween" racial position. In the eyes of the broader US society, the generally dark-skinned newcomers from the *Meridione* looked more similar to African Americans than to white Europeans.[17]

In particular, Italian travelers to the states of the former Confederacy often complained that their fellow countrymen were usually treated as if they were Blacks.[18] Common conditions of peonage and agricultural work back to back with African Americans on the sugar cane, cotton, and rice plantations ended up blurring the difference between Italian Americans and people of color.[19] Significantly, as late as 1922, a court in Alabama cleared an African-American man, Jim Rollins, of miscegenation charges on the grounds that

---

[15] For an in-depth and extensive study of the Italian-language press in the United States at the time of mass immigration, see Bénédicte Deschamps, "De la presse 'coloniale' à la presse italo-américaine: Le parcours de six périodiques italiens aux États-Unis," Ph.D. diss., U Paris VII – Denis Diderot, 1996.

[16] "Mob Kills Italian Renewing Race War."

[17] Bénédicte Deschamps, "Le racisme anti-italien aux États-Unis (1880-1940)," *Exclure au nom de la race (États-Unis, Irlande, Grande-Bretagne)*, ed. Michel Prum (Paris: Syllepse, 2000) 61-66; David R. Roediger, *Colored White: Transcending the Racial Past* (Berkeley: U of California P, 2002) 34-37, 142-44, 163, 167; Ferdinando Fasce, "Gente di mezzo: Gli italiani e gli altri," *Storia dell'emigrazione italiana: Arrivi*, ed. Piero Bevilacqua, Andreina De Clementi, and Emilio Franzina (Rome: Donzelli, 2002) 235-43.

[18] Matteo Sanfilippo, *Problemi di storiografia dell'emigrazione italiana* (Viterbo: Sette Città, 2002) 69-70.

[19] Pete Daniel, *The Shadow of Slavery: Peonage in the South, 1901-1969* (Urbana: U of Illinois P, 1972) 94, 103, 152.

it could not be proved that his Sicilian partner, Edith La-bue, was white.[20] In 1911, even several members of the Committee on Immigration and Naturalization of the US House of Representatives doubted that southern Italians were "full-blooded Caucasian" and the report of a Senatorial commission investigating immigration pointed to a likely "infusion of African blood" among Sicilians and Sardini-ans.[21] Similarly, testifying before a Congressional committee on immigration in 1890, a railroad construction boss con-tended that an Italian was not a white man but a "Dago," a slur immigrants from the peninsula were usually referred to at that time.[22] In the early twentieth century, the Italian am-bassador in Washington himself—Edmondo Mayor des Planches—acknowledged that newcomers from Italy "hold a racial middle ground between whites and Blacks."[23] Re-markably, in 1905, in one of the first academic studies about lynching that included a racial breakdown of the victims, James Elbert Cutler listed the statistics about the Italian casualties under the category, grouping people that were neither "negroes" nor "whites."[24]

While Italian Americans' full "whiteness" was generally denied and member of this immigrant minority were often associated with Blacks, it could be easily suggested that their

---

[20] Matthew Frye Jacobson, *Whiteness of a Different Color: European Immigrants and the Alchemy of Race* (Cambridge, MA: Harvard UP, 1998) 4.
[21] US House of Representatives, 62nd Congress, 2nd Session, Committee on Im-migration and Naturalization, *Hearings Relative to the Further Restriction of Immi-gration* (Washington, DC: GPO, 1912) 77-78; US Senate, 61st Congress, 3rd Ses-sion, *Abstracts of the Reports of the Immigration Commission: With Conclusions and Recommendations and Views of the Minority*, 2 vols. (Washington, DC: GPO, 1911) 1:250.
[22] Qtd. in George J. Manson, "The 'Foreign Element' in New York City," *Harper's Weekly* 18 October 1890: 817.
[23] Edmondo Mayor des Planches, *Attraverso gli Stati Uniti: Per l'emigrazione italiana* (Turin: Unione Tipografico-Editrice Torinese, 1913) 144.
[24] James Elbert Cutler, *Lynch-Law: An Investigation into the History of Lynching in the United States* (New York: Longman, Green, 1905) 181.

ambiguous racial status accounted for the fact that they became victims of the same excruciation and brutality that were usually reserved for African Americans as retribution and punishment for actual criminal behavior or alleged felonies. As in the case of Blacks, for example, committed or attempted rape of white women was a cause for lynching. This very charge resulted in the first lynching of an Italian immigrant, Federico Villarosa, in Vicksburg, Mississippi, in 1886. Accused of having tried to assault the thirteen-year old white daughter of the local postmaster, Villarosa was dragged out of the county prison and hanged by an angry mob while he was still waiting for a hearing in court.[25] Similarly, the lynchings of Italian Americans became public spectacles like those of African Americans.[26] For instance, after Albano and Ficarotta were killed in the evening, their cadavers were left hanging all night long and residents of Tampa went to the site where the two Sicilian immigrants had been assassinated by any means available. According to newspaper accounts, the crowd that gathered there reached roughly two thousand people by midnight.[27] Speranza's lynching was turned into a form of entertainment, too. Specifically, pictures of his corpse and prison cell went on public display.[28] Likewise, Daniel Arata—an Italian-American bartender who had murdered one of his patrons in Denver in 1893—was hanged twice to please the disappointed latecomers who had missed the real lynching and his body was dragged through the city's business district to the benefit of additional onlookers.[29]

---

[25] "Lynched by a Mob," *New York Times* 30 March 1886: 5.
[26] Grace Elizabeth Hale, *Making Whiteness: The Culture of Segregation in the South, 1890-1940* (New York: Pantheon, 1998) 199-239.
[27] "Italians Lynched in a Tampa Street," *New York Times* 21 September 1910: 10.
[28] Pulera 22-23.
[29] "Lynched by a Denver Mob," *New York Times* 27 July 1893: 1; Thomas Jacob Noel, *The City and the Saloon: Denver, 1858-1916* (Niwot: U Colorado P, 1996) 61.

Coeval sources argued that the failure to ascribe a white identity to Italian immigrants caused the resort to summary justice against them. A few newspaper accounts about the lynching of five Sicilians from Cefalù in Tallulah, Louisiana, in 1899, offered a case in point. The victims—the brothers Francesco, Giuseppe, and Carlo Difatta along with Rosario Fiducia and Giovanni Cerami—were killed after they tried to assassinate—but only managed to wound—J. Ford Hodge, the coroner of Madison parish, because, following an altercation, he had shot a goat that roamed freely around his house and belonged to one of the Sicilians.[30] The incident had all the ingredients to give good reason for the stigmatization of the Italians' tendency to overreact and employ violence in order to settle disputes. Yet some press reports focused on the racial perception of the newcomers. For instance, *Harper's Weekly* magazine commented that, in the minds of the local residents, the Italian newcomers deserved the same treatment of an African American who shot at or murdered a white man—namely lynching without trial—because they could be hardly classified as white people.[31] Likewise, the *New Orleans Times-Democrat* stressed that "the people [in Tallulah] believe that they were justified in the action they took" because the "maintenance of white supremacy at any cost" was at stake in the lynching.[32]

Similarly, in 1892, when the *Seattle Press-Times* published the news of the presumed lynching of four Italian railroad construction workers in Montecristo, Skagit County—which, in fact, never occurred—it made a point of ex-

---

[30] "The Italian Lynchings," *Outlook* 5 August 1899: 735; "The Lynching Affair at Tallulah," *Christian Advocate* 17 August 1899: 1294; Edward F. Haas, "Guns, Goats, and Italians: The Tallulah Lynching of 1899," *North Louisiana Historical Association Journal* 13.2-3 (1982): 45-58; Salvetti 55-58.
[31] Norman Walker, "Tallulah's Shame," *Harper's Weekly* 5 August 1899: 779.
[32] *New Orleans Times-Democrat* 25 July 1899, qtd. in Haas, "Guns, Goats, and Italians" 52.

plaining such an alleged murder by emphasizing that neither Italians nor Chinese were considered as belonging to the white race in Washington State because members of both minorities were forced to live in segregated residential areas.[33] Reflecting what Richard Hofstadter has called a "mystique" of white Anglo-Saxon superiority over southern- and eastern-European immigrant groups, even the reputable *New York Times* contended, with reference to the Sicilian newcomers who had been charged with the killing of police chief Hennessey in New Orleans, that "our rattlesnakes are as good citizens as they; our own murderers are men of feeling and nobility compared to them."[34] Likewise, a report to the Second Congress of the Italians Abroad, held in Rome in 1911, contended that the lynchings of immigrants in the United States in general and in Louisiana in particular were in part the consequence of both the newcomers' failure to distance themselves from people of color and their tendency to treat Blacks as equals.[35]

Scholars have followed suit. For instance, to historian George E. Cunningham, social intimacy and familiarity with African Americans was "a hindrance to white solidarity" in the states of the former Confederacy, challenged the racial order of a society that not only was unprepared for interracial relations but even antagonized them, and was eventually responsible for such intense hatred and hostility toward Italian immigrants that could eventually result in lynchings.[36] By the same token, John Higham has contended

---

[33] "A Murder Avenged," *Seattle Post-Times* 17 June 1892: 1.
[34] Richard Hofstadter, *Social Darwinism in American Thought* (New York: Braziller, 1959) 172; "The New-Orleans Affair," *New York Times* 16 March 1891: 4.
[35] Luigi Scala, "Poche considerazioni giuridiche e sociali su l'emigrazione italiana negli Stati Uniti e particolarmente in Louisiana," *Atti del Congresso degli italiani all'estero* (Rome: Tipografia Editrice Nazionale, 1913) 17-23.
[36] George E. Cunningham, "The Italian: A Hindrance to White Solidarity in Louisiana, 1890-1898," *Journal of Negro History* 50 (1965): 22-36.

that summary justice against Italian newcomers arose from the fact that they "violated the white man's code" because they associated with African Americans "nearly on terms of equality."[37] Likewise, Dominic Pulera has remarked that olive-skinned "Speranza died at least in part because he was visibly different from the native-born white majority in Johnston City. [...] The lynch mob almost certainly did not see him as a 'white' man, at least in the same way that the men of English, Irish, and German ancestry were considered white."[38] Explaining mob justice against Italian Americans in terms of ethnically-motivated intolerance because of their hazy racial classification between Blacks and whites matches scholarly interpretations that have stressed the marginality of Italian immigrants and their progeny in a society dominated by people of Anglo-Saxon extraction.[39]

According to conventional scholarly wisdom, World War II marked a turning point in Italian Americans' march toward their inclusion within US society and consequent acquisition of a fully-fledged white identity as revealed by their resentment toward African Americans on the occasion of race turmoil in Detroit and New York City during the conflict.[40] Nonetheless, even prior to that event, not everybody agreed that Italians did not belong to the Caucasian race and, thereby, deserved lynching in case they broke the law. An incident that occurred during a 1934 riot in Harlem offers an illuminating case in point. After an African-American mob made a fruitless attempt at lynching an Italian-American

---

[37] John Higham, *Strangers in the Land: Patterns of American Nativism, 1860-1925* (New York: Atheneum, 1981) 169.

[38] Pulera 23.

[39] Rudolph J. Vecoli, "Italian Americans and Race: To Be or Not To Be White," *'Merica*, ed. Aldo Bove and Giuseppe Massara (Stony Brook, NY: Forum Italicum, 2006) 94-109.

[40] "Nell'inchiesta risulta che i negri causarono tumulti," *La Tribuna Italiana d'America* 30 July 1943: 1; Studs Terkel, *"The Good War": An Oral History of World War II* (New York: Pantheon, 1984) 141-42.

baker who had been accused of short-changing a woman of color, the *Amsterdam News*—a local newspaper for Black readers—commented in amazement that it was "unbelievable that Negroes should threaten to lynch a white man."[41]

Against this backdrop, one could similarly reassess the inner reasons for the lynching of Italian Americans and argue that racial hatred was often nothing more than a pretext concealing other motivations. A re-examination of some of the cases already surveyed will help demonstrate such a point.

The five Italians lynched in Tallulah in 1899 were grocers who had been held up to public scorn because they had given their Black and white employees equal pay and had granted their patrons equal status regardless of race. They had, therefore, violated the cornerstone of the southern economy after the civil war, namely the principle that African-American workers were to provide cheap labor force by receiving lower wages than their Caucasian companions. Their success in business also provoked the antagonism of their local competitors of Anglo-Saxon ancestry.[42] A report by Italy's consular agent in New Orleans confirmed that ethnic hostility did not account for the murder of the five immigrants by itself. While he did not rule out that "racial hatred" had played a role in the lynching, he listed two additional causes that, in his opinion, made a significant contribution to it. On the one hand, he pointed to the jealousy of the native merchants for the victims' economic achievements. On the other, he stressed the increasing influence of

---

[41] Qtd. in Isabel Boiko Price, "Black Response to Anti-Semitism: Negroes and Jews in New York, 1880 to World War II," Ph.D. diss., U of New Mexico, 1973, 253-54.
[42] Haas, "Guns, Goats, and Italians" 45-46, 52; Vincent J. Marsala, "Italian Settlement in North Louisiana: A Preliminary Study," 1990, 3, unpublished typescript, Noel Memorial Library, Archives and Special Collections, Louisiana State University, Shreveport.

Italian Americans in local politics as a swing constituency that—albeit very small—could decide the outcome of elections in a township where registered voters were usually fewer than 150.[43]

Indeed, if lynching was among the means to intimidate the African-American eligible voters and disenfranchise them in post-Reconstruction southern states, one can reasonably envisage that the same strategy was also used to interfere with Italian Americans' suffrage in consideration of the proximity that these minorities held in the racial hierarchy of the US public opinion.[44] After all, especially in Louisiana, populism had begun to attract individuals of Italian ancestry by the early 1890s and, therefore, the Italian-American electorate seemed to pose a threat to the southern Democratic establishment like Republican-leaning Blacks.[45] As Kate McCullough has pointed out in much broader terms, "the lynching of the Italians produces an effect similar to the lynching of African Americans: it terrorizes the community under attack and reinforces the white population's sense of power."[46]

Business and politics intertwined in the New Orleans 1891 lynching, too. It is well-known and does not need further examination here that ethnic prejudice and the Mafia

[43] Natale Piazza to Emilio Visconti Venosta, New Orleans, 26 July 1899, Records of the Ministry of Foreign Affairs, Series P – Contenzioso, box 656, Archivio Storico del Ministero degli Affari Esteri, Rome, Italy.

[44] Terence Finnegan, "Lynching and Political Power in Mississippi and South Carolina," Under the Sentence of Death: Lynching in the South, ed. W. Fitzhugh Brundage (Chapel Hill: U of North Carolina P, 1997) 189-218.

[45] John V. Baiamonte, Jr., "Immigrants in Rural America: A Study of the Italians of Tangipahoa Parish, Louisiana," Ph.D. diss., Mississippi State U, 1972, 18-24; Andrew F. Rolle, The Italian Americans: Troubled Roots (Norman: U of Oklahoma P, 1984) 82; Vincenza Scarpaci, "Walking the Color Line: Italian Immigrants in Rural Louisiana, 1880-1910," Are Italians White? How Race Is Made in America, ed. Jennifer Guglielmo and Salvatore Salerno (New York: Routledge, 2003) 74.

[46] Kate McCullough, Regions of Identity: The Construction of America in Women's Fiction, 1885-1914 (Stanford, CA: Stanford UP, 1999) 77.

stereotype heavily shaped those events.[47] For instance, it was not surprising that Senator Henry Cabot Lodge (R-MA) seized the opportunity of the incident to advocated immigration restriction in order to prevent alien criminals from entering the United States and, thereby, igniting the natives' supposedly legitimate retaliatory violence.[48]

Sufficient is to say that Hennessey was killed during a prolonged conflict between rival Sicilian crime organizations, the Matrangas and the Provenzanos. The police chief, however, was hardly an innocent victim who had been assassinated while performing his duties. He, too, was probably involved in illegal activities and perhaps so corrupt that both gangs had him on their own payroll.[49] In any case, his alleged statement "the Dagoes did it" before dying triggered off a sort of moral crusade to sweep away the allegedly Italian-dominated criminal activities from New Orleans by means of bloodshed, regardless of the court verdict.[50] Significantly enough, the most authoritative local daily—the *Times-Picayune*—praised mob justice by arguing that "desperate diseases require desperate measures."[51]

Italian Americans' presumed involvement in the underworld did contribute to the carnage. Nevertheless, the resort to lynching in the struggle to uproot the supposed presence

---

[47] Barbara Boiten, "The Hennessy Case: An Episode in Anti-Italian Nativism," *Louisiana History* 20 (1979): 261-79; Cristogianni Borsella, *On Persecution, Identity, and Activism: Aspects of the Italian-American Experience from the late 19th Century to Today* (Boston: Dante UP, 2005) 57-58; Tom Smith, *The Crescent City Lynchings: The Murder of Chief Hennessey, the New Orleans "Mafia" Trials, and the Parish Prison Mob* (Guilford, CT: Lyons P, 2007).
[48] Henry Cabot Lodge, "Lynch Law and Unrestricted Immigration," *North American Review* 152.414 (1891): 602-12.
[49] John V. Baiamone, Jr., "'Who Killa de Chief' Revisited: The Hennessey Assassination and Its Aftermath, 1890-1991," *Louisiana History* 33 (1992): 117-46.
[50] Qtd. in David M. Reimers, *Unwelcome Strangers: American Identity and the Turn against Immigration* (New York: Columbia UP, 1998) 15.
[51] *Times-Picayune*, 15 March 1891, qtd. in Andrew F. Rolle, *The Immigrant Upraised: Italian Adventurers and Colonists in an Expanding America* (Norman: U of Oklahoma P, 1968) 103.

of the Mafia from New Orleans was also exploited to intimidate Italian Americans in order to break their monopoly
over the importation of tropical fresh fruits from Central
America, to snatch the control of the city's French Market
from their hands, to curb their inroads into the lucrative
fishing and oyster trade, to force them out of longshoremen
activities in the harbor's docks, and to hamper their rise in
local politics. Italian Americans' economic success and early
stages of involvement in civic affairs had aroused the envy
and fears of numerous native residents. By the time Hennessey was assassinated, the Sicilian immigrants allegedly
operated over 3,000 fruit and other food retail outlets in
New Orleans. Moreover, the rivalry between the Matrangas
and the Provenzanos involved mainly the control of both the
waterfront and ward politics in the Sicilian settlement.[52]

It was hardly by a chance that the defendants in the
case resulting from Hennessey's murder included such a
prominent leader of the local Little Italy as Joseph Macheca.
A wealthy Sicilian businessman with large interests in the
fruit commerce as well as in the seafood industries, as early
as 1868 Macheca had also organized many of his fellow ethnics into an association—the "Innocents"—that protected
his own economic activities but also got involved into politics
and eventually came to opposed the Democratic political
machine of Mayor Joseph A. Shakspeare.[53] As author Richard Gambino has concluded, the 1891 lynching was part of
a much larger struggle that the antebellum commercial and

---

[52] Humbert S. Nelli, *The Business of Crime: Italians and Syndicate Crime in the
United States* (New York: Oxford UP, 1976) 37-38, 61-62; Baiamonte 128-29; Michael Kurtz, "Organized Crime in Louisiana History," *Louisiana History* 24 (1983):
362-64.
[53] Melinda Meek Hennessey, "Race and Violence in Reconstruction New Orleans:
The 1868 Riot," *Louisiana History* 20 (1979): 77-91. For Macheca, see also the rather anecdotal account by Thomas Hunt and Martha Macheca Sheldon, *Deep Water: Joseph P. Macheca and the Birth of the American Mafia* (Bloomington, IN: iUni-
verse, 2007).

professional establishment of Anglo-Saxon and French ancestries had orchestrated to retain its economic, political, and social power in the face of the rise of recent newcomers such as the Italians in the late nineteenth century.[54]

Actually, for example, in the aftermath of the lynching, the City Council granted the business of unloading ships to a recently established Louisiana Construction and Improvement Corporation, whose president was James D. Houston, one of the leaders of the mob that had assaulted the prison in order to lynch Hennessey's supposed murderers. In addition, the Louisiana Construction and Improvement Corporation yielded to the request of the New Orleans Longshoremen's and Screwmen's Association that only the latter's members be employed on the waterfront. Remarkably, this union barred Sicilian immigrants from their ranks.[55] By the same token, Italian Americans were kept at the margins of politics until the late Senator Huey Long's Democratic machine handpicked Conservation Commissioner Robert S. Maestri—a wealthy businessman involved in shady deals who was the son of a poultry peddler and had been the financial backbone of the party's state organization—for the position of mayor of New Orleans in 1936.[56]

The Tampa incident added a further element of labor disputes to the lynching of Italian Americans. Albano and Ficarotta were killed during a six-month walkout of roughly 10,000 cigar workers who went on strike to push their employers into recognizing the Cigar Makers International Union, discontinuing the entrepreneurs' open shop policy, and complying with a plan of equalization that aimed at pre-

[54] Gambino, *Vendetta* 130.
[55] Baiamonte 137.
[56] Roger Biles, *The South and the New Deal* (Lexington: UP of Kentucky, 2006) 132. For Maestri, see Edward F. Haas, "New Orleans on the Half-Shell: The Maestri Era, 1936-1946," *Louisiana History* 13 (1972): 283-310.

venting plant owners from cutting wage rates.[57] Although the victims were not labor activists, rumors circulated that they were professional murderers whom the strikers' committee had engaged to retaliate against Esterling because the accountant for the Bustillo Brothers and Diaz Cigar Company had been involved in hiring scabs.[58]

The city's cigar-making entrepreneurs had relied on vigilantism to quell labor controversies since the turn of the twentieth century. For instance, in order to speed up the end of a previous strike in 1901, a self-proclaimed Citizens' Committee abducted thirteen union leaders and placed them on a boat heading for Honduras after threatening them with death in case they dared return to Tampa. The following year, something similar happened to Francisco Milián, the mayor of West Tampa and a revered *lector* at the Bustillo Brothers and Diaz Cigar Company. A peculiar institution in cigar factories, the *lector* was paid by workers to read to them and was an instrument for the latter's politicization. Accused of reading inflammatory materials aiming to pit the cigar makers against the plant management and owners, with the complicity of the police Milián was kidnapped, beaten and forced to leave Tampa on a steamer on its way to Cuba. Both the union leaders and Milián eventually managed to return to Tampa but their experiences offered evidence of manufacturers' resort to violence in fighting radicalism and workers' organizations.[59]

---

[57] George E. Pozzetta, "Italians and the Tampa General Strike of 1910," *Pane e Lavoro: The Italian-American Working Class*, ed. George E. Pozzetta (Toronto: Multicultural History Society of Ontario, 1980) 29-46.

[58] "A Lynching and a Lesson," *Tampa Morning Tribune* 22 September 1910: 6; "Il linciaggio di Tampa," *Il Progresso Italo-Americano* 27 September 1910: 1.

[59] Gary Ross Mormino and George E. Pozzetta, *The Immigrant World of Ybor City: Italians and Their Latin Neighbors in Tampa, 1885-1985* (Urbana: U of Illinois P, 1987) 98, 117; Armando Mendez, *Ciutad de Cigars, West Tampa* (Tampa: Florida Historical Society, 1994) 49, 93-94.

The 1910 strike was no exception to this pattern of behavior. Plant owners recruited squads in the adjoining rural areas and exploited such gangs in order to patrol the streets, to protect the strikebreakers, to assault the union members on the picket lines, and to disrupt any other activity in support of the walkout.[60]

According to the correspondent from Tampa of *La Parola dei Socialisti*, the mouthpiece of the Socialist Party of America for Italian immigrants, it was one of those groups of vigilantes that lynched Albano and Ficarotta.[61] The purpose of their murderers was less to retaliate against the two Italians for the attempted assassination of Esterling than to threaten the dark-skinned Cuban and Italian cigarmakers who had been on strike for roughly three months and to coerce them into going back to work. Especially Albano seemed to be tailor-made for the role of the designated victim. Indeed, before turning to selling insurance, he had been a tobacco worker and a member of Local 462 of the Cigar Makers International Union.[62] He, therefore, became the unintentional spokesperson for a warning to the strikers' most pugnacious faction. A notice was pinned to Albano's belt while his corpse was still hanging from the rope. Written in black ink, it read "Beware! Others take note or go the same way. We know seven more. We are watching you. If any more citizens are molested, look out—Justice."[63]

---

[60] Robert P. Ingalls, *Urban Vigilantes in the New South: Tampa, 1882-1936* (Knoxville: U of Tennessee P, 1988) 55-115.

[61] Giovanni Vaccaro, "Due operai linciati," *La Parola dei Socialisti* 1 October 1910: 3. For *La Parola dei Socialisti*, see Annamaria Tasca, "Italians," *The Immigrant Labor Press in North America, 1840s-1970s: An Annotated Bibliography*, ed. Dirk Hoerder, 3 vols. (Westport, CT: Greenwood, 1987) 3:97.

[62] C. Pugliesi, "Una lettera dal luogo del massacro," *Il Progresso Italo-Americano* 30 September 1910: 2.

[63] "Il linciaggio di due italiani a Tampa, Fla.," *La Tribuna Italiana d'America* 1 October 1910: 1, 5.

The meaning of such a desecrating insult could be hardly misunderstood. Not even the Italian vice-consul at New Orleans, Gerolamo Moroni, failed to realize that the intimidation of the striking workers was the main purpose of Albano's and Ficarotta's lynching. Notwithstanding a conservative judgment about the walkout, in his report to the Italian ambassador in Washington about the killing of the two Sicilian immigrants, Moroni pointed out that the aim of the double hanging was "teaching an awful lesson to the strikers of the cigar factories who had passed from quiet protest to acts of violence against the manufacturers."[64] After all, the postcards made out of the photographs of Albano's and Ficarotta's hanging corpses had captions reading "labor agitators lynched during the cigar makers' strike."[65]

The labor connection of the lynching was so strong and undeniable that both commercial and radical Italian-language periodicals agreed on it. For instance, *L'Italia*—a conservative weekly published in Chicago that was "read from the Atlantic to the Pacific, from Canada to the Gulf of Mexico"—and *La Parola dei Socialisti* stated in the early aftermath of the killing that both Albano and Ficarotta were labor activists involved in the walkout.[66] So did from Milan the *Corriere della Sera*, the most authoritative daily in Italy, which even contended incorrectly that Albano and Ficarotta were "the leaders of the strike."[67]

---

[64] Gaetano Moroni to Cusani Confalonieri, 11 October 1910, qtd. in Mormino and Pozzetta 120.

[65] James Allen et al., *Without Sanctuary: Lynching Photography in America* (Santa Fe: Twin Palms, 2000) 76.

[66] "Due Italiani linciati da una folla sanguinaria," *L'Italia*, 24 September 1910: 1; "Per i linciati di Tampa," *La Parola dei Socialisti*, 15 October 1910: 3. For *L'Italia*, see Humbert S. Nelli, *Italians in Chicago, 1880-1930: A Study in Ethnic Mobility* (New York: Oxford UP, 1970) 78, 158-60 (quote 160).

[67] "Il linciaggio di due italiani strappati in un agguato alla polizia," *Corriere della Sera* 22 September 1910: 2. In this article the *Corriere della Sera* mistakenly renamed Ficarotta as "Picarotta."

A labor connection can be perceived in other lynchings of Italian Americans. In Johnston City Speranza's allegedly actual target was the victim's son-in-law, a superintendent in a local mine who had been responsible for the discharge of numerous Sicilian immigrants and had consequently become abhorrent to the latter.[68] Speranza's lynching, too, therefore, was set against the backdrop of a labor conflict. It has also been suggested that the role of Italian Americans as unionized workers and labor agitators accounted for the lynching of five immigrants who had been rounded up in connection with the murder of a saloonkeeper by the name of Abner Hixon in Walsenburg in the wake of a strike in the Colorado coal fields.[69] A local newspaper highlighted the victim's previous function as a deputy sheriff during a walk-out that had taken place a few months earlier.[70] Yet a few scholars have disagreed about such labor-related interpretation or have even denied that the killings of the five Italians could be regarded as an ethnically-motivated lynching although the events were defined as such in authoritative periodicals like the *New York Times*.[71] On the other hand, business rivalries were somehow supposedly connected to the summary execution of Angelo Marcuso, Lorenzo Saladino, and Decimo Sorcoro in Hahnville, Louisiana, in 1896,

---

[68] "Miner Lynched by Illinois Mob," *New York Times* 11 June 1915: 8.

[69] Higham 91; Vincent N. Parillo, *Strangers to These Shores: Race and Ethnic Relations in the United States* (New York: Wiley, 1985) 98-99; Richard Gambino, *Blood of My Blood: The Dilemma of the Italian Americans* (Toronto: Guernica, 2000) 118.

[70] "A Brutal Murder," *Walsenburg World* 14 March 1895: 1.

[71] Conrad Woodall, "The Italian Massacre at Walsenburg, Colorado, 1895," *Italian Ethnics: Their Languages, Literature and Lives*, ed. Dominic Candeloro, Fred L. Gardaphe, and Paolo A. Giordano (Staten Island, NY: American Italian Historical Association, 1990) 297-317, esp. 311-12; Salvetti 43-48 (an account that draws extensively upon Woodall's research and conclusion); "Cruel Work of a Colorado Mob," *New York Times* 14 March 1895: 1; "Quiet Is Restored at Walsenburg," ibid. 15 March 1895: 13.

while they were detained on charges of murder in unrelated incidents.[72]

As in the case of Arata, cries of "kill the Dago" or "hang the Dago" usually mobilized the mobs that inflicted summary justice on Italian immigrants and the latter's murder by enraged throngs often occurred against the backdrop of white supremacists' backlash not only at Blacks but also at newcomers who were not of Anglo-Saxon stock.[73] Yet one cannot conclude that all the lynchings of people from Italian background resulted only from ethnic hatred and the victims' racial inbetweenness. At least the dynamics of retribution in the cases of New Orleans and Tampa demonstrate that the racialized perception of Italian Americans in the eyes of the broader US society was sometimes a smokescreen that masked other kinds of rivalries and antagonism. The fact that the dark-skinned Italian immigrants and their children looked more similar to African Americans than to white people did contribute to the resort of lynching violence in order to murder single Italian Americans and to intimidate their ethnic communities. Nonetheless lynchings also resulted from economic, political, and labor conflicts between the local establishment and Italian Americans and exploited the latter's alleged crimes as a excuse for bloody retribution that intended to sweep away competition in different spheres of public life.

---

[72] Anthony V. Margavio and Jerome J. Salomone, *Bread and Respect: The Italians of Louisiana* (Gretna, LA: Pelican, 2002) 200-202.

[73] Janet E. Worrall, "Adjustment and Integration: The Italian Experience in Colorado," *New Explorations in Italian-American Studies*, ed. Richard N. Juliani and Sandra P. Juliani (Staten Island, NY: American Italian Historical Association, 1994) 205-6; Noel 61; Bill Ong Hing, *Defining America through Immigration Policy* (Philadelphia: Temple UP, 2004) 57. For a rather popularizing account of Arata's lynching, see also Randy Perkins, "The Lynching of Danny Arata," *True West* 35.7 (1988): 37-39.

In Brooklyn, They Love the Guv'ner?
Italian Americans for George Wallace

MARIA C. LIZZI
University at Albany, SUNY

The air outside Madison Square Garden on the evening of October 24, 1968 was cool and crisp; inside, however, it was as hot as Alabama in mid-July. A crowd of 20,000 stood shoulder to shoulder, waiting for their hero of the evening, a little bantam-weight fighter named George Corley Wallace, to take to the ring. When Wallace stepped to center stage, a roar of joy penetrated the sweltering air. The crowd watched with pleasure as Wallace dodged the insults aimed at him by the clearly out-manned opposition, weaved from right to left in his rhetoric, and finally delivered his knockout blow:

> They've looked down their noses at the average man on the street too long. They've looked down at the bus driver, the truck driver, the beautician, the fireman, the policeman, and the steelworker, the plumber, and the communication worker and the oil worker and the little businessman and they say, 'We've gotta write a guideline. We've gotta tell you when to get up in the mornin'. We've gotta tell you when to go to bed at night.' And we gonna tell both national parties the average man on the street in Tennessee and Alabama and New York don't need anybody to write him a guideline.[1]

---

[1] "Stand Up for America: The 1968 Campaign Speech," in Lloyd Rohler's *George Wallace: Conservative Populist* (Westport, CT: Praeger, 2004) 153.

79

The New York crowd roared with delight, stamping their feet and clapping their hands to signal support. Leaving the arena that night, an Italian-American cabdriver who had attended the rally told a *New York Times* reporter, "He sounds like us."[2]

Perhaps Wallace did sound like working-class Italian Americans in the urban North. The George Corley Wallace with whom this cabdriver resonated in 1968 had left behind much of his blatantly racist rhetoric. He had made a calculated move away from his 1963 vow of "Segregation today, segregation tomorrow, segregation forever" and step back from the schoolhouse door, where he had once stood in defiance of federal government's orders to integrate the University of Alabama. Just as he had won the governorship of Alabama by solidifying his image as an arch-defender of segregation and State's Rights, he now sought to win enough votes to throw the election to the House of Representatives by casting himself as a Populist champion of those working-class Americans who felt abused and misused by an out-of-touch Federal government, upper-class intellectuals, and the privileged media.

Before his ill-advised selection of Curtis "Bomb Them Back to the Stone Age" LeMay as his running mate, Wallace was running one of the most successful third-party candidacies in United States' political history.[3] While political pundits viewed Wallace's success with white voters in the Deep South as a given, his success in Northern states such as New York, New Jersey, and Pennsylvania, shocked many.[4] There, Wallace had found support among many working-

---

[2] "Wallace Backers Say Why They Are," *New York Times*, October 25, 1968.

[3] George Wallace: Settin' the Woods on Fire, Daniel McCabe and Paul Steklar (PBS: American Experience, 2006).

[4] Edward Schneier, "The Scar of Wallace," *The Nation*, November 4, 1968, 454-457.

class white ethnic voters, including Italian Americans—the same people he had once referred to as "lesser breeds."[5] In light of this, Wallace support in areas such as the white ethnic outer-boroughs of New York City left political pundits of all stripes scratching their heads and searching for explanations.

Not surprisingly, the explanation on which they settled was literally black and white. Wallace could not be easily separated from his pro-segregationist stance, a fact that led many to dismiss his supporters as nothing more than racist bigots who used the coded language of class conflict to hide their true intentions. Historians and sociologists have subsequently accepted contemporary analysts' too obvious conclusion, and have continued to dismiss both the issues raised by Wallace's presidential campaigns and those who supported him.

It would be unrealistic not to give some credence to their findings that race played a role in a vote for Wallace. For example, over twenty percent of Italian Americans in race riot-ravaged Newark's North Ward voted for Wallace, while he garnered only nine to eleven percent of the vote in working-class Italian-American neighborhoods in Brooklyn and Queens. Undoubtedly, as this admittedly limited statistical evidence indicates, racial fears or concerns played some role in Italian Americans' support for George Wallace; those faced with tangible racial "threats" were more likely to cast their vote for Wallace. However, as Wallace's speech at Madison Square Garden suggests, those fears were tied to much larger issues that went far beyond racial antipathy or hatred.

While Newark's Italian Americans may have voted for Wallace based on their racial fears, two surveys taken during

---

[5] Robert Sherrill, *Gothic Politics in the Deep South* (New York: Grossman, 1968) 258.

the 1968 election year show that New York's Italian Americans may have held a different view of race relations. One survey on the advancement of African-American civil rights showed that sixty-two percent of New York's Italian Americans believed that the cause was moving "too fast."[6] This result seems to support the contention that Italian Americans held some racists views. However, another survey of New Yorkers conducted that same year revealed that only two percent of white, Roman Catholic so-called "backlash" voters would feel "uncomfortable if a 'black sat next to them at a lunch counter.'" Less than five percent of these New Yorkers had problems with other types of causal inter-racial contact, compared to more than double the number nationally.[7] These survey results suggest that Italian-American racism did exist in New York, yet it differed from that of other Wallace supporters. New York's white ethnics believed that segregation was not acceptable, but neither was seemingly rapid social upheaval. What they feared most was not African American advancement or even social change, but social turmoil that would threaten their own social, economic, and racial status.

In 1968, Italian Americans, like many other working-class white ethnics across the country, had woken up to discover that, as columnist Pete Hamill wrote, that "they hadn't made it after all."[8] In New York City, Italian Americans became the representatives of the increasingly disgruntled "middle American," who felt pressed, economically and socially, from above and below. They were tired of being told by both Republicans and Democrats that they were living the "American

[6] Joshua M. Zeitz, *White Ethnic New York: Jews, Catholics, and the Shaping of PostWar Politics* (Chapel Hill: U North Carolina P, 2007) 147.
[7] Joshua M. Zeitz, *White Ethnic New York*, 168.
[8] Pete Hamill's "The Revolt of the White Lower Middle Class" (*New York Magazine*, April 14, 1969.

Dream" and should, therefore, bear the brunt of social re-
forms, cast down upon them by a distant government. They
were, as Wallace stated in his Madison Square Garden
speech, tired of being looked down upon for their lifestyle
and work, while being simultaneously told they were too
well-off to qualify for many of the government's new social
programs. An Italian-American gas station owner in Long
Island City, Queens, who had immigrated to the United
States in 1956, summed up the feelings of many of his fellow white ethnics, when he asked: "I work like a horse and I
gotta pay taxes so those people can get welfare? I go home
every night at 10 o'clock and I gotta pay for those people?"[9]
Above all, Wallace supporters were tired of the existing political system, which had, apparently, left them without a
voice.

Wallace provided that voice. Ever the mimetic orator, he
reflected back to voters their fears and concerns in plain
language, the language of New York, spoken with an Alabama accent. However plain his language was, it was far
from straight-forward. Politicians and pundits on both the
left and right termed Wallace's call for a restoration of "law
and order" racially coded language. Although polar political
opposites, Richard Nixon and Robert Kennedy, employed
the same phrase, when Wallace referred to a return to "law
and order," non-supporters heard a pledge to maintain Bull
Connor's Alabama-style opposition to Civil Rights. Although
"law and order" contained an element of racialized fear, defining it simply as coded racist rhetoric, as many contemporary pundits did, detracted from the term's broader meaning. As American political historian Gary Wills wrote that

---

[9] "Humphrey is Gaining in Queens," *New York Times,* October 31, 1968.

The desire for 'law and order' is nothing so simple as a code word for racism; it is a cry, as things break up for stability, for stopping history mid-dissolution. Hammer the structure back together; anchor it down; bring nails and bolts and clamps to keep it from collapsing. There is a slide of things—queasy seasickness.[10]

For the Italian Americans of New York who clung to their neighborhoods, lawlessness seemed pervasive. In addition to the streets where they lived, they found a breakdown of "law and order" in the public schools their children attended, the colleges to which they fought to gain admission, and the political system in which they remained fringe members. Italian-American neighborhoods experienced not only violence, but blockbusting and redlining while the political elite stood by. By a variety of means, Italian Americans sought to insulate their communities from the effects of so-called hippie demonstrations, open sexuality on college campus, political assassinations, and the riots of the long, hot summers that occurred in their backyards, all the while their sons were being drafted into a losing war. Millions of Americans shared an abstract fear of the breakdown of social order, but urban Italian Americans experienced it as a reality.[11] In George Wallace, they found a politician who not only acknowledged their fears, but also made them visible and important.

Perhaps the answer to the question of why Italian Americans supported Wallace lies not in their perception of other races, but in how they perceived themselves and their political power. As James Lewis Canfield's study of Wallace cam-

[10] Gary Wills, *Nixon Agonistes: The Crisis of the Self-Made Man* (Boston: Houghton Mifflin, 1970) 51-52.
[11] Stephen Lesher, *George Wallace: American Populist* (Reading: Addison-Wesley, 1994) 422.

paign workers reveals, many staffers were attracted to the Wallace campaign because they believed that, through Wallace more than any other candidate, they could directly "influence governmental policy."[12] Throughout his campaign, Wallace, the born-again populist, made appeals to those Americans who felt they were powerless in the wake of big government and social change. The little governor and former bantam-weight boxer who had taken on the federal government now declared himself ready to "Stand Up for America." Wallace appeared prepared not only to listen to disaffected voters, but also fight for them, physically, if necessary.

More than anything, the white working class, both urban and rural, sounded afraid, and it was on fear that Wallace based his campaign. They feared the loss of "law and order" and apparent social stability perhaps because they held on so tightly to an idealized version of the American past.[13] These were the Americans who, as Hamill described them, longed for a return to an orderly and "fair" America, where hard work and determination defined who succeeded and who did not. But, above all else, as Hamill wrote,

> They wanted to return to a time in America when you lived in the same house all of your life and knew everybody you would ever care to know on the street where you were born.... A lot of people attracted to George Wallace are just people who think America has passed them by, leaving them confused and screwed-up and unhappy.[14]

[12] James Lewis Canfield, *A Case of Third Part Activism: The George Wallace Campaign Worker and the American Independent Party* (New York: UP of America, 1984) 41.

[13] For more on white working-class nostalgia for an idealized American past, see "The Troubled American" (*Newsweek*, October 6, 1969), Peter Schrag's "The Forgotten American" (*Harper's Magazine*, Agust 1969), and Pete Hamill's "The Revolt of the White Lower Middle Class" (*New York Magazine*, April 14, 1969).

[14] Pete Hamill, "Wallace," *Ramparts* (1968), 47.

For the Italian Americans of New York City, in particular, where forty percent of them continued to live in the same neighborhoods their parents had, Hamill described more than a nostalgic past; for them, this way of life was still very much a reality and they clung to it with ferocity.[15] Wallace, in his direct appeals to Americans' sense of cultural nostalgia, addressed not only their fears, but their hopes as well. He carefully orchestrated his campaign rallies to remind Americans of the "other" America; even the country music that was played reminded audiences of "families that loved and sacrificed for each other, communities that were safe, and homesteads where the old died among their children with dignity and respect."[16] Just as strongly as he had defended the "Southern way of life" in his 1963 inaugural speech, in 1968, Wallace defended a vanishing "American" way of life. However, rather than representing a "Southernization" of American values and culture, as historian Dan Carter contends in *The Politics of Rage: George Wallace, The Origins of the New Conservatism, and the Transformation of American Politics*, what the 1968 campaign did was normalize those values and the culture that white ethnics, especially Italian Americans, still lived. Instead of making specific appeals to individual ethnic groups, like the Italian Americans, Wallace instead appealed to them as the true representatives of what it meant to be a white American.

Republican Richard Nixon adopted Wallace's themes of "law and order" and cultural nostalgia. The Wallace and the Nixon campaigns differed not so much in what was said, but in who was saying it and how they said it. "Nixon may

---

[15]Levy and Kramer, 165.

[16] Dan T. Carter, *The Politics of Rage: George Wallace, The Origins of the New Conservatism, and the Transformation of American Politics* (New York: Simon & Schuster, 1995) 315.

say it," opined one Wallacite, "but Wallace means it."[17] As Canfield demonstrates in his case study of volunteers for Wallace's American Independent Party, around twenty percent of the campaign workers had been attracted to the party by the governor's persona.[18] This figure appears questionably low when it is remembered that, in 1972, when Wallace chose to run as a Democrat, the American Independent Party collapsed. Surely, "Wallace—the man," rather than any specific platform, the general direction of the country, or strong belief in the viability of third parties, was what drew people to vote for Wallace. By the same token, people also voted against the Wallace persona, preferring to support Nixon's presentation of eerily similar policies.

Wallace had many characteristics that made him a natural politician. In addition to his ability to zero in on those issues that had an immediate, visceral appeal, Wallace also had a quick wit and the ability express his emotions, including fear, without coming across as weak. While Humphrey ignored realities and claiming that his campaign represented the way politics ought to be in America, "the politics of happiness, the politics of purpose and the politics of joy," and Nixon tried to live down his literally shady appearance in 1960s televised debate against John F. Kennedy, Wallace came across as a "man's man," unafraid to be disliked and willing to back up his words with physical force. Wallace's masculine image appealed primarily to men, who made up the overwhelming majority of his supporters.[19]

Wallace's dealings with the press illustrate his level of comfort with the image he projected and, in fact, cultivated. When the national media accurately demonized him as a

---

[17] "Why They Want Him," *Time*, October 18, 1968, 2.
[18] James Lewis Canfield, *A Case of Third Party Activism*, 41.
[19]Jody Carlson, *George C. Wallace and the Politics of Powerlessness* (New Brunswick, NJ: Transaction Books, 1981) 88.

racist, Wallace smiled as he told crowds: "I guess you folks are sorta disappointed that I don't have horns after all you have read about me in the press."[20] During the campaign's swing through Pennsylvania, newsmen reported that a state senator asserted that Wallace was "a menace" to himself, Alabama, both political parties, and the entire United States; the senator concluded that "if (Wallace) bit himself, he'd die of blood poisoning." The next day, Wallace introduced reporters to his bodyguards, saying, "I have them here to keep me from biting myself."[21] Half man or half human, George Wallace was never dull and never appeared to cow-tow to the media.

Wallace was an expressive politician, something that Richard Nixon was not. He was, as Dan Carter wrote, "the perfect mimetic orator, probing his audiences' deepest fears and passions and articulating those emotions in a language and style they could understand."[22] Nixon, on the other hand, who once said of himself, "My strong point is not rhetoric, it isn't showmanship, it isn't big promises—those things that create the glamour and the excitement that people call charisma and warmth,"[23] was an instrumental politician. He focused on solving the causes of, rather than expressing, the rage of the people. But the men who supported Wallace wanted their anger heard and made tangible; they were not content to be recognized as the "silent majority." In addition, they wanted their candidate to sound like them. Wallace's Alabama accent may not have had much in common with typical Brooklynese, but Lureen

---

[20] Stephan Lesher, *George Wallace,* 277.
[21] Stephen Lesher, *George Wallace,* 401.
[22] Dan T. Carter, *The Politics of Rage,* 246.
[23] For a comprehensive analysis of differences between the political styles of Wallace, Nixon, and Humphrey, see Theodore H. White's *The Making of the President 1968* (New York: Atheneum, 1989).

Wallace correctly identified her husband's appeal to voters throughout the country: "When he's on 'Meet the Press,' they can sit and listen to George and think, 'That's what I would say if I were up there.'"[24] Presumably that was the thought in the minds of the thousands of locals who flocked to Madison Square Garden to hear Wallace speak.

Wallace, the pugnacious ex-boxer, had no qualms sparring verbally, or, by implication, physically, with his opponents, whereas Nixon left that dirty work to his own personal Southern ethnic, Spiro Agnew. Dozens of speech writers insured that Agnew was equipped with witty rejoinders and alliterative phrasing; Wallace relied on his own combination of wit, timing, and fearlessness, which made his idiomatic speech more pronounced. He dismissed intellectuals because they "couldn't park their bicycles straight." He addressed the long haired-hecklers that appeared at his rallies as "sweetie," regardless of their gender, and offered to autograph their sandals.[25] He declared unabashedly that "a good crease in the skull would stop some of this lawlessness."[26] He promised that, if elected president, "and a group of anarchists lay down in front of my automobile, it's gonna be the last one they ever gonna want to lay down in front of!"[27] Wallace gave as good as he got, was not afraid to use the threat of physical force, and articulated, in simple direct terms, the anger of his supporters. When he did employ coded racist language, namely in his discussions of "law and order," school busing and the protection of property rights, supporters argued that he was not referring to African Americans when he spoke in terms of "us" versus "them" because, if George wanted to say something, he came right

[24] Jody Carlson, *George C. Wallace and the Politics of Powerlessness*, 6.
[25] "Alabamian Given Lengthy Ovation," *New York Times*, October 25, 1968.
[26] Jack House, *George Wallace Tells It Like It Is* (Selma: Dalla Publishing, 1969) 68.
[27] Jody Carlson, *George C. Wallace and the Politics of Powerlessness*, 129.

out and said it. Only the "big men of society," stated Michael Novak, spoke to them "in code."[28]

Yet, "us" versus "them" was not a clear-cut, black and white issue. The "them" was far bigger than African Americans alone. More than anything, a vote for Wallace, concluded sociologist Jody Carlson, was a vote against a sense of "powerlessness," rather than an overtly racist stance.[29] All too often, Carlson writes, this sense of powerlessness did manifested itself as a fear of the rapidity of integration, a fear that often appeared inseparable from what Dan Carter calls a "casual and frightening racism."[30] But inherent racism did not motivate Italian Americans to support Wallace; their sense of powerlessness did.

According to political scientist Patrick J. Gallo, Italian Americans may have had more reason to feel powerless than a cursory examination may suggest. In his 1974 book, *Ethnic Alienation: The Italian American Case*, Gallo examines the role that Italian Americans voters played in three generations of American politics. Gallo concludes that Italian Americans, despite having several markers of ascribed status (a position that an individual inherits at birth), lagged behind many other groups in the hallmarks of achieved status (a position that is earned or accomplished). Gallo's findings illustrate that because Italian Americans had not achieved the same levels of education, movement into white-collar occupations, and, therefore, higher income levels as other groups, they felt a sense of alienation from the broader American political scene. Consequently, Italian-American voters often fell back on identity politics and would have been naturally attracted to a third-party candidate who

---

28 Michael Novak, "Politicizing the Lower-Middle," *Commonweal* (June 6, 1969): 343.
29 Jody Carlson, *George C. Wallace and the Politics of Powerlessness*, 124.
30 Dan T. Carter, *The Politics of Rage*, 375.

made direct appeals to their feelings of alienation. In his speeches, George Wallace validated their status anxiety and provided them with a way to overcome it. For Italian-American men who felt marginalized or abused by the government, as many in New York did, a vote for Wallace was a vote to improve their achieved status.

While achieved status can be controlled and modified, an individual's ascribed status should, in theory, be unchangeable. Achieved status is protected consciously, but the protection of ascribed status happens on a subconscious level. Traditionally, sociologists treated both gender identity and race as part of an individual's ascribed status, meaning they were fixed characteristics, the definition of which never varied.[31] When Gallo and Carlson examined the 1968 election, in 1974 and 1981, respectively, they treated both masculinity and whiteness as immutable characteristics and, therefore, did not factor them into their analyses of alienation and powerlessness. However, in subsequent decades, the fields of masculinity and whiteness studies have emerged, allowing historians to complicate their analysis of voting behavior.

In 1968, what did it mean to be a man? Wallace and his supporters viewed his opponents as nothing more than "goddamned, mealy mouthed sissy britches"; his opponents, on the other hand, dismissed Wallace and his supporters as hyper-masculine, "little men" who needed to continually prove their worth.[32] Wallace certainly projected a certain type of working class, Southern white masculinity, one that relied heavily on what Carlson called a show of "bravado." Bravado, she writes, was the Southerner's "way of dealing

---

[31] James M. Henslin, *Essentials of Sociology* (New York, 2006) 82.
[32] Dan T. Carter, *From George Wallace to Newt Gingrich: Race in the Conservative Counterrevolution, 1963-1994* (Baton Rouge: Louisiana State UP, 1996) 48.

with life that allows (him) to hide feelings of pain and inadequacy." Because he had less education and income than the larger white society, "the southerner was obligated to outdistance the northerner through devious means: by manipulating thought and logic and by projecting the threat of violence." [33] Italian Americans could relate to this sense of "bravado." As sociologist Richard Gambino wrote in *Blood of My Blood: The Dilemma of the Italian Americans,* the ever-present obligation for Italian-American men was "*agire da maschio*, to act in a manly fashion." For Italian-American men, the ideal manliness involved "protecting one's blood and advancing family, security, and power. One did this not by being noble, but by being clever, foxy, shrewd."[34]

However, by the late 1960s, both rural Southern white men and urban Northern Italian-American men were experiencing a crisis of masculinity, similar to the one that had swept over middle class, suburban WASPs in the previous decade.[35] By remaining on their old rural homesteads or in their urban ethnic enclaves, and retaining their working-class status, both groups had maintained their traditional sense of masculinity much longer than those who migrated to the suburbs and traded in blue-collar manual labor for the ubiquitous grey flannel suits of corporate culture. As the hallmarks of working-class white American culture shifted or disappeared entirely, so too did men's grasp on "traditional" masculinities, leaving them with a subconscious anxiety about their supposedly ascribed status. In

---

[33] Jody Carlson, *George C. Wallace and the Politics of Powerlessness*, 1.

[34] Richard Gambino, *Blood of My Blood: The Dilemma of the Italian-Americans* (Garden City, NY: Anchor Books, 1974) 121-122. For more on Italian American masculinities, see Fred Gardaphe's *From Wiseguys to Wise Men: The Gangster and Italian American Masculinities* (New York: Routledge, 2006).

[35] For comprehensive treatments of white masculinities in the 1950s, see KA Cuordileone's *Manhood and American Political Culture in the Cold War* (New York, 2005) and Michael Kimmel's *Manhood in America* (New York: Oxford UP, 2005).

Wallace, they found a walking, talking stereotype of traditional masculinity and their bond with their candidate quickly became what Dan Carter called, "the ethos of the locker room, of a man's world free from the constraints of women and their weaknesses."[36] A vote for Wallace was a vote against masculine anxiety and a gendered sense of powerlessness.

A vote for Wallace was also a way for Italian Americans to solidify their racial identity, another element that should have been part of their fixed ascribed status. Historians and sociologists, such as David Roediger, Thomas Guglielmo, and Matthew Frye Jacobson, have demonstrated that whiteness was something that immigrants from Southern and Eastern Europe had to achieve, rather than a characteristic that was inherent to their identity. While he may have once called Italian Americans and their ethnic counterparts "lesser breeds," in his 1964 and 1968 campaigns, Wallace proclaimed their full whiteness. As Carter writes, in his national campaigns, "[Wallace] never treated ethnic Americans of eastern and southern European ancestry with contempt; he embraced them as potential allies who shared his fear of blacks as well as his cultural conservatism."[37] Wallace's official biographer, journalist Steven Lesher, writes that Wallace instinctively understood that "ethnic groups were powerfully attracted to the message that the civil rights bill might adversely affect their jobs, their property values, the makeup of their neighborhoods, and children's school sites."[38]

On some level, Wallace also understood that these ethnics needed to be brought into the fold of whiteness. He accomplished this with campaign stunts and appearances de-

---

[36] Dan T. Carter, *From George Wallace to Newt Gingrich*, 27.
[37] Dan T. Carter, *The Politics of Rage*, 297.
[38] Stephen Lesher, *George Wallace*, 282.

signed to directly connect ethnic Americans to unquestionably white Americans. For example, as part of his campaign rallies, Wallace brought out what reporters disparagingly referred to as his "ethnic row" or "U.N. Squad" of Alabamian supporters of Italian, Polish, Greek, and Jewish descent.[39] In the South, these ethnics, regardless of their religion, had, often after prolonged discrimination and harassment, been adopted into the racial hierarchy as honorary whites and they voted as such.[40] Wallace could only hope that Northerners of questionable whiteness would recognize a chance to solidify their whiteness by voting for the unabashed icon of white power. To insure that they did, Wallace embraced what Matthew Frye Jacobson would later refer to as the central myth of "Ellis Island whiteness"[41]: "Other ethnic groups had suffered worse deprivation (than African Americans), Wallace argued, and they had responded by buckling down, going to work, and raising themselves by their own bootstraps."[42] This belief would become the central tenant of both the "white backlash" and the New Ethnic movement. By demonstrating that he considered them white, Wallace, the defender of whiteness, helped Italian Americas who still questioned their racial status gain a sense of identity and of belonging.

Any historian or sociologist who attempts to determine why voters supported George C. Wallace finds the words "segregation today, segregation tomorrow, segregation forever" to be inescapable. One must simultaneously acknowledge and condemn racist attitudes, while trying to explain

---

[39] Stephen Lesher, *George Wallace*, 305.
[40] For more on the assimilation and voting patterns of Roman Catholics in the South, see Andrew S. Moore, *The South's Tolerable Alien: Roman Catholics in Alabama and Georgia, 1945-1970* (Baton Rouge: Louisiana State UP, 2007).
[41] Matthew Frye Jacobson, *Roots Too: White Ethnic Revival in Post-Civil Rights America* (Cambridge, MA: Harvard UP, 2006).
[42] Dan T. Carter, *The Politics of Rage*, 304.

them without justifications. One must also avoid making the sort of judgments that Louise Kapp Howe encountered when discussing the collection of essays, *The White Majority: Between Poverty and Affluence,* which she edited. Howe writes that

> In discussing this book with a number of people—intellectuals of genuine compassion who would be the first to avoid any easy generalization about blacks or youth—I found many telling me the same thing about the average American: He's simply a boor and a bigot, a racist and a fascist. Later of course came the new view from the Potomac: He's the forgotten American, the silent member of the silent majority, the common man. I'm not sure which of these two attitudes is more offensive: the open contempt of the first or the condescension of the second. Both would seem to make understanding impossible in any case.[43]

The truth lies somewhere in-between contempt and condescension. Only by striving to reach that elusive middleground can we begin to understand why Italian Americans supported George Wallace. Evidence suggests that they may have been racist on some level. However, the evidence also suggests that, for many, fears and anxieties of which they may not have even been aware played as large a role, if not larger, than the very tangible fears they experienced on a daily basis. Their fear does not excuse their racism, but it helps us understand the appeal of a man like George Corley Wallace.

---

[43] Louise Kapp Howe, *The White Majority: Between Poverty and Affluence* (New York: Random House, 1970) 6.

Saint Expedito's Role in the Italian American
Community of Independence, Louisiana

KAREN WILLIAMS
Louisiana State University

As the supplicants of Our Lady of Guadalupe Church in New Orleans eagerly opened the package containing the new statue that was to grace the sacristy, a beautiful image of Our Lady, they were surprised to note that a second package of similar size had come to the same address. Puzzled, they read the bold letters EXPEDITE printed clearly on the outside. Opening the wrappings, they found a Roman soldier in resolute pose, both helmet- and sword-less, holding a palm branch in his left hand and raising high in his right hand a cross stating "hodie" (translated "today"). Quickly—the saint's name allowed no hesitation—the soldier's image was ensconced in the right hand corner, near the church's entrance. In New Orleans, the saint's popularity rose quickly, a patron for those needing help right away; concerns both sublime and ridiculous fell under Expedite's providence. Those praying for the end of warfare, those seeking a speedy redress in legal and personal disputes, those seeking immediate employment, those striving to break habits of procrastination—all wondered how they had done without St. Expedite.

This may be an interesting anecdote, but its authenticity is far from certain, although many New Orleanians who believe in Expedite's power claim it to be true. In looking for St. Expedite's origins, one finds a rich morass of history and culture. New Orleans claims the saint as its own—both

Catholic and voodoo followers—and remains unperturbed by its possible nascence in New Orleans. However, it is definitely not true that New Orleans has the only statue in the world as some sources claim or even the only statue in America. In fact, a number of churches in the United States as well as in Spain, France, Italy, Germany, and other countries contain the noted foot soldier, often titled Expedito; and opinion is varied as far as the authenticity of the saint.[1] In Louisiana studies Saint Expedite is an important figure that illuminates how a particular culture may claim a saint for its own. In New Orleans, St. Expedite's unofficial and questionable status came to be a part of its appeal as voodoo embraced the figure. In contrast, the Italian community in rural southeastern Louisiana celebrated St. Expedito with public demonstrations and feasting.

My first interaction with the saint, however, was in New Orleans at Our Lady of Guadalupe on Rampart Street, the oldest church building in the city, whose façade was completed in 1827. A burial chapel during yellow fever epidemics, Our Lady of Guadalupe was closed several times after yellow fever declined in the 1850s. In 1918 the Oblates of Mary Immaculate, an order of men dedicated to preaching to the poor, were invited to administer the mortuary chapel. After 1918, an interesting gallery of saints was installed, including St. Expedite, St. Michael, St. Raymond, and St. Anthony. St. Jude—the saint of the last resort—gathered much attention with only a small statue in a side niche. In 1995 a 17-foot image of the saint, the largest in the world,

---

[1] This story is a composite of the various tales about St. Expedito in New Orleans; note that the tales put the arrival of the statue some time in a distant past, but the statue was brought to its present resting place in Our Lady of Guadalupe in the 1920s. See "History of our Church." Our Lady of Guadalupe, New Orleans. <http://www.judeshrine.com/hist.htm> (accessed July 28, 2011).

was placed in the chapel's rose garden.[2] Our Lady of Guadalupe also hosts an outdoor grotto dedicated to Mary Immaculate in which hundreds of bricks state "thank you" for answered prayers. And one cannot leave the church proper without facing two compelling figures. St. Michael rises on the right, with his spear piercing a fallen Satan. On the left, Expedite stands firm, palm branch in hand, ordering the immediate end of strife.

As one leaves our Lady of Guadalupe, he or she may walk behind the church, across the street to St. Louis Cemetery #1, reportedly the final resting place of Voodoo Queen Marie Laveau. Accustomed to making a lingering impression, Expedite managed to work his way into Laveau's hybrid religion, which incorporated the important trappings of Roman Catholicism—statues of saints, prayers, incense, and holy water—into voodoo, making New Orleans Catholicism itself akin to certain African religious practices. For example, both African deities and voodoo spirits transform into Catholic saints, and in rare instances an opportune spirit will manifest itself for the first time.[3] Rather than a sinister Satan, Alegba appears. Worshiped at the opening of the voodoo dance, Alegba is the guardian of the entrance way.[4] As gatekeeper, Alegba is also identified with St. Peter.[5] Logically, Damballa, the dreaded serpent god, becomes none other than St. Patrick in this melding of African and European traditions.[6] St. Expedite himself is associated with Mercury, the messenger god of the Romans and with the "Af-

[2] "Super Naturally New Orleans." (pamphlet, Our Lady of Guadalupe Chapel, International Shrine of St. Jude, New Orleans, Louisiana).

[3] Karen Luanne Williams, *Images of Uneasy Hybrids: Carnival and New Orleans.* Unpublished Diss. (Emory U: UMI, 1992) 49.

[4] Melville J. Herskovits, *Life in a Haitian Valley* (New York: Octagon Books, 1964) 180.

[5] Jim Haskins, *Voodoo & Hoodoo* (New York: Stein and Day, 1978) 52.

[6] Herskovits, 315.

rican and Afro-Caribbean entities Elegua, Legba, Baron Samedi, Bonsu," which are messengers and tricksters.[7] St. Expedite, as you might guess, became a revered voodoo saint who, in keeping with voodoo custom—one must feed the gods—asked to be given pound cake for granting favors. A New Orleans tradition claims Sara Lee the dessert most preferred.

My questions at the church and its adjacent gift shop went largely unanswered. The woman working at the gift shop claimed to know nothing of St. Expedite, although prayer cards, small statues, and metals all bore the image of the saint, and offered more information about St. Jude, to whom the shrine is officially dedicated. She not only refused to verify St. Expedite's authenticity but declined to speak about the saint at all.

My Louisiana quest for the saint seemed to be at a dead end. However, driving on the back roads one day near the quiet town of Independence, Louisiana, I came upon a small chapel marked by the title St. Expedito. Independence is home to a significant population of Italian descent, whose ancestors made their way to the area's fertile strawberry fields after first sojourning in the port city of New Orleans. Researcher Harry Becnel, Jr. explains that between 1880 and 1920 many southern Italians and Sicilians left Italy because of unrest and poverty and settled in south Louisiana. Plantation owners were looking for labor after the Civil War, and the immigrants found work harvesting and refining sugar as well as jobs in labor and construction in New Orleans. Then, after saving their money, large numbers of the immigrants moved to Tangipahoa Parish to buy truck farms and work in the burgeoning strawberry industry. By 1920, 10 per cent of the population of Tangipahoa Parish (1805

---

[7] "Saint Expedite," <http://www.luckymojo.com> (accessed August 1, 2005).

inhabitants) was of Italian or Sicilian heritage. As I surveyed the chapel, I wondered if this Expedito could be the same figure. Unable to enter the locked door, I carefully pushed ajar a heavy window and peered into the quaint chapel. Near the altar, Expedito stands tall, crow underfoot and cross in hand, with all the standard features. A young Roman centurion, as mentioned earlier, has taken off his helmet and sword and instead holds aloft the cross stating "Hodie," today, in Latin. One recurrent interpretation is that Expedito wanted an immediate end to war, thus helmet and sword are laid aside, replaced by the palm branch. The figure appears stoic, calm and immobile; but his stance is belied by a second banner emblazoned with "Cras, Cras," emanating from the throat of a crow being stomped under the saint's foot. Why must the otherwise peaceable saint torment this prostate crow? Here Expedito shows his love of wordplay beyond his apt appellation. In Latin and Sicilian, the crow says "cras, cras" which means tomorrow; thus the crow is always croaking about the future. Stomping the crow, Expedite destroys the tendency to procrastinate.[8]

There was no mistaking this figure—so remarkably like his New Orleans' brother. Perhaps I would find a willing supplicant here in the largely Catholic community, especially since the whole chapel was proudly marked as St. Expedito's. Although the pavilion beside the building seemed somewhat in disrepair, the chapel remained intact, my limited view inside yielding a neat, well organized room. I drove to the main Catholic Church office in Independence to see if I could get any information. An elderly man stopped me before I entered, sensing I needed help, and told me the name

---

[8] Harry Becnel, "Customs, Traditions, and Folklore of a Rural, southern Italian-American Community." *Louisiana's Living Traditions*. Louisiana Division of the Arts, 1999. <http://www.louisianafolklife.org> (accessed July 28, 2011).

of the family who maintained the chapel—and little else. The church office had no more information for me about the chapel but did inform me that a young man had just chosen (this was 2005) St. Expedito as his patron saint, a common practice in Louisiana Catholicism where a person being confirmed could choose a saint to emulate or use as a mediator in personal devotion.

Driving back toward the chapel, I noticed a well-kept wood frame house across the street. I knocked on the door, to be greeted by Mrs. Carmella Marciano, a vibrant woman in her seventies, who happily acknowledged my interest in St. Expedito. Mrs. Marciano, whose father built the chapel in the late 1940s because of St. Expedito's help in a personal circumstance, told me of the celebrations that used to be held every second Sunday in June in honor of the saint.[9] Food, beer, and bands converged with friends to offer homage. In the 50s and 60s the pavilion was packed with people eating and drinking. Differing from New Orleans's custom of feeding the saint, the Italians made sure to feast with him, not limiting the food to one simple cake to leave for the saint's benefit, but feasting on hotdogs garnished with a local specialty, Hi Ho barbeque sauce, made in the community, along with soft drinks and beer, while the festivities included dancing and music by local bands like the Rhythm Kings, who played popular jazz numbers or current rock and roll. By the late 1980's, as membership in the St. Expedito society declined, celebrating the feast day eventually fell by the way, although the chapel was used for special occasions or for special intercessions. The family told me, however, that the larger society of St. Joseph is still quite active and a number of families as well as the church itself continue the St. Joseph Altar celebrations replete with homemade

---

[9] Carmella Marciano, personal interview with the author. August 20, 2005.

bread, cookies, and meatless specialties for the March 19 Lenten festival.

But while the St. Expedito society has dwindled, the chapel remains intact to this day, allowing curious visitors to enter. On October 17, 2009 Mrs. Marciano and family members were gracious enough to open the chapel, which her grandson, Johnny Lee, had recently taken possession of The Expedito statue is in excellent condition as well as other artifacts I will describe later. Mrs. Rosemary Lee talked of the St. Expedito Society, of which she was secretary for a number of years, describing the raffles and rock and roll dances that were held. Mrs. Janet Perise explained that a novena was recited in the chapel on the feast day; prior to that, the members would say the rosary for a week, ending with a mass Sunday at Mater Dolorosa Church in Independence. There would be bingo during the day and fireworks at night. On the feast day itself the Independence Brass Band would lead a procession to the chapel and pavilion. Mrs. Marciano remembered that the musicians were especially rewarded with Italian sausage and homemade bread with olives and oil.[10] The society was quite active, celebrating the feast day for eighty years. The society also tried to maintain ties to Italy, for example sending money for flood relief to Italy in 1952.

As I listened to the enthusiastic reminiscences of the family most responsible for observing Expedito's feast days, the continued veneration of the saint was apparent. This was a saint they could count on. Back in 2005, when I first asked Mrs. Marciano about the saint's story, she quickly told me that Expedito was a German soldier—she didn't

---

[10] Carmella Marciano and family members, including Johnny Lee, Rosemary Lee, and Janet Perise, personal interviews with author and with Dr. Francesco Fiumara, professor of Italian and Spanish, Southeastern Louisiana University, October 17, 2009.

know what war he fought in—but that he wanted an end to the war. "Today—stop the war today," she slapped her hands in the air emphatically. She then laughed at the story of the "postal" Expedite and had no doubts that he had been an actual soldier. The name Expeditus is mentioned in the "Hieronymianum" (an early Catholic document of Church martyrs) in two groups of martyrs, one group assigned to Rome, one to Armenia; but there is no tradition verifying either reference.[11] At the most, reference books of the saints list Expedito as one of a group of Armenian martyrs; and even the postal story has existed for centuries. One story claims that a saint's body was sent to a community of nuns in Paris in 1781. The corpse's case was marked "expedite" for "obvious reasons."[12] The nuns mistakenly believed Expedite to be the name of a martyr, and his cult became widely popular in France and other Catholic countries as news of the saint who quickly granted miracles spread. One problem with this story is that before this date St. Expeditus was established as patron saint of a town in Sicily in the seventeenth century.[13]

The origins of the saint remain hopelessly blurred while the visual renderings of the saint are remarkably consistent.[14] In her interview in August of 2005, Mrs. Marciano explained that before the chapel was built, a special room of the house was dedicated to the saint; her grandmother had

---

[11] "Catholic Online Saints," <http://www.catholic.org> (accessed August 12, 2005).

[12] "St. Expedite," <http://www.armeniapedia.org> (accessed August 1, 2005).

[13] "Expedite," <http://www.angelfire.com> (accessed August 1, 2005).

[14] Note that while the legend of the crated statue marked "Expedite" is told most frequently in relation to New Orleans (those receiving the statue mistakenly gave an unknown foot soldier a name) it is told in association with the Paris post as well as with the Independence post, although this rendition is fairly new to the Italian community in Independence. My research in the Independence community suggests this modern proliferation of the "postal" legend in Independence is due to influence from the more widespread New Orleans legend.

promised that if St. Expedito granted her a favor, she would get a special print of the saint. A second portrait was ordered by her father who later had a statue made in Germany, which he placed in the chapel when it was completed in 1947. When I asked Mrs. Marciano if I could accompany her to the chapel, she obligingly allowed me entrance to the sun-filled, orderly room with its immaculate white walls. After viewing the St. Expedito paintings and the by now familiar statue at the center of the chancel area, I concentrated my gaze back toward the side walls. Mrs. Marciano noticed my focus and asked if I wanted to see the eyes, hand, and two legs the saint had healed. "Yes," I said. Hanging near the back wall were plaster appendages, models of the limbs the saint had saved from diabetes and gangrene, while a model hand sat on the altar next to Expedito's feet. There was no embarrassment or hidden ritual involved in this community's veneration of the saint. Unlike the exclusivity or privacy of New Orleans's celebration of the saint, the feast days in Independence were public celebrations; and the praying to the saint for favors was a common, accepted practice.

A month later on September 16, 2005 I interviewed by phone Mike Correnti (an adult who had put off his confirmation) as he was driving up north moving goods to people after Hurricane Katrina.[15] He said he simply chose the saint as his patron because he liked what he stood for—which he couldn't really remember—and that he identified with the saint, who was known for his "expeditiousness" and his "good behavior"—qualities which Mr. Correnti certainly exhibited as he ventured forth from the little community of Independence, "expeditiously" driving through the night, hastening to deliver goods to those ravaged by Hurricane

---

[15] Mike Correnti, telephone interview with the author, September 16, 2005.

Katrina. He also said his priest was at first hesitant for him to choose this saint, but that the uncertain origins "piqued" his curiosity. He informed me that he had found the saint by looking at a list on the Internet.

In all the various stories there is one certainty—the use of wordplay arising from the saint's name. In all its various spellings-Expedite, Expeditus, Expedito, Spedito—those praying to the saint want immediate results and according to supplicants, that is the saint's driving force—the immediate answer to life's difficulties. Here follows a common prayer:

> Saint Expedite,
> Noble Roman youth, martyr,
> You who quickly bring things to pass,
>
> You who never delay,
> I come to you in need—
>
> Do this for me, Saint Expedite,
> And when it is accomplished,
> I will as rapidly reply for my part
> With an offering to you.
>
> Be quick, Saint Expedite!
> Grant my wish before your candle burns out,
> And I will magnify your name.[16]

"A prayer answered and a promise kept" is the motto to commemorate the St. Expedito Feast. In the Italian community of Independence, St. Expedito functioned not as a new saint who appeared when circumstance demanded, but

---

[16] "Saint Expedite," <http://www.luckymojo.com> (accessed August 1, 2005). Various versions of prayers to St. Expedito may be found online, all similar to pamphlets from Our Lady of Guadalupe in New Orleans and from the St. Expedito Society in Independence, Louisiana. All ask for speedy help in time of need.

as a continuance of an established tradition of seeking help and expecting and finding solace in community ritual. On October 17, 2009, as I revisited the shrine and listened to Mrs. Marciano's family recount their celebrations of the saint, I saw family traditions and values preserved remarkably well. As Mrs. Marciano stated, "St. Expedito is a true miracle saint. He's a good saint." In the society's donations to Italian flood relief, in Mr. Correnti's transport of materials to hurricane victims, in the strong and enduring traditions of family and faith, St. Expedito delivered time and again, finding a true home in this Italian-American community.

From *Cucina* to Kitchen
Italian Cooking *vs.* Italian-American Cooking in Tangipahoa Parish

ELISABETTA VIOLI LEJEUNE
Southeastern Louisiana University

Cultural traditions and cultural cuisines have a life of their own, and they can change according to the needs of the community and the resources available. While it may be difficult to say how some traditions and foods have become so popular and representative of Italian-American culture, we can discover how they may have evolved to become what they are today. In some cases, food traditions may be closely connected to religious celebrations such as the Saint Joseph celebration. On the other hand, they may be the result of contact with other cultures. They can be even prompted by the need to make adjustments to an environment with different resources than those found in the country of origin. It is important to know that most Italian food is regional, therefore dependent on local ingredients indigenous to that area. Often dishes are derived from a small community in Italy and are available only in that restricted area and not known in the mainstream of modern Italian culture. When immigrants came to the United States, they brought with them the cuisine and the traditions of their native villages and regions. As they adapted to new climates and environments, they strived to keep their cultural heritage, but they also faced many obstacles and challenges. Ingredients which were not readily available in the United States had to be substituted or eliminated. Consequently, some typical Italian American foods have become mostly adaptations of original dishes specific to a very restricted area. But if something was lost, a great deal was gained from the contact with other ethnic cuisines that were prevalent in Southern Louisiana, creating new traditions and new ways of cooking.

Contemporary Italians traveling to the United States will probably experience culture shock when visiting an Italian American community. They will not recognize some of the traditions celebrated by Italian Americans, nor most of the foods served in Italian restaurants located in Italian communities. Many aspects of the culture of Italians in America will not be familiar to native Italians because they do not exist anymore in Italy. In some cases, traditions, which originated in small villages in Italy and were later transferred to the United States took a new strength and a different meaning. As the community members were striving to maintain their cultural identity, they persevered in celebrating the festive occasions that are still celebrated in specific regions of Italy, but not in all parts of Italy. For example, in Sicily some traditions have changed as citizens relocated or communities' resources and needs also changed. Therefore, we often find that traditions celebrated by Italian American communities have developed a new identity accordingly with their main purpose of helping families and settlements to preserve their ethnic identity and heritage. So while most native Italians may not know of Saint Joseph altars or may have never eaten spaghetti and meatballs or fettuccine Alfredo, Italian communities of southern Louisiana maintain unchanged celebrations that were carried from Sicily over one hundred years ago. The religious and culinary identity that Americans of Sicilian heritage have developed in these areas resembles more of a nineteenth century Sicilian village than a modern Italian city. Until the late 1980's, in Italian settlements surrounding New Orleans, some foods that are now so prevalent in Italy, such as pesto or polenta or gnocchi, were virtually unknown. Now in the first decade of the twentieth-first century, many new varieties of Italian foods have become available in most supermarkets and are now better known in those communities.

One area that retains many cultural traditions brought and maintained by communities of Italian descent is located in Southeast Louisiana where immigrants arrived to the Port of New Orleans in large numbers at the end of the nineteenth century. The communities that were formed as a result of the 1880's and 1890's immigration waves settled first in or near the French Quarter in New Orleans. The vast majority came from Sicily and traveled from Palermo on the steamships that transported "Mediterranean produce, especially citrus fruit, that was then distributed northward through the Mississippi valley" (Dormon 16). They were attracted by the promise of work on sugar cane plantations located along the Mississippi River in South Louisiana. When the season for harvesting sugar cane was over in December, they returned to New Orleans or migrated to Tangipahoa Parish to help the strawberry farmers. Through hard work and a frugal lifestyle, they saved enough to purchase land. Many settled in Tangipahoa Parish, just north of New Orleans across Lake Pontchatrain, attracted by the agricultural and rural economy.

"Parish" in Louisiana designates political administrations that in other states are called counties. It also indicates the strong Catholic background, which must have appeared welcoming to those new Italian settlers. Tangipahoa Parish extends along Highway 51 that connects New Orleans with Chicago and along the railroad track that follows the same route. The Sicilian immigrants, drawn to the area by the possibility of acquiring farming land, settled in large numbers from the 1990's to the 1930's. Information from the Bureau of Census included in *Bread-and Respect* by Anthony Margavio and Jerome Salomone indicates that the population of foreign-born Italians in Tangipahoa Parish grew from 97 in the 1900's to 1,550 in the 1930's (38-40). That second number is the highest of all the Louisiana parishes with the exception of Orleans Parish, which includes the metropolitan area of New Orleans. The Italian settlement concentrated in the Township of Independence, Louisiana, which is located directly on the rail route, and in the Village of Tickfaw located four miles south. With them the Sicilians brought foods and religious traditions that have endured there almost unchanged. The population of Sicilian background is numerous in the area, and today second and third generation Italians are prominent in local businesses and government. They became involved in the local politics with the purpose of improving transportation and drainage to facilitate their farming economy. As a result, they have become prosperous by being laborious, but also by making sound investments in real estate.

In the late 1970's, the large number of Italian descendants prompted local school board officials to acquire state and federal grants to develop a bilingual program in public elementary and secondary schools. By that time, few children heard Italian spoken in the home and most grandparents spoke a Sicilian dialect that had assimilated English words and expressions. Although the Sicilian families had preserved and developed cultural traditions, they had neglected to teach the language to their children. Because of past discrimination, they feared economical disadvantages, by being recognized as Italians.

Although the beginnings of these new citizens were poor, they were willing to work very hard and were able to save their small earnings. Often very young children worked in the fields alongside their parents, and families helped each other. They faced discrimination and in some cases violent prejudice; therefore, they kept many of their traditions very private and refrained from contact with other sections of the parish population. Most traditions that have survived were closely tied to religious celebrations or to family events. Throughout the parish, we can still find today small chapels built by families that wanted to show their gratitude for fortunate events or for overcoming illness, disasters, or other tragedies. The religious celebrations also offered an opportunity to feast on food that reminded them of their native land. In fact, many Sicilians who settled in this part of the United States will state that they are Sicilians and not Italians. These remarks underline the fact that when their ancestors left Italy, Sicily had just become part of the newly unified Kingdom of Italy. There was no sense of national identity to connect these immigrants to the rest of Italy. In some cases, there was no sense of unity even in the Sicilian community as some of the immigrants came from groups such as the Albresh from Contessa Entellina who had migrated to Sicily from Albania. Even today, the population of Tangipahoa Parish celebrates two festivals to recognize their ethnic background: one in Independence, named the Sicilian Festival, and another named the Italian Festival in the Village of Tickfaw, located only four miles south of Independence.

As soon as they were able, the Sicilian immigrants acquired land and farmed to support their families and to earn income by selling fruit and vegetables in the near cities. They were truck farmers who traveled to the City of New Orleans to sell their produce. When farmers settled in the middle part of Tangipahoa Parish, they kept close ties to the city of New Orleans and developed business relationships that brought about changes in both communities. In the rural areas of Tangipahoa parish, Italians worked in the food industry, as producers and business owners. They soon became involved in the cultivation of strawberries and manufactured products such as ricotta, strawberry wine, Italian sausage, and tomato sauces. They also became owners and patrons of small grocery stores that offered a small selection of imported Italian foods otherwise not available locally, such as olive oil, olives, and Parmesan cheese. Now that Italian foods are widely available and the small groceries have disappeared, the Italian community brings forth their heritage in occasion of religious festivities and family celebrations.

Today, only a couple of restaurants in the entire parish claim that their menu uses an authentic Italian style of cooking. One of these is Gina's located in Independence, where we find spaghetti and meatballs, veal parmesan, eggplant parmesan, lasagna: all dishes that include tomato sauce to complement a main ingredient. These are the dishes that the local Italian grandmothers prepare every Sunday for their families. However, there are more than home cooked meals in the Italian community of this region. New Orleans' food is the result of many merging cultures: Spanish, French, African-American, Caribbean, German, Irish, Croatian, and of course, Italian. While the Italian foods of this region have borrowed ingredients and techniques from other ethnic groups, Sicilian cooking has contributed to the development of Louisiana's Creole and Cajun cooking.

Some dishes were created to satisfy the needs and demands of the Italian population, which was adapting to a very new environment. Others are creative adaptations of available ingredients. An item that combines many easily available Sicilian ingredients is the Muffuletta, a popular sandwich that can only be found in a very restricted area of Southeast Louisiana. It was developed by the owner of an Italian grocery store located in New Orleans' French Quarter, called "Central Grocery," which carries many Italian specialty products and it is still today one of the landmarks of Italian cooking in New Orleans. When it opened in 1906, it catered to the Italian farmers who traveled to the nearby French market to deliver their produce. When they purchased their lunch, which consisted of cold cuts, cheese, olives, and bread, they ate everything separately, as it is customary in Sicily, but had a difficult time balancing the meal while sitting on crates since the grocery did not provide a seating area. According to Marie Lupo Tusa, daughter of the founder of the Central Grocery, her father suggested "that it would be easier for the farmers if he cut the bread and put everything on it like a sandwich" (4). So the popular sandwich was born, and as its story shows, it did not originate in Italy, but was created in the United States to satisfy the needs of the Sicilian patrons of an Italian grocery store located in New Orleans. Certainly many of those Sicilian farmers were residents of Independence and Tangipahoa parish, and with them they brought the newly created Italian sandwich back to Tangipahoa Parish. The sandwich can be found in the Italian bakeries that make the typical sesame seed covered bread loaf. The ties between Tangipahoa Parish and New Orleans are still very strong today as many residents of Tangipahoa Parish travel to New Orleans to visit relatives and vice versa.

The availability of local fresh produce, or the lack of it, led to significant changes in the way some dishes are prepared. A typical item so common in the Italian-American style of cooking is Italian gravy, Italian sauce, red gravy, tomato gravy, red sauce, or spaghetti sauce. Whatever it may be called, it generally consists of olive oil, onion, and garlic with the addition of tomato paste, an equal amount of water, and canned sauce or peeled tomatoes. The sauce is then cooked for a long time, maybe four to five hours. The acidity derived from the use of the tomato paste is counteracted with the addition of sugar. As she explains in her cookbook *Marie's Melting Pot: Sicilian Style Cooking*, Marie Lupo Tusa adds baking soda to all the tomato-based dishes in her recipes (48). Other ways of reducing the acidity of the tomato paste based sauce may be to add a carrot or even a small potato. In general, the desired result is a rather thick sauce, which "sticks" to the pasta. The sauce can also be used in a myriad of dishes such as spaghetti and meatballs, chicken Parmesan, eggplant Parmesan, or pizza. The sauce itself served over pasta often includes the addition of other ingredients such as eggplant, anchovies, eggs, and even boiled potatoes.

This particular preparation of tomato sauce is not common in Italy where tomato paste or "concentrato" is used in very small amounts mainly to flavor soups or roasts. The need to preserve fresh tomatoes for the winter months has generated peculiar ways of preparing an "extract" that can maintain the flavor of fresh tomatoes and is easy to keep even unrefrigerated. In Sicily where tomatoes are plentiful in the summer, a very local artisanal product has been concocted. The result of drying crushed tomatoes in the sun on tilted wooden boards is the "elioconcentrato," or "strattu," a product rarely seen outside its area of origin. It is often homemade and locally consumed. It is reconstituted with water to make pasta sauces, and it is sparingly added to meat dishes or soup to flavor them. Even in Sicily its production is limited to a few areas that are closer to the drier and more ventilated coastal regions. It is possible that families which came to Louisiana from Sicily brought with them this very rare and unique tomato product. When the supply ended, the only easily obtainable close substitute was tomato paste, which is also very inexpensive and certainly more available than good fresh tomatoes for most of the year. During the peak of the summer it is difficult to grow good tomatoes in Louisiana because of the humidity and the extreme heat. We can now purchase good tomatoes year around, even in the middle of the winter if we are willing to pay a high price for produce transported from far away regions. However, even if good ripe tomatoes are obtained, they cannot be naturally dried in the sun in Louisiana because of the level of humidity. Therefore, in the early 1900s, the Italian immigrants had to cope with the difficulties of adjusting to their new life by substituting ingredients and assimilating elements of the local culinary tradition.

Often, the tomato paste, which is so widely used in Sicilian-American cooking, is "fried" or browned in the olive oil before it is diluted with water to prepare the sauce. The process is similar to the preparation of the roux so common in Creole and Cajun dishes. So in addition to substitutions of ingredients, we also notice the adaptation of cooking techniques often borrowed by other ethnic cuisines. With some variations, the red sauce or gravy has also become part of Southern Louisiana's other cuisines because the contact between the Sicilian population and other ethnic groups contributed to the development of new dishes. Consequently, these ethnic groups added new ingredients to the traditional Italian-American dishes. The cultural diversity of settlers in Louisiana makes New Orleans and the areas in its vicinity a wide ground for a range of culinary styles. The Creoles contributed elements of French and Spanish culture, the Africans, who came here from Haiti, brought new spices, and the Irish and Germans who also settled in Tangipahoa Parish added their own traditions. Just like their Sicilians ancestors who carried a heritage of so many mixed nationalities through the island's history, the Sicilians in Louisiana were in contact with many ethnic cuisines.

An interesting connection between the Sicilian immigrants and the African-American community is apparent in the feast of Saint Joseph, the most important celebration of Sicilian culture and food, which takes place on March 19. The festivities are often combined with the Irish celebration of Saint Patrick and the two communities come together with processions, which in New Orleans become parades with floats and many nonreligious connotations. In his book *The Joy of Y'at Catholicism,* Earl Higgins reviews and explains the religious beliefs and traditions of Catholic New Orleans. He mentions that "Perhaps the most exotic tradition of honoring St. Joseph is the appearance of the Mardi Gras Indians ... beginning in the nineteenth century ... groups of black working class men got the idea to dress as American Indians, form tribes and march through the streets on Mardi Gras in their costumes.... The Mardi Gras Indians saw that the Italians were cavorting and partying during Lent on St. Joseph Day and they decided to join in the celebrations...The Indians decided to hold a parade of all tribes on the Sunday before St. Joseph Day, referred to as Super Sunday" (Higgins 38). And they still do so today while wearing their elaborate and handcrafted attire. Another instance of this merging of culture is mentioned by Kerri McCaffety, who compiled *Saint Joseph Altars*, a beautiful illustrated book depicting Saint Joseph altars of New Orleans and surrounding areas. She remarks that "since the 1930's, African American Spiritual congregations have joined in the Saint Joseph's Day tradition, building altars in their churches and filling them with Italian foods. Here, Saint Joseph, as the patron of social justice, is associated with Black Hawk, the powerful Sauk Indian saint at the center of the Spiritual cosmology" (24). However, racial and political issues of the early years of Italian immigration created a dangerous environment for the Sicilians who, according to Cunningham, at first "were in a predicament. They could find sustenance and success only by disregarding the Southern mores, which made so much of racial background. Native whites classed them with Negros, because they did what the natives looked upon as Negroes' work" (71). Voting rights had also created controversy and disagreement in local politics. Therefore, Italians soon learned that "they better adopt the customs, prejudice, and way of life of white Louisianans as soon as possible.... Once they did so, the Italians could gain acceptance among the native whites" (Cunningham 71).

They certainly did so when they settled in Tangipahoa Parish. There, the Italians formed closely knit communities and developed a sense of ethnic pride. In *Community Life in the Italian Colonies of Tangipahoa Parish, Louisiana 1890-1950,* John Baiamonte reports that newspapers were published in the Italian language at least until World War II. The Catholic priests in Independence and Tickfaw spoke Italian and performed services in Italian. Sicilian communities formed societies of mutual help to assist elderly, sick, and those who had lost a family member. Sicilians also married other Italians and "double cousins" (siblings who married siblings of another family) were not uncommon. Because of the unity of the community, celebrations and cooking styles are very consistent. However, by the time the Sicilians migrated to Tangipahoa Parish, they had already assimilated information from other ethnic groups.

When working side by side at the sugar plantations or in the French Quarter in New Orleans, Sicilians were in contact with African Americans. Mary Lorini Connolly remembers that when she was growing up in the French Quarter her neighbor "Mrs. Simmons, a big black woman, wonderful woman, clean and lovely" would tell her "stories and things." She also recalls Mrs. LeBot, the wife of the black undertaker, who "three or four times a week was in our home. Now my mother couldn't talk to her because she did not talk English, but she could understand a lot, and my sister and her would be exchanging recipes and having tea" (Dormon 27). These contacts must have produced new ideas and stimulated the use of new ingredients and the practice of new techniques in the kitchen.

In her book *Cajun-Creole Cooking*, chef and author, Terry Thompson-Anderson dedicates an entire chapter to Creole-Italian cooking, whose signature dishes are spinach bread, "brucholoni," muffuletta, roux-based red gravy, meatballs, olive salad, Creole-Italian Tomato gravy, Italian baked oysters, and Creole Daube with red gravy. Some of these dishes with names of uncertain spelling are common on the menus of Italian restaurants in Southeast Louisiana and also in many households that are not of Italian backgrounds. In some cases, Sicilian cooking contributed the use of ingredients such as anchovies, basil, olives, and tomato paste. In other ways, it is the technique that produces unique results. In her review of Italian based recipes, Terry Thompson-Anderson notices that frying tomato paste "produces a specific taste without which you simply do not have authentic Creole-Italian tomato gravy. After the vegetables are sautéed in olive oil, tomato paste is added and, literally, fried before the liquids are added" (137). This common procedure prepares the foundation of so many dishes, but it also varies with each cook as to which vegetable constitute the "seasonings."

When asked about "seasonings," many Sicilian Louisianans cooks will mention onion, celery and bell pepper (the "trinity" as it is called in New Orleans) and, of course, garlic. The finely chopped vegetables correspond to an Italian *soffritto*, which includes carrot in place of pepper. This merging of ingredients and methods creates many dishes that are unique to the region of southeastern Louisiana, including New Orleans and surrounding municipalities and parishes. For example, one dish influenced by Italian contributions is shrimp Creole, which has a tomato and roux based sauce. Another dish with Italian ties is sauce piquant, a versatile Cajun tomato sauce which can be served with seafood, meat, or poultry. Its distinguishing characteristic is the addition of peppers. Another dish with a French name and a Cajun background is fish courtbouillon. The gravy in which the redfish or other seafood is stewed includes tomato sauce and many of the same ingredients common to the area of south Louisiana, such as the "trinity" and cayenne pepper. However these recipes, unlike the Sicilian gravy, always begin with a roux, and the Creole or Cajun dishes are always served with rice. A country version of red gravy is what some incorrectly call red eye gravy, often prepared in country settings to serve over biscuits. Although the traditional red eye gravy does not list tomatoes among its ingredients, a Southern regional version includes tomatoes and can be served over grits for a breakfast meal.

Another important component of Sicilian food prepared

for Saint Joseph altars or for special celebrations, such as birthdays and weddings, is baked goods, such as intricately decorated breads and cookies. These cookies have changed very little. They rely on specific ingredients such as sesame seeds, figs, almonds, and anise, which are not indigenous of this area. Many home cooks and some small bakeries in New Orleans and Tangipahoa Parish prepare them according to recipes passed from previous generations. Bread was baked in outdoor brick ovens and often covered with sesame seeds. In New Orleans and Tangipahoa Parish, sesame seeds on bread are synonymous of Italian bread. Some groceries call the sesame covered bread "Saint Joseph loaf" to distinguish it from French bread, which does not have seeds to coat its crust. Sesame seeds also cover the round loafs used for the Muffulletta sandwich. Pride in these domestic skills has prompted classes, exhibits, and demonstrations. So we can hope that the traditions of baking such beautiful and tasty treats will continue for generations to come.

Mrs. Lucy Ditta Mike, a 94-year-old resident of Tangipahoa Parish, is an exceptional Sicilian cook, who grew up on a sugar cane plantation. She is still very active in the Italian community and bakes cookies for many events and also to sell at farmers markets and festivals, such as the Jazz Festival in New Orleans. In a personal interview, she recalled that her parents used to dry cooked tomato sauce in the sun. She remarked that people do not do it anymore because they are "lazy." However, Mrs. Lucy still cans tomato sauce to use with tomato paste to prepare her "sugo," as she called it. Her tomato gravy consists of first frying the seasonings and the tomato paste in good olive oil for a long time before adding the home canned tomato sauce. When asked about the seasonings, she stated she uses "onion, garlic, and parsley." She proudly remembered that when she visited her relatives in New York, they wanted her to cook her gravy as they preferred it to their own "bland" sauce. She described their sauce as "long," insisting that good gravy must be thick and well-seasoned. The contrast that she established was "bland" versus "seasoned" and insisted that the seasoning must be fried a long time with tomato paste and sugar before the tomato sauce and water are added. The resulting thick gravy is preferable to the "long" gravy that goes through the spaghetti to the bottom of the plate. Of course, there are many variations to the preparation of this gravy as there are families and Italian grandmothers.

An example of the motivation to preserve Sicilian ways of cooking is found in Lafayette, about two hours west of New Orleans where two cousins of Italian background offer cooking classes, as Cherè Coens explains in her article "The Accidental Chef Cooking School" published in the July 2011 issue of *Country Road* magazine:

> The school is owned and operated by Macomber and Carlos Russo, her first cousin who's also from Abbeville. The two share a Sicilian background as well so classes range from the more traditional Louisiana fare such as crawfish étouffeé and chicken and sausage gumbo; to an Italian shrimp rosemary with garlic, artichokes and rosemary sprigs. Other Sicilian dishes include Italian Wedding Soup, Oyster and Fennel Capellini and Biscotti di Regina. (50)

The southeastern region of Louisiana is a "melting pot," and its original cuisine is the outcome of the contributions of many ethnic groups. We can conclude that the Italian American style of cooking in southeast Louisiana has its own characteristics and has maintained its own identity closely related to its Sicilian roots. Although it has assimilated elements from the local culture, it has developed its own identity which distinguishes it from other Italian-American groups who settled in other parts of the United States. The products of this way of cooking are original and firmly anchored in their tradition, so much that little variations exist in the community. This consistency has enabled the community to keep its own culinary traditions and at the same time has generated unique dishes that have maintained their original identity.[1]

WORKS CITED

Coen, Cheré. "The Accidental Chef Cooking School." *Country Roads.* Baton Rouge, Louisiana: July 2011: 50.

Cunningham, George E. "Italians: Hindrance to White Solidarity, 1890-1898." *Racial classification and History.* Ed. E. Nathaniel Gates. New York and London: Garland Publishing, Inc., 1997.

Dormon, James. "Striving for Success." *A Better Life: Italian-Americans in South Louisiana.* Ed. Gardner, Joel. New Orleans, Louisiana: American-Italian Federation of the Southeast, 1983.

Higgins, Earl J. *The Joy of Y'at Catholicism.* Gretna, Louisiana: Pelican Publishing Company, 2007.

Margavio, Anthony, and Jerome Salomone. *Bread and Respect. The Italians of Louisiana.* Gretna, Louisiana: Pelican Publishing Company, 2002.

McCaffety, Kerri. *Saint Joseph Altars.* Gretna, Louisiana: Pelican Publishing Company, 2003.

Mike, Ditta Lucy. Personal interview. July 14, 2011.

Thompson-Anderson, Terry. *Cajun-creole Cooking.* Tucson, AZ: HPBooks, 1986.

Tusa, Marie Lupo. *Marie's Melting Pot: Sicilian Style Cooking.* The Spielman Company, 1980.

---

[1] The author of this article has lived in Tangipahoa Parish since 1979, when she came from Italy as a graduate student to teach Italian language to the children and grandchildren of the Sicilian immigrants who had settled in the area. Many observations included in this paper stem from direct observation and contact with those Italian families.

"Dearer to me than any other"
New Orleans, the Massacre of 1891, and the Arrival of Sister Frances Xavier Cabrini

WILLIAM BOELHOWER
Louisiana State University

First Scene: On the night of October 15, 1890, New Orleans Police Superintendent David Hennessy was ambushed and mortally wounded while walking to his home on Girod Street. When his friend Bill O'Connor arrived on the scene and asked him who did it, Hennessy supposedly whispered the word "Dagoes."[1] As Richard Gambino notes in his study *Vendetta*, "No one but O'Connor heard Hennessy's whispered reply" (4). But by the time of Hennessy's death the next day, newspapers across the nation had begun to declaim the Mafia-style ambush of New Orleans' chief law officer and point to the Sicilian secret societies as the cause. It was the beginning of the country's ambiguous romance with that now familiar entity *Cosa Nostra*. What happened immediately after the shooting, however, was a well-orchestrated act of repression, which many scholars and historians have repeatedly sought to document and understand. From the hospital where Hennessy lay dying, the city's mayor Joseph Shakspeare sent the police out with these orders: "Scour the whole neighborhood! Arrest every Italian you come across, if necessary, and scour it again

---

[1] See Richard Gambino, *Vendetta*, 4; Giose Rimanelli, "The 1891 New Orleans Lynching: Southern Politics, Mafia, Immigration and the American Press," in Rimanelli and Postman, eds. *The 1891 New Orleans Lynching and U.S.-Italian Relations*, 74-6; Herbert Asbury, *The French Quarter*, 411; Joseph P. Cusco, *Imagining Italians*, 13-14, 155-157.

123

tomorrow morning" (Gambino 7). The neighborhood in question was largely Italian. As Gambino notes "At the moment of Hennessy's death, some fifty Italians had already been arrested, and between one and two hundred more were to be taken during the next twenty-four hours" (8). As a result, an entire people (in the language of the day, 'race') largely concentrated in the French Quarter's Little Palermo was declared outside the law. That is, the Italians living there (predominantly Sicilian) were stripped of any constitutional rights and indiscriminately subjected to a Hobbesian reign of terror.

In the highly political trial that concluded on March 13, 1891, none of the suspects in the Hennessy murder were convicted. Angry and frustrated, a number of prominent politicians, newspaper editors, and civic leaders stirred up thousands of people into a bloodthirsty mob, which marched on the prison where the men were still being held. The mob leaders then broke in, hunted down, and ritually poured shot after shot into nine of the Italians, and lynched two others who were still alive outside in Congo Square, where the mob could fully enjoy the spectacle. Afterwards, people stripped a piece of bark off the hanging tree and dipped their handkerchiefs in the blood of the victims for a souvenir. According to the official line that was used to justify New Orleans to itself and to the rest of the nation, it was the sovereign will of the people that demanded immediate justice (Smith 242). All of the authorities, from the governor of the state on down, openly approved.[2]

* * *

---

[2] See, for example, Tom Smith, *The Crescent City Lynchings*, chapter twenty-four, "'I Can't Arrest the Community,'" 233-240.

Second Scene: Barely a year later, in the spring of 1892, Sister Frances Xavier Cabrini, Superior General of the Missionary Sisters of the Sacred Heart, landed in New Orleans from Nicaragua, where she had gone to establish a religious house. Learning of the recent events and seeing the poverty, the degradation, and the demoralized condition of the Italian community there, she promised the bishop of the city and Father Gambera, both of whom begged her help that she would send some of her sisters to prepare for the establishment of a mission as soon as she could. After New York and Nicaragua, New Orleans was the third place in the Americas to witness and benefit from the community services, the charitable activities, and the spiritual example of this religious order totally devoted to serving the Italian immigrants.[3] It is this second scene and the symbolic order it established that I wish to discuss here, by connecting its significance to the series of events embodied in the police raids and killings that scourged Little Palermo after the murder of Hennessy. Historians of the 1891 killings invariably neglect to mention the arrival of Cabrini in connection with that mob action, largely because of the disciplinary challenges that such a linkage entails but also because of an unstated conviction that the realm of the sacred and of religion is ultimately beyond the representational capabilities of the middle range of historiography that academic scholars normally deploy. In short, what belongs to Caesar should remain Caesar's and to God, God's.

Thus, in their monograph *Bread and Respect. The Italians of Louisiana*, co-authors A.V. Margavio and Jerome J. Sa-

---

[3] On the activities of the Missionary Sisters of the Sacred Heart in New Orleans, see above all Mary Louise Sullivan, MSC, *Mother Cabrini. "Italian Immigrant of the Century,"* 117-128, 186-189; Segundo Galilea, *In Weakness, Strength. The Life and Missionary Activity of Saint Frances Xavier Cabrini*, 84-87; Theodore Maynard, *Too Small a World. The Life of Mother Cabrini*, 150-161.

lomone deal with "The Hunger of Justice" in one chapter and "Religion: The Quest for Beauty" in another, and never do the twain meet. Cabrini is discussed concisely in the latter chapter but not in the former. Although three of Cabrini's sisters arrived in New Orleans in July of 1892 and then Cabrini herself with four more in August, the authors fail to take note or meditate on the import of their coming. Even more to the point, the authors grumble, "When the biographers of saints stress the miraculous events, they perhaps do their readers a disservice. Would not the reader profit more from seeing a life-sized individual struggling with human limitations" (235)? But the question—the distinction—is beside the point. In 1890 Hennessy's martyrdom led, through popular acclamation, to his sanctification as a local hero, and although Hennessy and Saint Frances Xavier Cabrini are quite different figures, they belong to the same history of death and life in New Orleans.[4] What suggests that not only Hennessy and Cabrini, but also these two public figures and the eleven slain Italians, contribute to the making of the same historical constellation is their co-involvement in the literal and symbolic order of bloodletting or, even more figuratively central, the image of the bleeding heart. Indeed, Cabrini called her Order the Missionary Sisters of the Sacred Heart. She and her sisters literally arranged their lives of total sacrifice around the spiritual appeal of this religious icon.

By choosing to consider this highly charged anthropological emblem of the heart as a means to fathom the deeper meanings of the scenography outlined above, we as historians and cultural studies scholars can go below the line

---

[4] See here the useful essay by Michel de Certeau, "A Variant. Hagio-Graphical Edification," in his book of essays *The Writing of History*, 269-283. Joseph P. Cosco also discusses the New Orleans lynchings but fails to discuss Cabrini (155-157).

of middle-range narrative and historical explanation to what Régis Debray in his book *Cours de médiologie générale* calls the *mediographic dimension* (37-62). An appropriate example of this form of attention is the set of linguistic signs "A.M.G.SS.C.J" which Mother Cabrini wrote at the top of almost all of her letters. Spelled out in full, these signs mean *Ad Majorem Gloriam Sanctissimi Cordis Jesus*, To the Greater Glory of the Most Sacred Heart of Jesus. This dedication, in fact, was not only the Order's banner but also its mandate or marching orders. Albeit in a highly synthetic way, the symbolic order of the Sacred Heart explains Cabrini's presence in New Orleans in 1892 as a convocation which interfuses the sisters' apostolic mission with the beleaguered existence of the Italians of Little Palermo, as we shall see below. In short, the emblem of the Sacred Heart acts as a hermeneutical conduit that allows us to acknowledge the interworldly manifestation of the mundane and the sacred in the missionary activities of Cabrini's Order. Cabrini herself chose as her personal motto this verse from the New Testament: *"Omnia possum in Eo qui me confortat"* (Phil. 4:13); in English, "I can do all things in Him who comforts me" (see Jones 259). According to Cabrini biographer C.C. Martindale, Pope Leo XIII said to her in a private audience: "'Come, come, M. Cabrini,' said he: 'You have the Spirit of God: carry it to the whole world. I have consecrated the whole world to the Sacred Heart: you are the instrument God has chosen to carry this devotion forth'" (Martindale 55-56).

It was Glazer and Moynihan who in their important study *Beyond the Melting Pot* observed that ethnicity suffused all aspects of life and, our contention here, so does the dimension of the sacred. In point of fact, the French anthropologist Marcel Mauss already recognized the criteria by which such an observation becomes plausible in his classic study *The Gift*: "in this way of treating a problem there lies a heuristic principle we should like to bring out. The facts that we have studied are all, if we may be allowed the expression, *total* social facts" (78). By looking at the events of early 1890s New Orleans—Hennessy's assassination, the massacre of the Italians, and the arrival of Sister Cabrini—as elements of a total social fact, we can more readily see them as not only intertwined but also interdefined. As Mauss reminds us, "All these phenomena are at the same time juridical, economic, religious, and even aesthetic and morphological" (79). Perhaps more obviously, it is hard to deny the real effectiveness of what might otherwise be written off as imaginary when we consider that "every social structure is founded on belief or trust" (Paul Valery qtd in Debray 43). First, the Italians of Little Palermo and, secondly, the larger population of New Orleans came to place great trust in Cabrini and her Missionary Sisters of the Sacred Heart.

Undoubtedly, a total history of the 1891 lynchings in New Orleans would require us to consider extremely elusive cultural and anthropological issues, such as: the motives of mob action, the widespread fear of secret societies, a hunted race's sense of terror, political and juridical conspiracy and hearsay, blood lust and elementary passions, but also equivalent intensities normally associated with the establishment of Cabrini's New Orleans foundation—the sisters' radical charity, their vow of poverty, the sacrificial modalities of their religious zeal, their labor of desire, their fearlessness, and, above all, their quest for holiness through devotion to the Sacred Heart. What brings all of these passional configurations together is New Orleans as the site of their incorporation, and all of them require scholars to go beyond cognitive history to a more enfolding notion of felt history. Thus, through the transfiguring affectivity of these competing passional forces, the extremes of violence and love are interanimated by the common figure of the heart, often considered (through the substance of blood) as the source of life itself and of the deeply impersonal dimension of the sacred in each human being. In other words, it is the very emblem of the heart—including Cabrini's Sacred Heart—and its capacity to generate meaning figuratively that point to a more extensive and intensive historical order.

As Michel de Certeau explains in his essay on hagiography, "the Life of a Saint also points to the relation that the group holds with other groups" (273). Cabrini's activities were spatially inscribed in the life of the Southern Italians of Little Palermo. Her religious Order of the Sacred Heart expressed its public self-consciousness most succinctly by associating a *figure*, Mother Cabrini, with a *place*, the Italian ghetto of New Orleans. In the rest of this essay, therefore, I will turn first to the figure of Cabrini (literally, to the few photographs we have of her) as every now and then someone's camera captured her image as she passed fleetingly from one of her foundations to another, constantly on the move; then I will turn to the site of Little Palermo, where the religious order/Order of the Sacred Heart took visible form. Scholars and historians have shied away from this visual material to date, although they have regularly used photographs of Cabrini to embellish their subject, thereby revealing in an image or two what they could not express in thousands of words. My further considerations, in other words, will be entirely *mediographical* in that the photographs of Cabrini I will include below reveal again and again—each time in a subtlely different way—the very symbolic order that so often eludes those who wish to speak of her. It was Wittgenstein who said that what cannot be explained or is inexpressible still shows itself (6.522), and again, "What *can* be shown *cannot* be said" (4.1212). By studying Cabrini's figure in these mere handful of photographs, I hope to show how they can help us to clarify the history of the Order's collective bonds with Little Palermo and with New Orleans at large.

Frances Xavier Cabrini was acclaimed America's first citizen-saint by Pope Pius XII on July 7, 1946. The special quality of her holiness is based above all on her life and work among the Italian immigrants in the Americas and elsewhere (England, France, Italy, Spain) at the end of the nineteenth and the beginning of the twentieth century. There are now well over fifteen biographies, memoirs, and diaries—not to mention websites—that recount the life and activities of this universally acknowledged patroness of immigrants. In May of 2002 Mother Cabrini's Missionary Institute in Rome came out with a five-volume critical edition of her letters, which run from the years 1868 to 1917, the year of her death.[5] Given their importance for arriving at new insights into the Saint's life, I would like to use them to suggest the close relationship between her incredibly active life, one of the Italian immigrant communities that gathered around her and her Order, and her deeply mystical spirituality. Again, it is the emblem of the Sacred Heart that imposes a manifest symbolic nexus connecting these three aspects. In addition, the roughly seven or eight photos that are regularly included in the biographies or in writings by

---

[5] *Epistolario di Santa Francesca Saverio Cabrini* (1868-1917). Ed. Istituto Missionarie del Sacro Cuore di Gesù. 5 Volumes. Rome: Tipografia Miligraf, 2002. The previous edition of her letters was published in 1968 and contains about one-third of the letters included in this new critical edition, which has a helpful textual apparatus, an analytical index, and an end section in volume 5 of a very helpful appendix of 258 biographical notes.

her tell us a great deal not only about her but also about her vocational devotion to the Sacred Heart.

Invariably, Mother Cabrini signed her letters with the tag "*Affez. in SS.C.J.*" (Affectionately in the Most Sacred Heart of Jesus) and beginning with letter N. 675, addressed to Sister Cherubina Ciceri in Panama and dated Dec. 19, 1894, she also headed them with *A.M.G.SS.C.J.* (For the Greater Glory of the Most Sacred Heart of Jesus). Those who belonged to the Missionary Sisters of the Sacred Heart would take these six initials at the top of Mother Cabrini's letters to them as an immediate reminder of the life of sacrifice, service, and obedience they had publicly vowed to lead. The initials allude to the defining spirit of the Order's rapidly growing apostolate in the Americas as well as to the intimate spiritual goals of each of the sisters. The cardinals, bishops, and secular authorities Cabrini was constantly writing to for help or permission of various kinds—or merely to keep up good relations with those who had power over the fortunes of her expanding Order—would also read in these same initials the Order's special mission to the multiplying Little Italies in the Americas.

After a vanguard of three penniless sisters reached New Orleans on April 12, 1892, Mother Cabrini herself, accompanied by four more sisters from New York, arrived in early August, with the Foundress leaving for Chicago about three weeks later. During that time, however, she chose a *Casa* (house) for the seven sisters on St. Philip Street where the Order would take care of orphans, teach school, open a chapel offering mass for the Italian community, and eventually do pastoral work in the immediate neighborhood and in and beyond the city.[6] It also served as their living quarters, their convent. As Cabrini writes in a letter to Monsignor Serrati on August 10, 1892, "In ogni modo però la Missione mi piace piantarla in mezzo ai più necessitosi pei quali siamo qua venuti e può darsi che prenda la Casa in una via tutta di siciliani e calabresi ove succedono frequenti uccisioni. Questi poveri birbanti sono i nostri più generosi benefattori ed hanno una venerazione per le religiose che è una cosa mirabile" [Anyhow, I would like to plant the Mission in the midst of the most needy for whom we have come here and perhaps I will choose a House in a street inhabited entirely by Sicilians and Calabrians where frequent killings occur.] (Vol.2, lett. 515).[7]

In the same letter to Serrati, Mother Cabrini also mentions an immediate effect their presence had on the city at large: "Tutti ora parlano e si interessano di noi, ci fermano sulle strade, vengono a visitarci, scrivono sui giornali, ma con cuore e venerazione, tutti." [Everybody is talking about us and is concerned about us; they stop us in the streets, come to visit us, and write about us in their newspapers, but with heart and veneration, everybody.] She goes on to say that she hopes to please them (not only the Italians but also the people of New Orleans), and in doing so she notes in passing that she has been falling to sleep from sheer fatigue every evening. That she is fulfilling her vocation of self-abandonment and total devotion to the Sacred Heart becomes obvious when she subsequently intimates, "ma sempre più mi cresce la voglia di travagliare a costo pure

---

[6] In a letter to Monsignor Serrati (Vol.2, lett. 515) she mentions that they were granted permission to use the tram in New Orleans for free, an obvious gesture of respect and gratitude to the sisters.

[7] Monsignor Antonio Serrati was the parish priest at Codogno, in Lombardy, where Mother Cabrini founded her Institute. Serrati was her spiritual guide during her first steps as founder of a new religious order. For an account of her actual arrival, see Vol.2, letter 511.

della vita" [but increasingly the desire to torment myself, even to the point of death, is growing in me]. In an earlier letter from New Orleans to Teresa Zanoncelli (Sister Virginia), dated August 8, 1892, Mother Cabrini reminds her that she should take heart and be a soldier of Christ (a *miles christi*) and that the value of a soldier is measured in battle (Vol.2, lett. 513).[8] On the same day as her letter to Zanoncelli, Mother Cabrini also wrote to Sister Bernardina Vallisneri, the Provincial of New York who later became Mother Superior at New Orleans for a short period, asking her to send an image (or statue, it is not clear) of the Sacred Heart for the chapel on St. Philip Street (Vol.2, lett. 511); and in her next letter dated August 23, she writes, "Oggi è arrivato il Sacro Cuore, molti accorsero a vederlo ed un giovane scapestrato l'ho veduto piangere" [Today the Sacred Heart arrived and many hurried to see it and I saw a young rake break out in tears.] (Vol.2, lett. 518).

By the time Cabrini left for Chicago at the end of August, her Institute was firmly established on 81 St. Philip Street not only as a site characterized by the sisters' devotion to the Sacred Heart, but also popularly recognized as a highly visible new presence in the city: "Tutti ci vogliono tanto bene, nessuno contrario che non par vero essere negli Stati Uniti" [Everybody loves us so much and without exception that it does not seem that we are really in the United States.] (Vol.2, lett. 519). Back in Rome some months later, Mother Cabrini wrote to Sister Domenica Bianchi, the first Director of the *Casa* at New Orleans, "È la più bella lode che io possa fare di voi a Roma col dire che siete in

---

[8] Cabrini often reminded her sisters that they should be soldiers of Christ; see, for example, her letter to Sister Cherubina Ciceri, Director of the *Casa* in Granada: "Le Missionarie del Sacro Cuore sono vere soldatesse, così scriveva un giornale di New Orleans, e per fare il bene noi superiamo immense difficoltà. Dunque procurate essere le vere soldatesse [...]" (Vol.2, lett. 519).

mezzo a tale gente e che sapete colla carità del Cuore SS. di Gesù attirarli al suo santo Amore" [It is the highest praise I can offer in your behalf here in Rome by saying that you are in the midst of such people and that with the charity of the Most Sacred Heart of Jesus you know how to attract them to his holy Love.] (Vol.2, lett. 565). In short, it is the effects of this symbolic order that provide us with an indexical sense of the intense religious passion now at work in New Orleans' Little Palermo. And in letter after letter, Mother Cabrini draws the sisters' attention to a code of behavior embodied in their Rule and created specifically for the stoking of their missionary devotion to the Sacred Heart. Again and again she reminds her sisters how before leaving for their Mission they said to each other that they would call that day blessed in which they would suffer much (Vol.2, lett. 590). The code, as this letter mentions, is that of *imitatio Christi* (the imitation of Christ), with its requisite virtues of poverty, humility, and self-denial. Writing to Domenica Bianchi on May 30, 1893, Cabrini says of the *Casa* in New Orleans, "un posto difficile, appunto per questo ci devono stare bene le Missionarie del Sacro Cuore che hanno ditto solennemente che per lui darebbero il sangue e la vita" [a difficult place, precisely and for this reason the Missionaries of the Sacred Heart should feel at home, having solemnly declared that for him they would give both their blood and their life.] (Vol.2, lett. 573). Here Cabrini is using the language of sacrifice—etymologically, *sacrum facere*, or making holy by giving one's blood and ultimately one's life. The Sacred Heart is a bleeding heart; it is what the sisters had in common with the murdered Italians, with police chief Hennessy, and even with the blood-thirsty mob.

Mother Cabrini and six other sisters (cofounders she called them) set up the Order's first house in Codogno, a small town in Lombardy, Italy, in late 1880. After she went to Rome to establish a foundation there and get her Order and rule officially accepted by the Church, she converted the Codogno site into the Order's novitiate. Cabrini's letters, and there are a good 2,056 of them, are full of information about her travels, her work opening new Houses, her religious enthusiasm, advice to the sisters at various foundations, and news about the Order's many activities. As these letters demonstrate, the material and spiritual spheres (the secular and the sacred) were totally fused in Cabrini's life and thought. She was constantly running up against stiff opposition from bishops and prelates who were skeptical about the effectiveness of her Order, but she always exuded an extreme sense of calm, confidence, and vocational determination. Although she was under five feet tall and of frail health, she crossed the Atlantic a good nineteen times between the years of 1889 and 1917.

The letters are the most extensive, detailed, intimate, and largely unexplored source of information about Cabrini's heroic life and works that we have. Thus, in a letter to Monsignor Rota from New Orleans, dated June 1904, she says, "Ultimato che abbia qui, farò ritorno in Colorado, ove per secondare il desiderio del Vescovo apriremo un orfanotrofio; di poi repasserò in Chicago per visitare le nostre due case e quindi per New York ove spero imbarcarmi alla volta di Italia" [Once I have finished here, I will return to Colorado, where, to carry out the wishes of the Bishop we will open an orphanage; then I will head back to Chicago to visit our two houses there and then on to New York, where I hope to embark for Italy.] (Vol.4, lett. 1393). As she informs him, she is writing from "queste remote contrade dove ormai mi trovo da quasi due anni, pellegrinando di Stato in Stato sempre più occupata che mai." [These remote regions where for almost two years now I find myself, journeying from state to state, always busier than ever.] For that matter this is the pace she set for herself and which her devotion to the Sacred Heart obliged her to follow. A totally modern woman, at the head of a burgeoning spiritual army of equally aspiring religious sisters (most of whom from Italy), Cabrini adopted a rhythm she often referred to in her letters as "slancio" (drive, devotion, zeal). Thus, in a letter to the Director of the *Casa* at Denver, dated April 23, 1909, she typically writes "Sono a Chicago; lunedi vado a New Orleans, poi a Los Angeles, indi a Seattle e poi a Denver e starò una settimana e mezzo in ciascun sito" [I am in Chicago; Monday I'll go to New Orleans, then to Los Angeles, from there to Seattle and then to Denver, and I will stay a week and a half at each site.] (Vol.5, lett. 1695). As the years passed, the number of Cabrini's foundations (orphanages, hospitals, schools) continued rapidly to increase and she insisted heroically on visiting all them, either to help solve the myriad of problems that sprung up here and there or to familiarize herself with the spiritual and material conditions of each of them.

The reason Cabrini was so well informed about the specific problems (both material and spiritual) that arose in the various houses and could address them as if she herself were there, on the spot, is that she insisted on reports being sent to her by her many directors. "Scrivimi sempre almeno ogni 15 giorni," she writes to one of them on October 2, 1903 [Always write me at least every fifteen days] (Vol.4, lett. 1348); and two years later she writes from Chicago to Sister Gesuina Diotti, Mother Superior of the house in Rome: "Mi piacerebbe sapere perché non mi scrivi. Se fossi anche malata al letto, dovresti prendere una carta e una matita e almeno ogni settimana scrivermi" [I would like to know why you are not writing me. Even if you were sick and in bed, you should pick up paper and pencil and write me at least once a week.] (Vol.4, lett. 1464). And three months later, from Denver, Colorado, she scolds Sister Rosario Marchesi, the Director of the house in San Paolo, Brasil: "Perché ora scrivi così di rado? Nel tuo orario speciale ci deve essere un'ora ogni settimana per scrivere alla Madre. Te lo dò per obbedienza e così non mancherai. Io vivo sempre collo spirito in mezzo a voi e puoi immaginare quanto desidero essere informata su tutto" [Why do you now write me so rarely? In your special schedule there must be an hour every week for writing to Mother. I give you this as an act of obedience so that you will not forget. I live always in spirit in your midst and you can imagine how much I desire to be informed about everything.] (Vol.4, lett. 1483).

Since the novitiate in Codogno was where most of her future spiritual daughters were trained, Cabrini writes to Mother Maddalena Savaré on March 12, 1895, in the very midst of her efforts to prepare the new building of Columbus Hospital, New York: "Dirai alle Sorelle che rammentino tutte quando mi scrivono di mettere nella sottoscrizione il nome da Suora, quello della loro famiglia e del loro paese perché, tra nuove e vecchie, mi fanno un poco di confusione mettendo solo il nome proprio" [Tell every one of the Sisters to remember that when they write me they should put at the bottom their name as Sister, that of their family and their town because, between the new and the old, they create a bit of confusion for me by putting only their proper name.] (Vol.2, lett. 690). By now the Order was growing by leaps and bounds, and Mother Cabrini anxiously wanted to know each sister individually, even if only by letter. On the other hand, by 1907, when she was fifty-seven years old, she had already founded some sixty-seven institutes on three continents and had built up her Order to over 1,500 missionaries.

As no biography can, the letters tell us where Mother Cabrini is, what she is doing, and what the spiritual and material concerns of the moment are in the various houses and in her mind. Above all, they help us to map her incessant movements back and forth across the United States, Europe, and the Atlantic and have a sense of the incredibly nomadic life she lived as head of the Order right up to her death in Chicago on December 22, 1917. We see her encourage and scold and command; we watch her assess character, give spiritual advice, repeatedly spell out the heroic virtues that would lead her daughters to become not only good missionaries but also holy. Indeed, time and again she exhorts her sisters to become saints ("*fateve sante!*"), and this she does in a variety of epistolary styles, depending upon the occasion. She often writes with humor, a touch of irony, fervor, and generally with persuasive gentleness. She also demands total obedience and stresses humility and self-abnegation as ways to obtain it. What consistently shows through is her unflagging strength of character, her unfailing trust in God, and her readiness to give all of herself all of the time. Frequently in the letters we are given glimpses of her frail health; particularly in New Orleans she suffered the heat and humidity of the Gulf climate and was bed-ridden several times, either with fever or with rheumatism ("*reuma*," she called it). Early on she was inflicted with malaria and this often kept her in bed and several times near death. Still, the sisters could rely on her for their every need, both spiritual and practical. Taken as a whole, her letters form a broad and deep record of a modern saint's life at the dawning of the twentieth century.

Little is said or known about the photographs of Mother Cabrini that I will discuss below. We do not know who took them or when. Nor have her many biographers cared to consider them as important sources for the study of her character, her spirituality, and her foundations as we are dealing with her here.

Figure 1

According to Segundo Galilea, a recent Cabrini biographer, in this first photograph [Figure 1] Mother Cabrini is in her early thirties, although she may be younger if we place the occasion at the time of her investiture of the religious habit.[9] It is the first public image, and perhaps the best, that we have of her. Although the background chosen for it is stark and nondescript, and the bare table (or predieu) and chair are simple and rustic, the photo may be taken as a

---

[9] See Galileo 32; he designates the time of the photo as "the time of the founding of the Institute."

celebration of her becoming the foundress of a new Order, with its own convent building and rule.

In that case the date would be November 14, 1880, now considered the birthday of the Institute.[10] But the photo may have been taken some four years earlier, when she first donned the religious habit and had still not taken her vows. At any rate, in this photo she is, in her own way, sitting at attention. She is serene but intense, sitting forward and upright in her chair rather than leaning back in it—with the air of a recruit! In effect, the purpose of the photo is officially to testify to her calling. The left hand, placed over the wrist of the right arm (holding a prayer book), helps to make the pose formal and suggests resolution. If Segundo Galilea's dating is right, it may also allude to the new missionary—rather than diocesan—pact between her and the Sacred Heart. All the signs of her vocation are present: the religious habit, the prominent crucifix on her breast, her prayer book, and above all her rosary which not only girds her waist but ends with a medal portraying the Sacred Heart.

Her hands in particular are illuminated, along with half of her countenance and her pectoral crucifix, so that implicitly they come to suggest the symbolic work of giving and service. Both hands and habit indicate her vocation, but only the former express the personal dimension of expenditure. And then there are her eyes, set rather deeply in a perfectly oval and utterly charming face. She has turned her head slightly in order to look straight at the camera and us. There is not a trace of the scarlet fever she had in childhood. As for the habit, compared to those of other religious orders of the day, it is made of a rough heavy cloth,

---

[10] See Sullivan 36, all of chapters 3 and 4. Sullivan dates this first photo 1880 (44).

extremely simple, uniformly black, and appropriate for the kind of inner-city work among the poor her Order would become famous for. As a uniform its purpose is to negate the figure of the person wearing it. Note, too, how it is made to cover the arm of the chair in order to keep her more prominently in the foreground. This is a modern woman ready to go out into the world, but one who has taken the vow of poverty. Thus, there is nothing fancy about the habit, unless one considers the bow under her chin a concession to religious fashion. On the other hand, the vows she took included those of poverty, humility, chastity, obedience, and charity, one she herself insisted upon.

Although, because of her frailty and poor health, Mother Cabrini was rejected by two different religious orders when she was young, the figure we see in the photo, half-smiling and alert, expresses nothing of this.[11] Her exposed hair, with the light catching it, reminds us that she is a young woman, perhaps even somewhat romantic and idealistic, as one should be who is just starting out on a long heroic journey into self-abnegation. Its manifestation, however, may suggest that she has not yet taken her final vows. While her posture clearly indicates she is ready to fare forward and meet the many challenges of missionary life, the prayer book and rosary remind us where her true strength lies. She is a soldier of the Sacred Heart, as her reading of Thomas à Kempis' *The Imitation of Christ* continued to teach her to be. Although a thoroughly modern and extraordinarily active woman, Mother Cabrini succeeded in living a highly contemplative life. As her book of resolutions and her letters demonstrate, she was also a mystic whose chief yearning remained union with God through the emptying out of self (*kenosis*).

---

[11] See Jones 260.

The second photograph [Figure 2] was taken around the time Mother Cabrini left for the United States for the first time in March of 1889 and now appears on the cover of her book *'Pensieri' e propositi,* published in its entirety in 1982. It is accompanied with no explanation.[12]

Figure 2

Here we are presented with a quite different Cabrini. This noticeably edited but familiar cameo pose strips her of her body and there is no competing background or corporeal detail to distract from her visage, except for the uniform black that blends in with her veil. The focus zooms in on her face alone, but above all on the eyes, which are looking steadily before her—into the providential future. Note, too, her mouth, which is slightly opened, expressing perhaps a sense of expectation. Her hair is now completely covered and the fabric of her veil is patently coarse. Once again, the eyes, with their pinpoint of light, are highly expressive; her

[12] In Sullivan's biography this photograph is dated 1889 (148).

gaze is fixed, wide-open, candid, inspired, and intimates her ardent zeal. *This* Cabrini is ready for her first Atlantic crossing and is therefore already grave.

It is fitting that she be presented in a less conventional pose than that in the first photograph, for there is simply no time for it in a missionary's life. She is also a bit older here and spiritually no longer a child. Evidently her apostolate has begun in earnest and the photo captures her unique strength of character. This is Cabrini at her most visionary, in the sense that the future lies entirely before her. In fact, she is about to embark on a life of travel and trials that will only end with her death. On one occasion she writes to her charges, "Hurry, hurry, my daughters, and happily. The world is too small for us to limit ourselves to a single point: I would like to embrace the whole of it and go everywhere" (*'Pensieri'* 36). And again: "I feel that the whole world is too small to satisfy my desires, and I will not rest until the sun no longer sets on the Institute, so that I can offer continual praise to the Sacred Heart of Jesus" (Ibid. 36-37). It is this passional tension that so obviously began to radiate from St. Philip Street in New Orleans following upon that August morning in 1892 when she arrived there to found an Institute. But on the verge of her first oceanic voyage she is still an almost private figure, except that six like-dressed sisters were always gathered around her now. Far more impressive on that maiden voyage out of Le Havre was the presence of some 1,500 immigrants in the hold of the ship. And yet, knowing beforehand of the impact she was about to have in the Americas, it is possible to catch a glimpse of that famous Cabrini style, as gayly modern as it was charismatic.[13]

---

[13] Segundo Galilea characterizes this style as her absolute trust in God, which led her time and again to begin her foundations without a penny to her name, counting instead on gifts and donations in order to succeed (42). Such was the case

This fascinating and heroically momentous group photo [Figure 3], with Mother Cabrini and another sister forming a focal point in the middle of three tiers of sisters, captures the second team of reinforcements that arrived at New York in June of 1890.[14]

Figure 3

Cabrini had made her second voyage to America already in April of that year and in a short period of time the New York mission had grown so rapidly that the orphanage alone cared for over four-hundred children. At this early stage all the sisters came from the novitiate in Codogno and hailed mostly from the small towns around Lodi, in northern Italy. The photo represents a *tableau vivant* (a living picture) and Mother Cabrini evidently wanted to use the occasion of the sisters' arrival both to make official the Institute's growing presence and to allude to the current of spiritual authority pulsing through it. The idea of handing a book to one of the sisters who is standing slightly behind her and receiving it with coyly averted eyes mines an age-old trope. The Order has taken root across the Atlantic and its apostolate abroad is growing so fast that now Cabrini must delegate someone

with the Institute in New Orleans, where in the first years the sisters went out daily into the immigrant neighborhood to beg for alms.
[14] Sullivan dates this picture June, 1889, but that simply cannot be (77). As Galilea correctly points out, in June, 1890, nine sisters arrived at the New York mission from Italy—four for the school in and five for the orphanage (70).

to run the foundation in New York in her absence. The book is either a bible or a prayer book or the Order's Rule. Passing it on signifies continuity, fidelity, growth, and the confirmation of an abiding fervor.

In her letters Cabrini constantly reminds the sisters to attend diligently to their spiritual exercises and obey the Rule which was written by her and finally approved by the Vatican on July 12, 1907. After all, it was this Rule (*Regula*) that would guarantee and preserve the founding spirit of the Order long after the passing of the founding generation. Behind the sisters reigns the statue of the Sacred Heart, given prominence by the focalizing action between Cabrini and another sister. This centripetal action opens up a spatial vista through which we recognize in the background the presiding presence of the statue of the Sacred Heart. As we saw in New Orleans, a version of this statue graced the chapel there, but it could be found wherever the Order established itself. Here, too, the country faces of the sisters and the various informal ways in which they pose their hands stir endless curiosity about the nature of the vineyard from which Cabrini harvested so many vocations. Thrown into the midst of one of New York's several Italian colonies, these simple young women, these soldiers of the Sacred Heart, appear suddenly to be ill-equipped and vulnerable, but also so patently determined to give entirely of themselves in the many Italian ghettos of the Americas where they will end up spending the rest of their lives. It is not at all surprising that a journalist who observed the sisters living and working in the heart of the Italian colony on the Lower East Side in mid-1889, would write the following in the June 30 edition of *The New York Sun*:

In these weeks, a group of women, of brunette complexion, dressed like Sisters of Charity, have been seen walking through the streets of Little Italy, climbing up narrow and dark stairs, going down basements and even risking to enter certain corners where not even the police dare to set foot. They were a habit and a veil different from those of others. Few speak English. It is an Institute which looks after orphans and all its members are Italian. The five or six sisters who have settled in this city are the pioneers of the congregation in the United States. They are led by Mother Frances Cabrini, a woman with large eyes and an attractive smile. She does not speak English, but she is a woman of firm determination. (Galilea 68)

The next photo [Figure 4] gives us a Cabrini at the height of her powers. It appears on the front and back covers of volume 2 of the critical edition of the letters, which covers the years 1891 to 1896.[15]

Figure 4

---

[15] Each volume of the letters features the photograph of Cabrini that best represents the period covered in that volume. Thus, there are five distinct photographs in all, but in none of the volumes is there a gloss providing contextual information on the photographs. Very likely this information has not survived.

This is how she would have appeared to the Italians on St. Philip Street in New Orleans in 1892. Facing the camera in a three-quarters pose, she appears healthy, commanding, and austere. In short, a public personage. Her gaze is penetrating and her face, with its peculiar texture and tones whitened out, more closely resembles the first photo discussed here than the second. Above all, she exudes the ministrating authority and stature of an ambassador or a person of rank. Already by 1891 she had developed a personal acquaintance with Pope Leo XIII and soon would be able to command a private audience with him. By 1891 she was habitually meeting with cardinals, bishops, presidents of foreign countries, and city dignitaries.

Also by 1891 her Order already counted one-hundred and fifty sisters and a steady influx of novices. Shortly she would also be known as a great administrator, one who built hospitals (in New York, Chicago, and further west) and made them turn a profit even while serving the poor for free. People so admired and trusted her that they were willing to contribute financially to her projects no matter how thin the shoe string. They would invariably get caught up in her spirit and become infected by her vision, her stillness, and her "*slancio*" (her inimitable drive). This Cabrini is portrayed as a worldly woman of action and of rare accomplishments, but not at the expense of her otherworldly aura of piety. The shiny silk band around the edge of her veil enhances and even intensifies her radiance, and its reflected light intermittently repeats the more brilliant band of halolight surrounding the crown of her head. Her figure also reminds us that we are looking upon the Foundress and Superior General of the Missionary Sisters of the Sacred Heart of Jesus.

When Sister Carolina Bertoli, then Director of the House in New Orleans, wrote alarmingly to Cabrini that the Mississippi was about to flood their neighborhood and the Institute, Cabrini writes back on March 18, 1903: "Scongiurate le acque, figliuole mie, con atti profondi di santa umiltà e con semplicità; [...] abbandonatevi nel Cuore SS. di Gesù [...]. Verrò tra voi e faremo una festa di ringraziamento a quel caro Gesù che vi avrà spero tutte liberate dai pericoli temporali e liberate ci avrà spero tutte dalle passioni ancora più pericolose delle anime nostre" [Exorcize the waters, my daughters, with deep acts of holy humility and simplicity; ... abandon yourself to the Most Sacred Heart of Jesus.... I will come among you and we will have a thanksgiving celebration in honor of that dear Jesus who, I hope, will have saved you from temporal dangers and, I hope, freed all of us from the still more dangerous passions of our souls.] (Vol.4, lett. 1290). Evidently, Cabrini wants her daughters above all to gird themselves spiritually, for it is the human passions that remain the chief threat and not the waters of the Mississippi. But, of course, she also promises to join them as soon as she possibly can and mentions that the sisters in New York are praying for them.

Four days later, when the danger of flooding seems to have subsided, Cabrini writes to Bertoli again: "Quando avremo la casa a Long Beach allora nei pericoli fuggirete colà; per ora invece fuggite nella caverna sacra cioè nel Cuore SS. di Gesù" [When we will have the house at Long Beach (on the Gulf coast of Mississippi) then when danger comes you will be able to flee there; but for now take refuge in the sacred cavern, that is, in the Most Sacred Heart of Jesus.] (Vol.4, lett. 1294). Ultimately, it is this inner sanctum that made the *Casa* on St. Philip Street *sacer*, that is, a place set apart—not a place of banishment now, as the neighborhood was after the murder of Hennessy, but a place of attraction protected by an equally inviolable sanction.

The next photo [Figure 5], far and away the most popular one of Cabrini, appears on the front and back covers of volume four of the critical edition of the letters, which covers the years 1902 to 1907.[16]

Figure 5

Apparently, it was taken on February 26, 1905, the day Archbishop Quigley dedicated Columbus Hospital in Chicago.[17] Again, we find a seated Cabrini with deep-set eyes now buried in shadow, and a mature and heavier face. The pose is frontal. The chair engulfs her and, being small, she sits forward in it, leaning her elbows on the arm rests. It is worth

[16] This photo also appears on the cover and opposite the title page of both Theodore Maynard's biography *Too Small a World. The Life of Mother Cabrini* and Lucille Papin Borden's *Francesca Cabrini: Without Staff or Scrip*; and as the only photo in Martindale's *Mother Francesca Saverio Cabrini*.

[17] This information is given as a caption to the photo in Sullivan (221), who also uses this photo for her cover.

comparing this image with the one from 1880, which is also a sitting portrait. Twenty-five years have passed and her folded hands are now thickened with age. It is evident from the eyes that she has suffered and she seems physically tried. She now has intermittent bouts of malarial fever, and constant intercontinental traveling has taken its toll on her. Yet her gaze is strong and steady as she looks directly into the camera. The photo is candid and does nothing to embellish the moment, although the occasion is triumphal. Mother Cabrini is not smiling here as she did in her 1880 picture, but she betrays her famous calm.

The picture already seems historical; a photo that speaks of someone who has lived fully and has persisted. Arguably, it is her vocation alone—and not her physical stamina—that now leads her on and the cross she wears is the one that she has carried a good many years. Directly below her hands is another of the Order's insignia, a large medal of the Sacred Heart. As she writes on March 13, 1899, to Sister Bernardina Vallisneri, now Director of the *Casa* of New Orleans, "Meditando ora la Passione di Gesù mi immagino che sarete divenute tutte sante. Oh! sì è pei meriti del Sangue di Gesù, dei suoi patimenti che ci ha meritato la vocazione, dono sopra ogni dono" [Now that you are meditating on the passion of Jesus, I imagine that you will all become saints. Oh! It is thanks to the effects of Jesus' blood, his sufferings, that he has won for us our vocation, the gift above all gifts.] (Vol.3, lett. 955). Cabrini was suffering from an attack of malaria from the beginning of January through March of 1899 and was unable to travel.[18] After admitting to her poor health, however, she goes on to draw strength from her very weakness. Writing from New Orleans on May

18 See Vol.3, lett. 965 of the critical edition of the letters, dated April 24, 1899 (817 St. Philip St.).

8, 1899, to Sister Gesuina Diotti, Director of the *Casa* of Rome, she confesses, "[S]ono diventata proprio un poco delicata, però [...] non mi manca la fibra del coraggio e vado avanti sempre con più fiducia, perché ove meno posso io può di più Colui che mi conforta" [I have become a little weak, but (...) I don't lack the fiber of courage and I go on with ever-increasing trust, because where I can do hardly anything He who comforts me can do more.] (Vol.3, lett. 966).

Immediately after, she recites her dearest motto: "*Omnia possum in eo qui me confortat*," and goes on to draw from it a spiritual lesson for the sisters in Rome: "Oh quanto è bello questo motto della Missionaria del Sacro Cuore di Gesù. Ogni giorno più mi pare di scorgere in quel sublimissimo motto una miniera inesauribile di tesori inestimabili. Ripetetelo frequente, o figliuoline mie carissime, e meditatelo che ne sentirete i sublimi effetti" [Oh how beautiful is this motto of the Missionary of the Sacred Heart of Jesus. Every day that passes I seem to glimpse in that most sublime motto an inexhaustible mine of priceless treasures. Repeat it often, oh my dearest little children, and meditate on it until you feel its sublime effects.]. Towards the close of the letter she adds one more counsel, which helps us better to understand the spirit of place which the Foundation in New Orleans' Little Palermo incarnated: "La Missionaria deve aver sempre molto da lavorare e morire in fine sul campo senza mai dire basta, né far scelta sulla qualità del lavoro." [The Missionary must always work hard and finally die in the field without every saying enough, or choosing the kind of work.]

Written from New Orleans, the lesson has additional force, for in 1897 (and later in 1905) the city was hit hard with yellow fever, and Little Palermo was at the very center of the epidemic, with the greatest number of victims.[19] On both occasions the sisters on St. Philip Street acted as intermediaries between the terror-stricken victims and the often intrusive public health officials. As the sisters' annals relate, their House became a small hotel for convalescents. They succeeded in penetrating places where the priests themselves could not go. Mother Saverio De Maria, Cabrini's earliest biographer, recounts that Cabrini asked the sisters "if they felt disposed to sacrifice themselves by going to the aid of the stricken."[20] Needless to say, they acted heroically and tirelessly throughout the crisis. They were given free access to the hospitals at any hour, assisted the dying at home, and helped make funeral arrangements for the family of the victim. Remarkably, all the sisters survived the epidemic as did the orphans in their charge. The word *sanctus* in Latin was originally used in reference to Christian emperors and, later, to the office of bishop. When, as she often did, Cabrini spurred her sisters on with the exhortation "*fatevi sante*" (become saints), she meant the words in the old sense, as a title of honor attributed to martyrs and confessors.[21] This photo of Cabrini from early 1905 has none of the gloss or affability of the photo from 1880, where her habit so fully dominated the foreground. Here we immediately sense a life of sacrifice and service, and the dignity she bears is the dignity of a life of charity and prayer. This image of her represents a different kind of authority than that portraying Cabrini as Mother General of a host of foundations. Here her authority is merely spiritual. But what other kind of prestige can there be for a Missionary Sister of the Sacred Heart who will soon be acclaimed a saint?

---

[19] See here Sullivan (126, 184-89); McMain (152-59).
[20] See Sullivan (186).
[21] See Gajano (5).

Of all the photos of Cabrini, I think this last one is the most eloquent [Figure 6], or perhaps we should say the most moving.

Figure 6

Like the others, its staging is intentionally severe and was probably taken at the insistence of the sisters of one of the foundations, as a favor to them. The argument would have been that, after all, the more time passed the less they saw of her, as she trekked forward on her endless rounds, visiting her Institutes in eight different countries in an attempt to encourage the sisters with her exhilarating presence. And what that presence was we can get a sense of here. For the first time, we have an almost full-length shot of her, and she is all religious habit again, except for her beatific countenance. Not even her hands are in sight now, as if her will alone were enough to found a new hospital or school or orphanage. In New Orleans in June of 1904, she succeeded in

winning a donation of $75,000 from Captain Salvatore Piz-
zati, a Sicilian, who made his fortune in shipping. At first,
Pizzati offered Cabrini a donation of $10,000, but her reply
was that what she really needed was a new orphanage. In
the end she succeeded in getting him to see himself as a
kind of patron of the orphans. And once this step was tak-
en, she even got him to oversee the building of it.[22]

The photo, you will note, has two centers of light: one
enclosed by her veil and the other deriving from the crucifix
she is wearing. Both sources testify to a life of sacrifice, and
she stands before us as one who has given more than she
herself has to give. Writing from New Orleans to Sister
Filomena Ajani, Provincial for the United States, on February 8, 1906, Cabrini responds to what must have been a
complaint of sorts: "Forse voi non pensate che potete morire
da un momento all'altro ed è forse per quello che tutto vi
pare pesante e grave. Se pensaste di avere sempre solo un
giorno allora sareste felici di patire per Cristo" [Perhaps you
don't think that you can die from one moment to the next,
and perhaps this is why everything seems heavy and bur-
densome to you. Were you always to have but one day left,
then you would be happy to suffer for Christ.] (Vol.4, lett.
1507). It is this kind of happiness that the photo captures
in her winsome countenance. In this last photo, then, she is
what she has become; life has marked her with its inescapable mortality and has left her with a full, disarming smile.
By this time she had founded some sixty-seven Institutes in
two hemispheres, and her Order was still rapidly growing.

In a sense this image of her is already spectral; and perhaps for this reason there is an aura of charity about her.
The ancient Greek work *kharis*, from which we derive our
word charity, spells out the link existing between the active

---

[22] See Vol.4, letters 1379, 1398, 1399, esp. 1400 (July 1, 1904), 1504, 1506.

force of giving and the effect of the gift—or *charisma*—on those who receive it. In ancient Greek culture *kharis* is always associated with beauty.[23] The aura of charity that surrounds Mother Cabrini represents a peculiarly spiritual beauty and derives from the communal space of her Order and that of the poor Italian immigrants in Little Palermo. Ultimately, it is foundations like the one in New Orleans and their surrounding communities that embody the visible place of grace which Mother Cabrini's charisma so poignantly intensifies. Rather early on (October 18, 1897), she wrote the following from Codogno, Italy, to Sister Vallisneri, the Director of the Casa of New Orleans: "Io in quest'anno conto andare a New York e quindi a New Orleans, città a me carissima sopra ogni altra. Mai parlo di codesta Missione senza sentirmi commossa al pensiero del come è avvenuta e del come è stata benedetta dal Cuore SS. di Gesù e pel bene che vi si può fare" [This year I plan on going to New York and then to New Orleans, the city which is dearer to me than any other. I never speak of this Mission without feeling moved by the thought of how it originated and how it has been blessed by the Most Sacred Heart of Jesus and of the good that can be done there.] (Vol.3, lett. 845).

So special was the Foundation on 81 St. Philip Street that she began recommending it to the other Institutes as a model for them to follow. Writing to Sister Giuseppina Pisoni in Paris on July 1, 1904, Cabrini tells her about Salvatore Pizzati's donation as follows: "Sono due mesi oggi che sono a New Orleans [...]. È una grazia del Sacro Cuore concessa a questa Casa dove si è sempre conservato un grande spirito di semplicità, di osservanza e di obbedienza [...]. Saluta tutte e tutte si studino alle belle virtù di questa Casa" [Today two months have passed since I came here to New

---

[23] See Hénaff (325ff).

Orleans (...). It is a favor of the Sacred Heart granted to this House, where a great spirit of simplicity, observance, and obedience has always remained intact. Give my greetings to everyone and may they all study the beautiful virtues of this House.] (Vol.4, lett. 1400). Eight days later she would write much the same thing to Sister Marchesi, Director of the House at San Paolo, Brasil: "Qui io credo che tale grazia è piovuta perché questa Communità si è sempre conservata molto semplice, umile, obbediente e molto osservante. Se voi fate lo stesso, io credo che avrete presto la stessa grazia" [I think that such a favor descended on this Community because it has always remained simple, humble, obedient, and very observant. If you do the same, I think you will soon have the same favor.] (Vol.4, lett. 1406). And on March 11, 1910, she writes to a sister in New Orleans saying, "Io sono sempre con voi in ispirito" [I am always with you in spirit.] (Vol.5, lett. 1748).

From the letters we know that over the years Mother Cabrini visited New Orleans at least six times and was in constant touch with the community there through a regular exchange of letters. The above mediographic discussion of her charismatic figure, accompanied by commentary from her letters, demonstrates the stages of her growing involvement and fame in Little Palermo and New Orleans at large. During her lifetime and after, the edification of her image helped to rally her communities and consolidate them around her example. As Michel de Certeau reminds us, however, it takes a community to create a saint, whose life, moreover, is not a temporal sequence so much as "a composition of places."[24] The Cabrini House on St. Philip Street (and later others in various parts of the city) was a special place. When the sisters set up their foundation

---

[24] See de Certeau (280-282).

there, they immediately introduced a new order of charity (based on community service, free schooling, liturgy, and Italian culture). Although directly motivated by the massacre of 1891, their presence there was totally gratuitous and unexpected. By this I mean, the Cabrini sisters gave of themselves spontaneously, freely, and wholeheartedly, according to an otherworldly logic. In point of fact, we can consider Cabrini's foundation in the midst of the Italian community above all as a cartographic point of mediation and intersection between two radically different orders, one secular and the other sacred. But even more than a point of intersection, it was a site of transformation, for a number of reasons.

As an instance of a special way of inhabiting the world, Cabrini's Order was a place set apart, consecrated by a set of spiritual virtues, which the presiding icon of the Sacred Heart so efficaciously symbolized. The House on St. Philip Street introduced a new point of view (a view from a point) in the blighted, poverty-stricken neighborhood of Little Palermo. In a very brief time, this House became inextricably tied to it as the sisters set about to weave the convent and the neighborhood into a single donative structure. In doing so, they turned their House into a community center. Writing to Sister Bianchi (the Director of the House in New Orleans) on October 29, 1892, Mother Cabrini tells her of her private audience with the Holy Father in Rome and of his intense interest in the New Orleans mission. Barely two months after she herself left New Orleans, Cabrini writes "Di costì gliel'ho ditto che siete in mezzo a Calabresi e Siciliani che contro ogni aspettativa si lasciano tanto bene maneggiare e che già ve li avete radunati tutti intorno [...]. Insomma io sono assai contenta di codesta Missione" [I told him, that there you are surrounded by Calabrians and Sicilians who, contrary to all expectations, allow themselves to be easily handled and that you have already gathered them around you. In sum, I am very happy of this mission.] (Vol.2, lett. 530).

Through ascesis and community service, therefore, the new Order took on the site-specific affinities of the besieged immigrant neighborhood. If the sisters radiated holiness, the process of their sanctification derived from the surrounding community. Cabrini was made holy by her role in behalf of the immigrants, and contemporaneously the House on St. Philip Street became a *locus religiosus*, a new byword in Little Palermo but also in the city. For that matter, Cabrini's body was itself a vector of transformation—of victory over violence, terror, racism, poverty, and abjection. Such was the scenography of New Orleans when she first arrived in St. Philip Street. Her holiness—and that of the Missionaries working in Little Palermo—was a consequence of her charitable life. Writing from New Orleans to Sister Maddalena Savaré, Director of the House at Codogno, she points out that hate "è la più grande rovina alla Carità, che è il soave e dolce legame che, unendoci come corpo compatto, ci unisce pure al Bel Cuore di Gesù. [...] mancando il quale manca tutto e più niente appar buono" [Hate is the greatest ruin of Charity, which is the gentle and sweet bond that makes us into a compact body and also unites us to the Beautiful Heart of Jesus.] (Vol.3, lett. 970). As de Certeau in his essay on hagiography notes, "We encounter here a *poetics of meaning* that cannot be reduced to an exactitude of facts or of doctrine" (274).

Allow me, then, to make a few concluding observations regarding historical method and historical consciousness which a consideration of the appropriate "poetics of meaning" begs us to raise. The two opening scenes involving the

Italian community of New Orleans mentioned at the outset are more than casually related. In effect, the sudden presence of the Missionary Sisters of the Sacred Heart in the city's Little Palermo is a *direct effect* of the ritual killings and lynching of eleven juridically innocent Italian immigrants. I have assigned these apparently quite different scenarios to a single historical constellation in order to provide a more inclusive narrative of this immigrant enclave within the city at large. In doing so, we can immediately see the heuristic advantages in aspiring to a 'total' narrative of both sequences. In multiple ways the latter manifest a doubling pattern that links them linguistically, semantically, and ethically.

Numerous books and articles have already been written on the first sequence of events (the murder of David Hennessey, the police raids into Little Palermo, the politically rigged trial, and the following massacre of the exonerated Italian immigrants). Therefore, I have chosen to focus on the little-known intimate rapport of Cabrini and her missionary sisters with New Orleans by exploring the critical edition of her recently published letters—above all, those to and from the Order's *Casa* on St. Philip Street. I have also sketched a biographical profile of Mother Cabrini based primarily on the rare photographic images we have of her. This profile alerts us to the language and concepts that motivated the sisters' missionary actions in New Orleans. Evidently, it is the problematical yoking of this material and the historical sequences of 1891 to a single hermeneutic project that forces us, as historians and cultural studies scholars, to foreground the radically different scales of representation and spectrum of values involved in narrating it. Nevertheless, it is our decision to do so that creates the unique heuristic tension necessary to shed full light on their significance.

A further purpose of this composite constellation is to promote a shift in interpretation of our historical understanding of the moments under discussion, moments that require us to reflect on the very nature of historical consciousness. By linking the two scenes in a single narrative, we are thereby compelled not only to call on but also to ponder and deploy different historiographical sensibilities. In the case of our two intertwined scenarios this project proves altogether advantageous as we seek to construct a version of Marcel Mauss's total social fact. Thus the doubling action that I mentioned above delineates a shared, albeit polysemic, language of martyrdom, sacrifice, kenosis, passionate action, community, vendetta, honor and shame, and ultimately naked life (existentialism's being-towards-death). By putting the Italian immigrant community and its imprisoned victims temporarily outside the law, the various leaders and people of New Orleans in effect created the scapegoats they needed in order to restore internal order to a blatantly corrupt, violent, and white-supremicist regime.

As our focus on the letters and life of Cabrini and her missionary order in New Orleans reveals, Cabrini and her sisters resemanticized the same anthropological language used racially to banish and terrorize the entire Italian enclave and, in a very short period of time, they recast it in a totally positive light, according to a donative vocation motivated by other-worldly values. As we have seen, in her letters Cabrini passionately evoked the language of martyrdom, kenosis, and sacrifice as a normative part of the spiritual aspirations of her Order. Moreover, the city authorities, the press, and a good portion of its non-Italian citizens (many of whom were Catholic) were quick to appreciate what we might call the Cabrini effect not only on Little Palermo but also on New Orleans at large. As I have tried to demonstrate in this essay, the two antithetical historical scenarios converge in their common appeal to the metaphorology of the sacred heart (universally considered the organ of life) and its running dialectic of life and death. In the light of this linguistic and semantic doubling activity informing both scenarios, scholars should readily acknowledge the representational and ethical challenges our historical constellation presents by providing as complete a description as possible of its singularity.

Thus, the scholar as interpreter is called upon to construct an appropriate methodological horizon in order to foreground the full range of epistemological tensions the constellation hosts. For when studying the extraordinary intersection of events and careers of 1891 and 1892, we are not simply faced with a set of actions requiring explanation; rather we are already *involved* in them as interpreters. In short, interpretation itself is a narrative "mise en acte" that is far from being neutral. Together, the ritual massacre of eleven Italian immigrants and the gratuitous life of service offered by Cabrini's sisters to the immigrants of Little Palermo and the city as a whole, create the interpretative horizon that best explains the cultural and economic tensions between the immigrant enclave and the surrounding city as a single narrative site. Ethically involved as narrator, the historian of these sequences must not only divine their sense but also sense the divine in them. Indeed, as I tried to do here, we must construct our hermeneutic task precisely around the occasionally untranslatable exchanges between the secular and religious dimensions of reality, both of which are radically imbued with the impersonal dimension of sacred life.

Some weeks into her first visit to New York in 1889, and after considerable stress and indifference from those who should have come to her aid, Mother Cabrini finally found rooms in "*bassa città*" (Lower Manhattan). On the first day that she went to take possession of them, she found outside the door a statue of the Sacred Heart given to her by an Italian craftsman, and at its feet there was also a loaf of bread. As Sister Umilia Capietti bent to pick up the bread with the idea of taking it with them, Mother Cabrini said to her, "No, leave it there. It's a sign that we will never be wanting." Events in themselves don't exist or mean anything. They happen and must be semanticized and explained. History does not have a threshold of knowledge; nothing that has happened is outside its bounds.[25] The killing of eleven juridically innocent Italian immigrants by a lynch mob in New Orleans in 1891 was an event that exploded from out of the uniform plane of everyday life. It made a difference. So did the sudden arrival in New Orleans of the Missionary Sisters of the Sacred Heart a year later, thereby heroically pitting the effects of charity against those of passionate hate and fear.[26]

WORKS CITED

Asbury, Herbert. *The French Quarter. An Informal History of the New Orleans Underworld*. New York: Thunder's Mouth Press, 2003 [Orig. pub. 1936].

Boesch Gajano, Sofia. *La santità*. Bari: Laterza, 1999.

Cabrini, Francesca Saverio. *'Pensieri' e propositi*. Rome: Centro Cabriniano, 1986.

Cosco, Joseph P. *Imagining Italians. The Clash of Romance and Race in American Perceptions, 1880-1910*. New York: SUNY Press, 2003.

---

[25] See Veyne (26-27).
[26] I would like to thank Sr. Lina Colombiani, MSC, Sup. Generale, Istituto delle Missionarie del Sacro Cuore di Gesù, Rome, for the privilege of being able to cite from the letters and reproduce five photographs of Mother Cabrini.

De Certeau, Michel. *The Writing of History*. Trans. Tom Conley. New York: Columbia University Press, 1988.

Debray, Régis. *Cours de médiologie générale*. Paris: Gallimard, 1991.

Galilea, Segundo. *In Weakness, Strength. The Life and Missionary Activity of Saint Francis Xavier Cabrini*. Trans. Colette Joly Dees. New York: Missionary Sisters of the Sacred Heart of Jesus, Stella Maris Province, 2004.

Gambino, Richard. *Vendetta. The True Story of the Largest Lynching in U.S. History*. Toronto and Buffalo: Guernica, 2000.

Glazer, Nathan and Moynihan, Daniel P. *Beyond the Melting Pot*. Cambridge, MA: M.I.T. Press, 1963.

Hénaff, Marcel. *Le prix de la vérité: le don, l'argent, la philosophie*. Paris: Seuil, 2002.

Jones, Kathleen. *Women Saints*. Maryknoll, New York: Orbis Books, 1999.

Mauss, Marcel. *The Gift*. Trans. W.D. Halls. New York & London: W.W. Norton, 2000.

Margavio, A.V. and Salomone, Jerome J. *Bread and Respect. The Italians of Louisiana*. Gretna: Pelican Publishing Company, 2002.

Martindale, C.C. *Mother Francesca Saverio Cabrini. Foundress of the Missionary Sisters of the Sacred Heart*. London: Burns Oates & Washbourne Ltd., 1931.

Maynard, Theodore. *Too Small a World. The Life of Mother Cabrini*. Milwaukee: The Bruce Publishing Company, 1953.

McMain, Eleanor. "Behind the Yellow Fever in Little Palermo," *Charities and Commons* 15 (1905): 152-159.

Papin Bordon, Lucille. *Francesca Cabrini. Without Staff or Scrip*. New York: Macmillan Company, 1946.

Rimanelli, Marco and Postman, Sheryl Lynn, eds. *The 1891 New Orleans Lynching and U.S.-Italian Relations. A Look Back*. New York, Bern, Berlin: Peter Lang, 1992.

Sullivan, Mary Louise, MSC. *Mother Cabrini, 'Italian Immigrant of the Century.'* New York: Center for Migration Studies, 1992.

Yeyne, Paul. *Comment on écrit l'histoire*. Paris: Seuil, 1996.

Wittgenstein, Ludwig. *Tractatus Logico-Philosophicus*. Trans. C.K. Ogden. London and New York: Routledge & Kegan Paul, 1988.

Tutto è burla
Humor and Identity in Italian American Culture

JOHN LOWE
Louisiana State University

In 1892, Giuseppe Verdi, Italy's greatest living composer, was persuaded by his collaborator, Arrigo Boito, to embark on a final opera, a comedy based on their beloved Shakespeare's *Falstaff*. As Verdi wrote, "What a joy! To be able to say to the Audience, 'WE ARE HERE AGAIN!!'" (Phillips-Matz 700). They came to refer to Falstaff as "Big Belly," and after the opera's premiere at La Scala in 1893, Verdi, now 79 years old, sent an autograph score to his publisher Ricordi, and inserted a note: "The Last notes of Falstaff. Everything is finished! Go on, go on, old John.... Go on down your road as far as you can.... Entertaining sort of rascal eternally true, beneath different masks, all the time, everywhere!!" (Phillips-Matz 718-19). In a letter to the conductor Edoardo Mascheroni, he wrote of both his joy in the opera's success and of his sadness at concluding his career: What 'we, 'what 'art'.... We? Poor supers with the job of beating the bass drum until they say to us 'Shut up over there. '*Tutto nel mondo è burla!*" (Phillips-Matz 718-19). The United States premiere of *Falstaff* was mounted at the Metropolitan in 1895, where it had been eagerly awaited by Verdi's Italian immigrant countrymen. Although the play that inspired it was English, Boito's libretto and Verdi's music made it their own, as did that "big belly" of Falstaff's that is the subject of so many Italian jokes dealing with excess, be it by a greedy priest, a thieving merchant, or a wily robber.

The opera's success at home and abroad put Verdi in excellent humor, and he wrote, again to Mascheroni, "What marvelous comedies are born all the time in the theatre and outside it too" (Phillips-Matz 700). And indeed, Italian literature and culture offer one of the world's richest repositories of humor of all sorts, from high to low, as Henry Spaulding's delightful anthology *Joys of Italian Humor* demonstrates. A text by one of my favorite Italian authors, Leonardo Sciascia, offers a convenient bridge between Italy and Little Italy. "The Long Crossing" concerns a group of Sicilian immigrants who gather to board a boat one night, en route to America. The man who has engaged their passage, "some sort of traveling salesman," promises to land them on a New Jersey beach, thus avoiding immigration. "The cunning ones ... had borrowed from the money-lenders with the secret intention of defrauding them, in return for the hardship they had been made to endure over the years by the usurers 'greed'" (18). After a voyage of eleven days, they are put ashore, as promised, on a beach. But the first car that passes looks like a Fiat. No problem: "They use our cars for fun, they buy them for their kids like we buy bicycles for ours" (20). But then the road sign reads SANTA CROCE CARAMINA—SCOGLITTI. "I seem to have heard that name before.... Perhaps one of my family used to live there ... before he moved to Philadelphia ... we don't know how the Americans read it, because they always pronounce words in a different way from how they're spelt.... I shall stop the next car ... all I've got to say is 'Trenton? '... they'll point or make some kind of sign.... The Fiat came round the bend ... the driver braking.... 'Trenton? 'the man asked. '*Che?* 'said the driver. 'Trenton? "*Che trenton della madonna,* 'the driver exclaimed, cursing. The passengers look at each other, thinking, 'seeing that he speaks Italian, wouldn't it be best to tell him the whole story? Cursing, the driver leaves, and one passenger says 'I've just remembered ... when the crops failed ... my father went to Santa Croce Carmarina 'to work.' 'There was, after all, no need to hurry back to the others with the news that they had landed in Sicily" (23).

Of course those who actually landed in America might well have felt they were in Sicily too, especially if they wound up in one of the many Little Italy neighborhoods, where for some time life, lived in a tightly knit ethnic enclave, continued to resemble the one they had left behind. Part of the baggage they brought with them that proved to be life-sustaining was their comic conventions, tales, modes of discourse, and wise sayings, products of an oral culture that continued to circulate as long as the wick of memory flared.

Comedy was being created on the streets of New York at this time too, and in its theatres. Edward Harrigan, American actor, manager, and playwright, was born in 1844 in New York on the lower East Side, the son of an Irish immigrant who had originally settled in Canada, and a Virginia-born mother. As a result, most of his characters were Irish, but many others were black, German, Chinese, and yes, Italian. "It was from my mother that I learned most of my Negro business and songs" (Koger 1). After a life at sea, Harrigan wound up in San Francisco and was lured to the stage, playing in minstrel and variety shows. Soon, finding ethnic sketches were popular, he was mining his Irish/Southern roots. On tour in Chicago, he met a talented 16-year-old singer, Anthony Cannon, who excelled in women's parts. Renaming him Tony Hart, Harrigan and his protégée began a vaudeville team, specializing in ethnic sketches. Moving to New York in 1872, they had their own theatre by 1876. They portrayed virtually every type of ethnic American in these early years, specializing at first in "Dutch"

(German) acts and minstrel black face sketches—in one, Harrigan portrayed Uncle Tom to Hart's Topsy. Eventually Harrigan moved up to full-length comic plays with music; his first great success, *The Mulligan Guard Ball*, 1879, led to an entire series of "Mulligan" plays with repeating characters, with most plays set in the multiethnic "Mulligan's Alley" on the Lower East Side. Harrigan wrote all the plays, most of the lyrics to the songs, and usually played an Irish hero opposite Hart's drag characterization of either the heroine or the leading black female figure. The team split in 1885 after their theatre burned. Harrigan then leased the Park Theatre and produced a string of Hart-less hits such as *Old Lavender* (1885), *The Leather Patch* (1886), *The O'Reagans* (1886), *Pete* (1888), and *Waddy Googan* (1888), a play about Italian Americans. James Dormon has speculated that Harrigan's Italians are not that clearly fo-cused because the southern Italian exodus was fairly recent: as Harrigan said in an interview, "some day there'll come a man who will...do things with the Italians as I did with the Irish and the Negroes. But not yet. We aren't well enough acquainted with them yet" (cited in Dormon 32). Although Harrigan painted sympathetic portraits of Italian women, he relied on stiletto bearing, rough Italian men—some members of the mafia—to provide menace in his plays. An Irish bartender in *The Leather Patch* states that "I carry me life in me hands behind me bar. I'm patronized by Italians who carry stilettos and nagurs with razors" (18). Of course he keeps a shillelagh himself for such encounters.

Harrigan also employed the stereotypical Italian dialect. In *Last of the Hogans*, the Irish gang imitates the Italians as they brandish their razors, yelling "Cutta. Soona. Quicka." (cited in Dormon 33), in yet another reference to the ever present stiletto. On the other hand, Harrigan also favors hard-working junk dealers, organ grinders, or fruit stand operators, all of whom demonstrate exuberant humor and a fondness for song, a staple in all of Harrigan's plays, for which he and John Brahm wrote hundreds of songs. The tenement setting featured by Harrigan is what Bakhtin calls the public square. Everything is made public—especially personal peccadilloes. As Bakhtin asserts, it is "necessary to liberate all these objects and permit them to enter into the free unions that are organic to them, no matter how monstrous these unions might seem from the point of view of ordinary, traditional associations" (169).

Harrigan's comedies had a hopeful energy to them, in that rather than bemoaning, as Henry James did when he visited the Lower East Side, the apparent Babel that America had become, the plays celebrate the carnivalization of culture, where no one language—since all are in dialect form—constitutes a standard. Here we find a play of all immigrant utterances, with all constituting both masks and signs. Harrigan appropriates dialects, yes, even commodifies them, but at the same time he legitimizes them and, to a certain extent, refuses to hierarchize them. The plays of Harrigan, like many classics of Italian American literature, are often situated around feasts or celebrations, and eating and drinking play prominent roles in both the plots and the modes of characterization. This is in keeping with the premise that the characters are "becoming," for eating and drinking are manifestations of the unfinished nature of the body and its interaction with the world. As Bakhtin indicates, this rending of food and incorporating it into the body suggests an incorporation of the world, a joyful triumph, in fact, over the world. Eating the bounty of America symbolizes becoming America. A joke could also be said to be a kind of eating—an incorporation of something orally, blending it with an unexpected opposite. Bakhtin also states that a festive occasion inevitably suggests looking into better days to come (286).

How does this relate to comic literature actually written by Italians? Their written record began immediately after they arrived here; the greatest numbers came during what has been called the "Mediterranean-Slavic" period of immigration (1890-1914), when over twenty million people arrived; five million were Italian. From the beginning, Italian Americans wrote mostly about the family and alienation, and that has not changed, really, over the past century. The best known until the past few decades were Paul Gallico, Bernard De Voto, Mario Puzo, and Lawrence Ferlinghetti. Scholars such as the ones in our organization alongside Italian writers themselves began to champion figures such as Pietro Di Donato, John Fante, Jerre Mangione, and Tina Di Rosa. Helen Barolini's novel *Umbertina* (1979) and her path-breaking anthology, *The Dream Book* (1985), brought about a second renaissance for Italian American writing through its women, which continues unabated to this day. That movement was vastly accelerated through the equally path-breaking critical work of Mary Jo Bona, Edvige Giunta, and others who helped us understand new novelists such as Josephine Hendin, Mary Cappello, and Diana Cavallo. With a few exceptions, however, these writers and critics don't often employ, or discuss, humor.

As Rose Basile Green notes, many early Italian American novels paralleled others in parallel ethnic traditions, which depicted immigrant heroes adapting the American model of self-help to achieve upward mobility, often by ruthlessly exploiting other members of their group. An Italian American example would be Garibaldi Marti Lapolla's *The Grand Gennaro* (1935), which echoed other ethnic classics in this vein such as James Weldon Johnson's *The Autobiography of an Ex-Colored Man* (1912) and Abraham Cahan's *The Rise of David Levinsky* (1917). These books had been conceived as more serious versions of the popular WASP volumes of Horatio Alger, and books by more prominent figures, such as William Dean Howells's *The Rise of Silas Lapham* (1885). Christie Davies also notes an opposite tradition in jokes about Italians Sicilian born Mafia figures, who come off as brave, ruthless, loyal, and organized. Indeed, Ronald Reagan got in trouble telling one such joke:

> How do you tell the Polish one at a cock-fight?
> He's the one with the duck.
> How do you tell the Italian?
> He's the one who bets on the duck.
> How do you tell the Mafia is there?
> The duck wins. (Davies, 202)

We see many other comic traditions, however, in the pages of the Italian American novel. In an interview with Fred Gardaphé and Anthony Bruno, Jerre Mangione was pessimistic about the future of Italian American literature. He did think, however, that at least four major texts would always be taught and read: Pietro DiDonato's *Christ in Concrete* (1939), his own *Mount Allegro* (1943), Mario Puzo's *The Fortunate Pilgrim* (1964), and Tina di Rosa's *Paper Fish* (1980) (Gardaphé and Bruno 54).

An old Italian proverb states that "a wise hen does not cackle in the presence of the cock," and as Italian American humor theorist Regina Barreca has written, until recently, women in the community told jokes—many of them about me [Barreca]—only in the kitchen. Di Rosa's text broke that silence and began a secondary renaissance of Italian American women's writing; *Paper Fish* deserves its legendary status as a revolutionary novel, one filled with rage and sadness, rather than humor. As many theorists have noted, revolutionary writers in the political and social sense rarely demonstrate much humor; revolt is serious business. And indeed, many early classics of the wider feminist/womanist movement are similarly humorless; it was only after some advances had been won and a critical mass of voices achieved that women could afford to indulge in levity and to explore the possibilities of subversive, liberating humor.

Accordingly, I will here consider the neglected humor in two of the "classics" Mangione named, beginning with *Mount Allegro*, then proceeding to *The Fortunate Pilgrim*. In 1906 Edward A. Steiner, an immigrant himself, and a man who made his career out of writing sympathetic books about immigrants, nevertheless characterized "the Italian emigration, the largest which we receive from any one source" as coming largely from the "crowded cities" of Southern Italy "with their unspeakable vices; the smallest number of emigrants come from the villages where they have all the virtues of the tillers of the soil. The most volatile of our foreign population, and perhaps the most clannish, they represent a problem recognized by their home government" (28). He then notes these dirty Southerners "had lost the romance of their native land but not the fragrance of garlic. They quarreled somewhat loudly and gesticulated wildly; but were good neighbors during those sixteen days.... All Italians are not alike...they do not look alike, and ... they are not all Anarchists" (28). Sicilians suffered more than most from such analyses, as they were already burdened with a special onus *within* the Italian community, one which increased with their exodus to America, where all of them were presumed to be members of the mafia, or uneducated, primitive peasants, or both. Jerre Mangione, a member of that community whose nine published books include four memoirs, was determined that "at last, the Sicilian immigrants, the most maligned of the Italian Americans, would be presented as I knew them to be, not as the criminals projected by the American press" (*Ethnic* 242-43).

But how was one to reverse negative perceptions of one's ethnic group without lecturing, and thereby turning off one's audience? One way was to capitalize on the tremendous interest in ethnic life by writing apparently benign, but actually corrective versions of their communal life into the consciousness of "mainstream" Americans, and the engine that drove such ethnic texts was frequently humor. Autobiography proved particularly useful in this experimental project, for as James Olney has pointed out, there are no rules or formal requirements for the writer, or for the critic of autobiography (3). Moreover, both the genre and the discourse of humor annul the distance between speaker and audience/ reader, creating warmth, intimacy, and new perspectives. Subjects at a distance are not comical, but brought near they may be satirized, toppled, or even transformed.

Mangione chose a key cultural moment for the publication of his personal *storia*, when Americans were dedicating themselves to a redefinition of their purpose and identity, during World War II. The fact that Italian Americans were dying for their country in battle against their ancestral homeland demanded attention. Mangione also wrote other autobiographical texts, *Reunion in Sicily* (1950) and *An Ethnic at Large* (1978), which echo and extend the themes of *Mount Allegro*.

When *Reunion in Sicily* was published in 1950, *The Boston Post*'s reviewer said that Mangione had an "American eye" and a "Sicilian heart." For Deidre Bair, the book offers the narratives "of a young man of two worlds who wishes to understand and be able to live with ease and acceptance in both of them" (xii). Mangione's account of duality, his desire for acceptance, and his preference for scientific perspective all helped foster the clarity and balance of his account. In fact, he more or less operates as a self-taught sociologist and ethnographer in Sicily in his memoirs. This meant acquiring a certain kind of detachment; in 1983 Mangione told an interviewer that *Mount Allegro* was designed to describe Sicilian American life, but also to chart his own "Pilgrim's Progress" from being a "kind of confused Italian-American living in two cultures, to observing them and writing about them objectively, as I came to understand them, as I grew older and more mature—and also from a distance. If I had never left Rochester, I would never have been able to write about them as I have.... I could also contrast them with the non-Sicilian and non-Italian world in which I found myself" (Mulas 75). We should remember that in 1943, *Mount Allegro*'s sunny nature made it an alternative to wartime despair and thus contributed to the needed national unity. Moreover, it was an opportunity to disarm readers' fears, and charm them with the joyous creativity, humor, and wit of Italian Americans.

Mangione has stated that *Mount Allegro*'s characters took on a life of their own: "The book was intended to be ... informative, ... sedate. It did not work out that way ... before long my ... protagonists were asserting themselves in a manner that exceeded the etiquette of the conventional memoir" (302). Their irascible and frequently comic behavior made them, instead of caricatures, human; Mangione claimed to have received hundreds of appreciative letters, including many from Anglos, who identified pleasurably with his Sicilian relatives. On the other hand, boundaries are maintained through humor; thus pressures from without the group and from within operate in determining identity, and they often take the form of jokes or corrective kidding.

Freud always maintained that the basic comic unit involved a forced juxtaposition of opposites. Bakhtin saw that this was also the opening gambit in dialogism. And in fact, one of Mangione's favorite narrative modes is the comic confrontation; when people collide in a quarrel they create entertainment, but also, frequently, a resolution that reveals a truth. Mangione describes a comic scene in Sicily; he's crowded inside a taxi with his uncle, five cousins, and luggage. "In bickering over the fare, insults and personal data were exchanged freely. The driver told of the number of mouths he had to feed, of the exorbitant prices he paid for rent, gasoline and repairs, and called us 'extortionists.' My uncle countered with a recital of the large number of children he had to support, his wife's recent illness, the tiny salary he earned, the exorbitant price of bread and macaroni, and called him a 'dirty capitalist.' The haggling was still in full swing when we drew up in front of my uncle's place.... I though surely that the argument would lead to blows. But after ten more minutes of insults, they suddenly settled ... and courteously bade each other good morning" (*Reunion* 32). This exchange operates on the border of joking and insult, and is akin to the custom in African American culture of the dozens, where adolescent boys verbally duel, usually hurling insulting comments about the opponent's female relatives, especially "yo mama." Ordinarily, a joking relationship permits exchanges to occur which create sham battles, as with the taxi driver, which thus avoids real conflict. As Radcliffe-Brown comments, such a situation affords each person safe conduct through what is otherwise hostile territory (107). In Mount Allegro or Sicily these codes are understood; but sometimes, when boundaries of identity shift, as it does when Mangione visits his Sicilian relatives, they must be reinterpreted, renegotiated.

As late as World War II and beyond, books like Mangione's were welcome attempts to create understanding and even intimacy between Americans, and to offer vital portraits of real people that would flesh out the desiccated histories of the period. As part of that program, ethnic life narratives were liberally studded with miniature stories, literary fruitcakes bursting with flavor. In Mangione's books, these tales are told amid the feasting and drinking of Amoroso family get-togethers on Sundays and have a similarly festive and nutritive quality. Mangione asks "what better means of consolation are there than people and wine?" and tells us that "a meal was more than a meal; it was a ritual and ... adults ... were the high priests" (17). Bakhtin says that "no meal is ever sad," and these never are. Here, and in the one comic chapter in Di Donato's *Christ in Concrete*, "Fiesta," tale tellers use vulgar gestures, noises, obscene puns, a whole arsenal of Rabelaisian humor, in telling tales in which, as in African American stories, the lowest peasant prevails, scheming aristocrats are punished, and love conquers all. As William Boelhower comments in his brilliant analysis of such scenes, "It is the social voice alone that is able to talk down the private written word of the American autobiographical tradition, thus celebrating its own subaltern condition" (Boelhower 205). Mount Allegro's houses, streets, and shops, with their relentless sifting of the community's characters through gossiping tales, replicate the congested Sicilian villages and the communal viewing and reviewing of the *passeggiata*, the long evening strolls around the square, where one sees and is seen, comments and is commented on. As we get to know Mangione's relatives (significantly renamed by him as the Amoroso family), we increasingly appreciate the subtleties of their individual comic modes of narration, and begin to perceive them as representative of American Sicilian culture, a people keenly and equally alert to their joint history and social nuance.

Comic tale-telling and verbal dueling are not the only modes in the book. Mangione alternates between the earthy, pointed, body-oriented humor of comic exchanges, and brooding, often tender reflective passages. For instance, describing his father and partner Uncle Nino playing *briscola*, in the days before they tellingly "became Americanized enough to learn poker," Mangione notes, "you would have had to go a long way to see a signal system as complicated as the one my father and Uncle Nino used. They would tweak their noses, belch, purse their lips, scratch their heads as though they really had lice—in fact, go through any gesture, permissible or not in decent company, that would tell their partner what cards they held an at the same time confuse their opponents to such an extent that they could not keep their thoughts straight" (14). Alternately, like the relatives he celebrates, Mangione may wax poignantly poetic: "Sometimes, at night, the sickly yellow glow of the factory was in the sky like a smouldering ceiling of sulphur. Underneath it my relatives sang and played guitars and, if they noticed the sky at all, they were reminded of the lemon groves in Sicily. They were stubborn poets" (*Mount Allegro* 41).

Moreover, Mangione stitches together scene after scene that fosters carnivalization of communal discourse, thereby giving a voice to every member of the community and creating an encyclopedic gaze. Rather than operating as aggressive, selfish individuals, community members seek each other out for joking, feasting, and gossip. Much of the joking and gossiping would be corrective. Mangione introduces this concept by demonstrating how the women, sewing near the *briscola* table, handle disorderly conduct: "The disadvantage of playing with children who were related was that any of the mothers sitting within striking distance felt she had the prerogative of delivering stinging slaps with the back of her hand, regardless of whether the target was her own child or not. Of course, if your own mother reached you, the slap was likely to be twice as stinging because she loved you more" (15). There is an ironic comment here, but beneath, one suspects, an actual truth. And the situation speaks metaphorically for the less physical processes of correction that joking and kidding initiate, as members of the extended family use their wits to hammer away at deviance from group norms and expectations. It is interesting that most Italian American writers—and for that matter, critics—have ignored the subject of many jokes told about the Italians—namely, their supposed cowardice during the two world wars. As Christie Davies notes, wartime humor often consists of mocking, non-patriotic humor that critiques top brass, crazy rules, and evinces a desire to get back home. In this sense the role of Italians in cowardice jokes is not only understandable, but perhaps admirable as well. Further, although Davies doesn't consider this factor, many Italian American writers hailed from Southern Italy and Sicily, regions traditionally treated badly and joked about by northern Italians, a tradition that has a venomous counterpart today in the Lega Nord party.

An example of such jokes: "What does the Italian battle flag look like?" "A white cross on a white field." Another joke depicts Mussolini on a balcony asking a troop of soldiers for volunteers for a dangerous mission. No one does, so he declares the feather he is dropping will land on a future hero's head. An hour later, he looks out and all the soldiers are still puffing the feather up as hard as they can. Or this one:

"How do you train Italians to be soldiers?" "First teach them to raise their hands above their heads" (Davies 174-75). Or, "What was the name of Mussolini's flagship?" "Chicken of the Sea." Many of these jokes have a second dig embedded against southerners: "What do you call a Neapolitan with a war medal?" "A thief" (Davies 197). Such jokes have also been told about Egyptians after their defeat by Israel, and have counterparts in Spain about Galicians, in Pakistan about Kashmiris and Bengalis, and in Iran about Kashis. Davies explains, too, that "The Italians failed to develop a sense of unity or of commitment to their new nation-state, and the poor performance of the Italian army in the Spanish Civil War, and both World Wars was a result"; as he asserts, "there is no reason to believe that Italians are as individuals, cowardly or disordered, but historically they have been reluctant to place their bravery and capacity for organization at the service of the state, which has often been seen in the South as insignificant and/or illegitimate" (Davies 189). He also notes that loyalty to family and kin became more important because of such feelings, and we may go further and look to this as the reason for the prominence of *la famiglia* in both Italian and Italian American literature.

Along these lines, in *Reunion in Sicily* at Easter, a risen Christ is revealed in the church, usually holding a red flag. Mangione is puzzled when this year it's white. It seems in the recent election campaign the communists had spread the story that Christ had been a Communist; as proof they cited the red flag he holds in resurrection. So a white flag is substituted, but "some of the priests objected to this on the grounds that a white flag signified surrender. As one of them argued, a Christ who gave up easily was almost as undesirable as a Communist Christ. For a while the clergy reached a compromise: Christ should not carry any flag. But the prelates overlooked an important factor—Christ, without a flag, looked as though he were giving the Communist salute, clenched fist and all.... 'And now, 'Andrea said, 'the Communists are claiming that the priests are sabotaging Christ by making him look like weakling instead of the militant comrade which they are certain he is'" (183). The story amuses, but also contains some rather obvious lessons about religion, politics, and semiotics, while also commenting in a guarded manner on the forbidden topic of stereotypical Italian cowardice.

Another humorous tradition, however, one prominent in Italian literature through the ages, receives no such silencing. The Catholic Church in general and Priests in particular get the comic needle more than once, perhaps most memorably in Mangione's section on language and dialect. Uncle Luigi tells of an American priest who speaks perfect Italian, and travels through Italy taking confession. Northern Italy's sinners prove boring, but he understands them. As he moves increasingly South, however, he has more and more problem communicating. "It must have been very annoying when he got to Naples, 'my uncle said, 'for Neapolitans are some of the most fascinating sinners in the world." An ethnic slur or possibly a tribute, marking distinctions between the larger group of Italians. When the priest hits Sicily, however, he can't understand a word and has to conduct confessions in sign language. Mangione provides the kicker: "when anyone who had not heard the story was gullible enough to ask Uncle Luigi how that was possible, he would gleefully grab the opportunity to show off his histrionic talents and act out a sin or two in pantomime. Invariably, of course, they were sins of the flesh" (53-54).

Uncle Luigi's comic saga has sequels as well. His daughter Teresa, like her four siblings, follows her father's command and becomes a Baptist; the others proselytize and convert their spouses too, even though fickle Uncle Luigi has moved on to other denominational ties. Teresa, however, dreams of going to Sicily to explore her past, even though she knows little Italian; when she embarks, she takes with her a life of Daniel Boone, an Italian-English dictionary, and pink American underwear for her aunt—signifiers of frontier myth, history, language and hedonistic materialism. Once there, despite the linguistic problem, she meets and marries an Italian dreamboat who joins her in America, but only when she agrees to revert to Catholicism! This mini-parable offers humorous but human proof of the ebb and flow of change in immigrant life. Teresa isn't the only Italian-American to go to the old country; as the text and historical records reveal, others go back for good. Teresa's former evangelism comically segues with an Americanizing mission; the way Mangione describes her dogged journey to the Old World makes it clear that she in her own way is just as much a pioneer entering the wilderness as Daniel Boone was, a reverse current in the flow West that will nevertheless end up with another new American. Her reversion to Catholicism, of course, sets an ironic twist to Uncle Luigi's antics, and provides, in a curiously satisfying way, continuity, both to Old World traditions and New World romance and progress. The newlyweds, of course, will form a new branch of the extended family.

I have written at greater length on Mangione's memoirs elsewhere (Lowe 1993, 1996), so I will now briefly point out that humor can also be used more sparingly, when a tragic narrative requires comedy to underline its major epic themes. Puzo has claimed, in fact, that "every tenement was a town square.... Audacity had liberated them; they were pioneers, though they never walked an American plain and never felt real soil beneath their feet. They moved in a sadder wilderness, where the language was strange, where their children became members of a different race. It was a price that must be paid" (8-9). Then too, the tenement was for the Jewish American who became U.S. Senator, Jacob Javits, the equivalent of the frontier's log cabin, where American virtues were learned, absorbed, and passed on to a new generation. Di Donato's *Christ in Concrete*, another classic text of Italian American literature, possesses a high degree of tragic seriousness. Yet like Greek tragedy, its pathos is set side by side with laughter and parody. As Bakhtin notes, "antique tragedy did not fear laughter and parody and even demanded it as a corrective and a complement," since plays by Sophocles were followed by satyr plays (*Rabelais* 122-123); as Bakhtin asserts, "True ambivalent and universal laughter does not deny seriousness but purifies and completes it.... Laughter does not permit seriousness to atrophy and to be torn away from the one being, forever incomplete. It restores this ambivalent wholeness. Such is the function of laughter in the historical development of culture and literature" (123).

Accordingly, before the tragedy of Geremio's death tears apart his workplace and his family, we see him and his workers make their backbreaking work bearable through bawdy, combative humor. While I cannot treat it here, the extended chapter "Fiesta" flares up comedically amid the more general despair and suffering of the novel, as the people of the community celebrate a wedding with feasting, taunts, comic duels, ribald sexuality, eating contests, and even comically celebrate the stripped stump of a man's leg. Significantly, Pietro Di Donato joined the American Communist Party on the night that Nicola Sacco and Bartolomeo Vanzetti were executed (Gardaphe 67). A strict concentration only on the grave, tragic, and ideologically serious leads to partial vision.

Mario Puzo's *The Fortunate Pilgrim* (1964) begins in 1928, the year before the onset of the Great Depression, and ends during World War II, as the Angeluzzi-Corbo family prepares to leave their Manhattan tenement for a new home on Long Island. The time span of the novel neatly encompasses the last years of the Twenties boom, the Depression, and the prosperity that came to Italian Americans with the economic uplift of the war years. The family, clearly, is meant to be representative of Italian American culture in general, much more so than the Corleone family of Puzo's more popularly conceived *The Godfather*. Like virtually all classic Italian American texts, *Pilgrim* utilizes the *famiglia* formula, in this case featuring a strong matriarch, who presides over the struggles of her very different but uniformly emotional sons and her bitter, although beautiful and intellectual daughter. Although her children eclipse her in education in several instances, there is never any doubt as that Lucia Santa's old world wisdom, honed through suffering and wily scheming, trumps them all. Robert Viscusi accurately reminds us that it her son Larry's "sterling masculinity" and acquisition of a godfather that enables them to leave Tenth Avenue. As Viscusi notes, this aligns Larry with other sons in Italian American literature, such as Paul in *Christ in Concrete* and Michael in *The Godfather*, who must replace their fathers (Viscusi 49), but Larry's strength and dedication to the family surely come from Lucia Santa rather than his two fathers, who both fail the family. It must be said too, that Lucia Santa emerges here as a woman of words, one who can signify, cajole, threaten, and scandalize with a crook of her hand and a twist of her wicked tongue. In this respect, the novel closely follows the script of Lorraine Hansberry's

A Raisin in the Sun (1959), whose tightly knit black family similarly "moves on up" into a house through the inspired, and vocally expressed determination of their mother, Lena, who is significantly described by Hansberry as "full of strength. She has ... wit and faith" and the bearing of "the women of the Hereros of Southwest Africa" (39), just as Lucia Santa's qualities, shaped in Italy, have been transformed and strengthened in her new "village" of Tenth Avenue.

As in many other classic ethnic texts set in Manhattan, the book concentrates on its Italian neighborhood, but also features other ethnic characters who live cheek by jowl with the Angeluzzi-Corbos in their Tenth Avenue enclave. The streets—particularly Tenth Avenue—become a version of Bakhtin's village square, and Harrigan's Mulligan's Alley; the old *passeggiata* in Sicily becomes replaced by gossiping women leaning out of windows, stoop-sitters, and children playing in the streets. As such, the novel strongly echoes Elmer Rice's stirring drama *Street Scene*, which used the dialogics of multi-ethnic life so effectively that it became a natural choice for the libretto Kurt Weill used for his opera with the same name. Puzo tells us, early in *Pilgrim*, "Each tenement was a village square; each had its group of women, all in black, sitting on stools and boxes and doing more than gossip. They recalled ancient history, argued morals and social law, always taking their precedents from the mountain village in southern Italy they had escaped" (9).

Many ethnic writers portray immigrants cursing the evil ways of their new country, often comically. The Jewish Girl in Abraham Cahan's *Yekl*, undone by the newfangled ways of her adopted country, utters a curse against Columbus. In Italian enclaves, Puzo tells us that

It was a favorite topic, the corruption of the innocent by the new land. Now: Felicia, who lived around the corner ... what type of daughter was she who did not cut short her honeymoon on new of her godmother's illness.... A real whore. And a son ... who could not wait another year to marry when his father so commanded? Ahhh, the disrespect, *Figlio disgraziato*. Never could this pass in Italy. The father would kill his arrogant son; yes, kill him ... and the daughter? In Italy—Felicia's mother swore in a voice still trembling with passion, though this had all happened three years ago, the godmother recovered the grandchildren the light of her life—ah, in Italy the mother would pull the whore out of her bridal chamber, drag her to the hospital bed by the hair of her head.... At the end of each story each woman recited her requiem, *Mannagia America!* (9-10)

These exaggerated, operatic outbursts are typical of the comic *sprezzatura* of Italian American writers, who often indicate this over-the-top orality is the spice that animates communal life, even when it comes at the expense of one's own children.

In many portions of the novel, characters travesty religion—a favorite imprecation is *porca Maria*, similar to the Old English "zounds," which began as "God's wounds." In European peasant culture, "the jargon of clerics, monks, schoolmen, judges, as well as popular speech were filled with travesties of religious texts, prayers, proverbs, and sayings of common wisdom" (Bakhtin *Rabelais* 86). In Italian American literature, we see this in. New World versions, as in popular jests. When one is asked something that is obvious, such as "are you hungry," a person might reply, "Is the Pope catholic," or more vulgarly, "can a bear shit in the woods?" This has now merged into the nonsensical, "can the Pope shit in the woods?" which harks back to the European travesty practiced widely in Italy.

One of the great comic scenes in *Mount Allegro* portrays "the unholy three"—Jerre's father Peppino and his brothers-in-law Nino and Luigi, playing *briscola* with Uncle Minne. Bakhtin states that games draw players "out of the bounds of everyday life, liberated them from usual laws and regulations, and replaced established conventions by other lighter conventionalities" (235). We might posit that both *Mount Allegro* and the early portions of *The Fortunate Pilgrim* are set in what we might call a "festive age," when the ethnic community is still intact and is drawing on the general prosperity and hope of the surrounding culture. The Depression dampened this festive moment, but hopes were revived by the economic renaissance of the forties.

Sex and the body find ample expression in the raucous humor of the wise elder Zia Louche Another old woman tells the story of a "villainous young Italian girl (born in America, naturally)" (16) who is dancing with another man when her young husband unexpectedly drops dead. "Does she rush to the side of her beloved?...She cried, 'no, no.... I will not look at it.' Slyly Zia Louche, her tongue rolling up both meanings, said, 'Ah! You may be sure she looked at it when It was alive" (17).

Near the end of the novel, speaking to her now-married daughter Octavia, who despite her refined education, speaks bawdily while at home, Lucia Santa tells her "With a husband I thought your mouth would get cleaner as the other got dirty." Octavia flushed deep red. Lucia Santa was pleased. Her daughter's surface vulgarity, American, was no match for her own, bred in the Italian bone" (210). This comic duel is capped, as it should be, by the older woman, whose age sanctions her more outrageous but also corrective humor.

Similarly, Lucia Santa, commenting on her Lothario son Lorenzo complains that he never comes home: "all the girls are off the street except those little Irish tramps on Ninth Avenue. 'She added with mock fervor, 'Thank Jesus Christ he only ruins good, decent Italian girls. 'She smiled with a touch of pride" (27).

Even when parents are quite serious and upset, they use humor in their over-the-top pronouncements. Angry at her son Gino for never being around, "being invisible," Lucia Santa threatens him with her club-like *Tackeril*: "By Jesus Christ, I'll make you visible. I'll make you so black and blue that if you were the Holy Ghost you could not vanish" (59). Like Mangione's parents, Lucia Santa has a pragmatic view of religion that stems from her sense of *destino*: "She herself had long since ceased to think of God except to automatically curse his name for some misfortune. There was no question: when she died she would prudently take the last rites of her church. But now she did not go to Mass even for Christmas or Easter" (91).

This bitter humor about religion can take other forms as well. Larry, the family's first born son, eventually lands a job collecting "dues" for Mr. di Lucca, which are really protection money extorted from businessmen. When Larry beats up a nasty German who not only refuses to pay but insults him, di Lucca, who has paid off the police, wishes Larry was his son, and tells him "do you know what it is to be born in Italy? You are a dog and you scratch in the earth like a dog to find a dirty bone for supper. You give eggs to the priest to save your soul, you slip the town clerk a bottle of wine merely to bandy words. When the *padrone*, the landowner, comes to spend the summer at his estate, all the village girls go to clean his house and fill it with fresh flowers. He pays them with a smile, and ungloves his knuckles for a kiss.

And then a miracle, America. It was enough to make one believe in Jesus Christ" (183).

In a telling moment, Larry switches his mother's Italian language *romanze* off the radio, in favor of an American station, even though he likes the other: "They always sounded as if they were killing each other.... It was nothing like the American soap operas. Here blows were struck; parents were not understanding but firm and intolerant; men killed the lovers of their wives on purpose, and not by accident. Wives poisoned their husbands, and usually with something that caused horrible pain, and there were screams to go with it. Their torture was a comfort for the living" (186-187).

Ancient prejudices find comic expressions. Lucia Santa stretches her money by buying black market food from thieving longshoremen: "these people dealt more honestly with you than the shopkeepers from Northern Italy who roosted on Ninth Avenue like Roman vultures" (189). Very often the narrator lets the anonymous communal voice take over. When they learn that Octavia is engaged to a Jew, they call it a "scandal," not because this heathen is a Jew, "but because he was not an Italian.... Where did she find a Jew, in Christ's name? For blocks uptown and downtown, east side and on the western wall of Tenth Avenue, there were only Catholic Irish, Polish, and Italians. But then, what could be expected of an Italian girl who wore business suits to cover her breasts?" (189).

Still, Puzo cautions us that "It is easy to laugh at the prejudices of the poor, their reasoning springs from a special experience. How irritating to hear some thieving Sicilian rascal say, "If you seek justice, put a gift in the scale." How insulting to a noble profession when the sly Teresina Coccalitti whispered, "When you say lawyer, you say thief." Lucia Santa had a saying of her own. "They who read books will let their families starve" (190).

It is both ironic and fitting that one of the most remarkable novels of the new Italian American Renaissance, Mark Binelli's *Sacco and Vanzetti Must Die!*, goes back to the most legendary tragic heroes of Italian American history to construct a raucous, postmodern comedy. As Jerre Mangione predicted to Fred Gardaphe, "The more Americanized the new generations of Italian-American writers become, the less likely they are to write about Italian Americans, uncles they begin writing historical novels with heavily fictionalized themes. This could lead to what you have called a renaissance" (Gardaphé and Bruno 54).

And in fact, Binelli could hardly have chosen a more "fictionalized theme," as he daringly transforms perhaps the most sacred tragic *storia* of Italian American life into a raucous comedy.

In the 19th century, Italian immigrants were viewed as little better than animals, their Catholicism feared as a contagion, and their peasant background a sign of their ignorance—unless they were linked with socialists and Communists, like Sacco and Vanzetti. Because many immigrants from Italy hailed from Reggio Calabria, Basilicata, and Sicily, then the poorest regions, they were also scorned by other immigrants from northern Italy, and all parties identified the Sicilians with the Mafia. Flannery O'Connor said, "To the hard of hearing, you shout." Apparently in agreement with this sentiment and these types of writers, Marc Binelli has recently taken a radically new approach to Italian American culture through the device of the postmodern novel. His title, *Sacco and Vanzetti Must Die!* operates on several different registers. First, it signals an irreverent, even revolutionary tone, and thus catches our interest. As we soon learn, he has "killed" the pair himself in a way by reinventing them as a comedy team active during the golden age of vaudeville, silent movies, and then the talkies. Binelli grew up worshiping Abbott and Costello, and he refashions the radical martyrs in that vein, also taking routines and gags from other comics and vaudevillians of the period, such as Buster Keaton, Charlie Chaplin, Harold Lloyd, Fatty Arbuckle, Laurel and Hardy, and Jack Benny, even Helen Keller, most of whom have cameo appearances in the novel. Mixing real and fictional characters is a staple of the postmodern novel, as is Binelli's scrambled chronology, use of pastiche (we consider newsreels, diaries, journals, interviews, movie out takes, vaudeville routines along the way) and above all, his exuberant embrace of parody. One of the most useful such parodies is Binelli's excerpt from the fictional Hylo Pierce's scholarly work, *A Funny Thing Happened on the Way to Mr. Mayer's Office.... Revisiting the Golden Age of Film Comedy* (1988), which tells us that the team has been rediscovered by the academy, and that one scholar has seen a gay thematic in pictures such as *You're Schvitzing Me* (which takes place in a bathhouse), *Jacks in the Box,* and above all their 1943 forgotten classic made with Bing Crosby, *Take it Like a Man!,* a comic prison film set on Devil's Island. Hylo is skeptical, however, as Sacco apparently was married four times, and indeed, throughout the novel, he comes across as quite a sexual athlete, includeing an acrobatic tumble with one of the Andrews sisters in a sleeping car.

On the other hand, Binelli sees to it that we get the straight facts—sort of—that he is parodying. In section labeled "Supplemental Material," he gives us mock-Wikipedia like mini-essays on various topics, including the real historical figures he features, such as the boxer Carnera, but also several that deal with the real Sacco and Vanzetti.

These inserts create a remarkable tension in the book, and draw attention to Binelli's willful intervention into history in the fictional portions, while simultaneously adding to the humor of irony.

As should already be clear, Binelli's technique and S&V's chaotic, often nonsensical comic routines resemble the aims and motives of anarchists, whose methods Binelli wants us to see as parallel to those of cutup comics. Along the way, we learn the etiquette of pie throwing, runaway car gags, racial and ethnic humor of the time, and most significantly of all, the art of knife throwing.

Binelli grew up in outside Detroit, where he worked in his father's knife-sharpening shop. The Binellis hailed from Pinzolo, which specialized in knife grinding, and in a tribute to the town, he has his duo visit it in 1965, when they are filming a comic encounter with Hercules, *Labor Pains*, in which Sacco and Vanzetti play the help at the Augean stables. This Sacco and Vanzetti, while successful in Vaudeville, really take off in the movies when they start a series of knife-grinding/knife-throwing comedies, which includes *The Daily Grind*, *Whichever Way You Slice It*, *A Couple of Cut-Ups*, and *Sacco and Vanzetti Take One More Stab*, and *A Couple of Wops in a Jam*, a comic allusion to the real S&V, but we also learn this movie was a parody of the popular Charlie Chan movies, with Italian stereotypes substituted for the Chinese.

In his fiction, however, although we never lose sight of the comic duo's ethnicity, Binelli seems much more interested in pyrotechnic writing, which he clearly sees as similar to the high-risk knife-throwing acts the pair perform as a complement to their comedy routines. As he puts it, "I took cartoonish movie characters and tried to make them somewhat 'real,' but neglected to remove them from their cartoonish movie scenarios" (McDermott 5).

Binelli's list of admired writers interestingly includes most of the names valued in creative writing classes today, but only one of them, Don DeLillo, has an Italian background. However, a reader who knows the Italian American literary canon will see some influences here and there. In one scene we encounter a boxing match with a kangaroo, which of course has to have been lifted from Paul Gallico's 1970 novel *Matilda*. Binelli went to graduate work at Ann Arbor and at Columbia, and made good use of the anarchist collection at Michigan while writing his novel. He has stated he decided to write about a comedy team first, and admiring the way the Coen brothers play with genre, he decided to focus on a comedy team working in film, a genre he could "subvert" himself. When it occurred to him that Sacco and Vanzetti would be a great name for his duo, he immediately started thinking about the links between anarchy and slapstick humor, and "how the comics tended to play working-class types, and how they would often end up foiling bosses, cops, and various authority figures and high-society types. The Three Stooges, the Marx Brothers, all of them; how often they would they end up at some ridiculously fancy party, trashing the place? ... the connections just proved endless" (McDermott 2). An interviewer asked Binelli if he ever thought he was going too far with these "martyrs to liberalism," to which he replied "I'm tweaking their historical image, which has become—for people who've even heard of them; and many haven't, these days—so one dimensional. From the start, even their supporters turned them into caricatures.... People overlook the violence of their cause, and romanticize their otherness.... Upton Sinclair wrote an eight-hundred-page novel about the trial called *Boston*, in which the Vanzetti characters speak in a phonetic broken English, literally stuff like, "I younga man, I washa da deesh'.... It's like *Amos and Andy*!" (McDermott 3).

Accordingly, Binelli shows his film stars being pressured into speaking this kind of dialect, or as Sacco puts it "Some kind of Chico Marx shit, 'Atsa good, Doc!" (21). Yet on the other hand, Binelli employs ethnic slurs himself, as one of their movies is entitled "A Couple of Wops in a Jam." Some years Salvatore Lagumina also seized the stereotype and un-packed it in great detail—his cover, however, had a ridicu-lous picture of a fedora clad Mafia warrior gobbling spaghetti and meatballs under the bold letter title of the book, *WOP!* This in-your-face presentation of course means dealing directly, if satirically, with the stereotype. As Binelli defends this by pointing to other ethnic writers such as Flan O'Brien, whose over-the-top Irishness takes back con-trol of the stereotype by embracing and mocking it.

Although Binelli reports sitting around family kitchen tables while relatives yelled at each other in Italian dialect, he feels current day Italian Americans have in fact assimi-lated so successfully that the feeling of otherness—which can apparently, for him, be both good and bad—has largely been lost, so much so that other ethnics regularly refer to Italian Americans as "Guidos," even though these liberals would never call a Latino "Pedro." But he thinks the success of Italian Americans makes the "Guido" label okay, and thus his own appropriations of old slurs is permissible too (McDermott 3).

While Binelli would admit that most of the comics he references here are Jewish, he creates routines for his duo and the other comedians in the book that employ the kind of slapstick that was originated in the *commedia dell 'Arte*, which we know Binelli studied, as he makes overt reference to Mel Gordon's classic book on the subject, *Lazzi: The Comic Routines of the Commedia dell'Arte* which resurrects the hushed-up scatological and sexual antics of the classic genre. Early on in the novel, Bart tells us "we worked in a classical tradition. The *commedia*. Speed plus incongruity equals funny. It's especially compelling for us, as Italians, because we're working in a tradition that can be traced back to the Ren-[aissance]" (21). As in that tradition, his Sacco and Vanzetti, because of the nature of their art, play many roles in many venues. They are picaresque figures who crisscross the country when in Vaudeville, and their movies give them a fantastic variety of roles and zany situations. Binelli feels that his attraction to this aspect of performance stems too from his prior career as drama critic, which segued with his interest in metafiction, with "characters winking at the audience, playing different roles, witching scenes on a dime. So many different levels (the character, the actor, the stage, the audience) can allow for an interesting fluidity, when you're telling a story." What he doesn't say here, however, is that fiction of this nature places extreme demands on the reader, who might well get exhausted early on.

As in Mangione, although the focus is on Italian Americans, the other acts S&V travel with in vaudeville is diverse: Borrah Minevitch and his Harmonica Rascals, the magician Ching Ling Soo, and Barbette, the French cross-dresser and trapeze artist, and El Brendel, a Swedish dialect comic, and Aunt Jemima, a black face singer (who turns out to be an Italian named Teresina sporting shoe polish), an Irish crooner, and some kid with the name of Durante. His many references to the role African Americans were playing in American musical comedy and vaudeville at the time often reveals that he sees strong parallels between that culture and his own.

The theatre tradition I detailed earlier involving Harrigan had a parallel in the variety shows that became known as vaudeville (the term comes from the French Voix de Ville). Many of the acts that were strung into an evening's entertainment involved ethnic "sthticks," acted out by actual or pretend ethnics. The classic example of the pretend kind of presentation was of course generated by the other precedent for this tradition, the minstrel show. Vaudeville proper began in 1865 with the opening of Tony Pastor's Opera House in the Bowery. Off-color material was purged, creating a famiglia-oriented format, which featured melodramatic and comedy sketches, dance routines, and stand-up comedy, which was more often than not delivered by a duo. Racial comics, James Dormon explains, "simply exaggerated the primary ascriptive qualities to the point of caricature in order to render the stereotype more comical" (4). Hebrew dialect performers were the most popular, but so were "Dutch" and "Irish" acts.

At one point a discussion about an ethnic group's use of slurs against them compares black and Italians, with agreement that accepting and then using the terms is taking away the white man's most powerful weapon, words. Ultimately, this relates to the lines of connection Binelli makes between the duo and blacks who were performing—sometimes in black face—"coon" songs, such as "All Coons Look Alike to Me" or "No Coon Can Come too Black for Me." They were popular because they were often accompanied by nimble dancing, comic pratfalls, done against the rhythms of the new syncopated music. Blacks, like the famous team of Bert Williams and George Walker, billed as "Two Real Coons," were also famous for their comedy routines. The Coon Song, however, could be subversive: "The Mormon Coon" bragged of his harem: "I've got a big brunette, and a blonde to pet / I've got em short, fat, thin, and tall / I've got a Cuban gal, and a Zulu pal / They come in bunches when I call"

(Dormon, 459). S&V similarly sing songs about WOPS and embrace the stereotype in order to subvert it.

Binelli isn't far from the truth here. No vaudeville bill would be considered complete at the time without an Italian character actor and an Italian dialect song. In staging instruction for his "A Sunny Son of Italy, Harry Newton required "Rough sack suit, trousers rather short; large shoes; blue shirt; red bandanna handkerchief tied around neck; black slouch hat; brass rings in ears..., black wig; small black mustache ... make-up face dark" (Dormon, 10). "Antonio Spaghetti" might be a day laborer, a peddler, or more often, a street musician, such as a singing organ grinder. Costume, gestures, and dialect—which led to the character Chico Marx played—make for an entertaining "type." Dormon suggests that the character's relatively benign qualities of naiveté, simplicity, and ignorance, deflected fears, while their striking physical difference suggested they would never be real Americans, also a deflection of fear. Ironically, however, this comic relation bred intimacy, and ultimately helped real Italians acculturate.

Just as Binelli brings in cameos by real people, so do his comic duos; their films feature roles for the celebrated Italian boxer Primo Carnera, and Mussolini's trophy airman, Italo Balbo, "the Italian Lindbergh," in his case in a hilarious movie (much of which is featured in the novel) about his kidnapping by the duo. Paul Ricoeur has noted that "every culture cannot sustain and absorb the shock of modern civilization. There is the paradox: how to become a modern and to return to sources." Binelli's novel, while concentrating on Italian folk traditions, slapstick and burlesque, also refers to the futurists, early aviation heroes, and modernist painters of Italy, while simultaneously ransacking both Italian and Italian American history to make contemporary points. Binelli's form of comic historical metafiction places him in the company of Fuentes, Marquez, Pynchon, and especially, Doctorow, whose *Ragtime* this novel strikingly resembles, in many ways. The comedy of this necessary revisitation and questioning of the past is part and parcel, in fact, of postmodernism, in that in Umberto Eco's words, such a move be done "with irony, not innocently," (67) and irony, perhaps the dominant form of humor in *S&V*; this irony is achieved through the imposition of different kinds of readings of the past, methods that have been facilitated recently by feminists, gays, and ethnic critics of all types. Part of the impulse to sift through the past comes from unhappiness with the present. As Bart tells us at one point, the mayhem the pair create makes them like the itinerants of the period; "they would or would not adhere to the discipline of the new industrial order ... the alternative was acquiescence. Comfort equals collaboration" (165).

Jean-François Lyotard states that the postmodern "invokes the unpresentable in presentation itself, that which refuses the consolation of correct forms, refuses the consensus of taste permitting a common experience of nostalgia for the impossible, and inquires into new presentations" (15), a concise description—albeit one that does not consider the comic—of Binelli's apparent intent and method, as he pillages the past to make statements about ethnicity, identity, and the affinities between destruction and creation, tragedy and comedy, anarchy and slapstick.

To return to Falstaff: Nic half completes a gag book, and notes within: "One dreams [of] ... the great titular roles, the Kings and Moors and ever-pondering Danes. But then one realizes, in a powderflash of epiphany, that the name Falstaff has been indelibly inked upon one's certificate of birth, and that placing a crown upon one's head, or blackening up, it'll merely makes on *more* what, in fact, he already 'tis" (227).

The novel ends with Sacco dead, and Vanzetti living alone with his memories, but Binelli can't resist one final, revealing parody. In an apparent flashback to one of the pair's movies, we get a parody of the classic Sydney Poitier/Tony Curtis movie, *The Defiant Ones*, where the two stars, escaped criminals who hate each other, are handcuffed together. This hilarious romp is also highly symbolic, as it underlines the lifelong bond between the two men, and their *destino* to be always dreaming up gags, always on the run. They wind up on a movie set, where extras representing virtually every ethnic group are milling about, en route to their sets. The chief set is a town square, taking us back to Bakhtin, Harrigan, and the origin of all narrative, folk culture. Sacco and Vanzetti, transformed through the lens of postmodern parody, leave us not only as a pair, but as part of the jostling, posing, and entertaining population, just waiting for their time on America's screen, and a possible place in their heart. Binelli's Italian comedians, ever anarchic, ever creative, paradoxically bring people together in a better way, helping transform an agreement to agree on *dissensus* into *e pluribus unum*.

WORKS CONSULTED

Bair, Deidre. "Introduction to the Morningside Edition." *Reunion in Sicily*. By Jerre Mangione. 1950. New York: Columbia UP, 1984.

Bakhtin, Mikhail. *The Dialogic Imagination: Four Essays*. Ed. Michael Holquist. Trans. Caryl Emerson and Michael Holquist. Austin: U of Texas P, 1981.

Bakhtin, Mikhail. *Rabelais and His World*. Trans. Hélène Iswolsky. Bloomington: Indiana U P, 1984.

Barolini, Helen, ed. *The Dream Book: an Anthology of Writings by Italian American Women*. New York: Schocken Books, 1985.

Boelhower, William. *Immigrant Autobiography in the United States:*

Four Versions of the Italian American Self. Verona: Essedue Edizioni, 1982.

Davies, Christie. *Ethnic Humor Around the World: A Comparative Analysis*. Bloomington: Indiana UP, 1990.

Dormon, James. "Ethnic Cultures of the Mind: The Harrigan-Hart Mosaic." *American Quarterly* 33.2 (1992): 21-40.

Dormon, James. "Shaping the Popular Image of Post-Reconstruction American Blacks: The 'Coon Song' Phenomenon of the Gilded Age." *American Quarterly* 40.4 (1988): 450-471.

Eco, Umberto. *Reflections on The Name of the Rose*. Trans. William Weaver. London: Minerva, 1994. 67-68.

Gardaphé, Fred L. and Anthony Bruno. "An Interview with Jerre Mangione." *Forkroads: A Journal of Ethnic American Literature* 5 (1996): 43-55.

Gardaphé, Fred L. *Italian Signs, American Streets: The Evolution of Italian American Narrative*. Durham, NC: Duke U P, 1996.

Gordon, Mel. *Lazzi: The Comic Routines of the Commedia dell 'arte*. New York: Performing Arts Journal Publications, 1983.

Hansberry, Lorraine. *A Raisin in the Sun*. 1959; rpt. New York, Signet, 1988.

Harrigan, Edward. *The Leather Patch*. Typescript, 1886. Manuscript Division, New York Public Library.

Koger, Alicia Kae. *A Critical Analysis of Edward Harrigan's Comedy*. Doctoral Diss., U of Michigan, 1984. Ann Arbor, MI: University Microfilms International.

Lowe, John. "Humor and Ethnicity in Ethnic Autobiography: Zora Neale Hurston and Jerre Mangione." *Cultural Difference and the Literary Text*. Ed. Katrin Schwenk and Winfried Siemerling. Iowa City: University of Iowa Press, 1996. 75-99.

Lowe, John. "Humor and Identity in Jerre Mangione's *Storia*." *VIA (Voices in Italian Americana)* 4. 2 (1993): 31-50.

Lyotard, Jean-François. *The Postmodern Explained: Correspondence, 1924-1998*. Minneapolis: U of Minnesota P, 1993.

Mangione, Jerre. *An Ethnic at Large*. New York: Columbia UP, 1978.

_____. *Mount Allegro: A Memoir of Italian American Life*. New

York: Harper, 1943.

———. *Reunion in Sicily*. Boston: Houghton Mifflin, 1950.

McDermott, Theodore. "Interview with Marc Benelli." *Context* 18 (2009): 1-6.

Mulas, James. "A MELUS Interview: Jerre Mangione. *MELUS* 12.4 (1985): 73-83.

Olney, James. *Metaphors of the Self: The Meaning of Autobiography*. Princeton, NJ: Princeton U P, 1972.

Phillips-Matz, Mary Jane. *Verdi: A Biography*. New York: Oxford UP, 1993.

Puzo, Mario. *The Fortunate Pilgrim*. New York: Bantam, 1964.

Radcliffe-Brown, Alfred Reginald. "A Further Note on Joking Relationships." *Structure and Function in Primitive Society*. London: Cohen and West, 1965.

Sciascia, Leonardo. "The Long Crossing." *The Wine-Dark Sea*. Trans. Avril Bardonni. New York: New York Review, 2000. 17-26.

Spaulding, Henry D. *Joys of Italian Humor*. Middle Village, NY: Jonathan David, 1980.

Steiner, Edward Alfred. *On the Trail of the Immigrant*. New York: Revell, 1906.

Viscusi, Robert. *Buried Caesars and Other Secrets of Italian American Writing*. Albany: SUNY P, 2006.

Italia Sacra
San Severino Marche, Orvieto, Bevagna[1]

JOHN PAUL RUSSO
University of Miami

THE PEACE OF SAN SEVERINO MARCHE

Sea breezes, sea memories, the cathedral on the promontory with a portal like a nun's white coif: Ancona. Scenes from Luchino Visconti's *Ossessione*, shot here in the early 1940s, captured the brio of a port city and its equivocal air. But now I was heading inland. A local train was taking me through the hills of the central Marche and my thoughts kept drifting from the outer to the inner landscape. Every so often the train shook to a stop. Most stations on this line are nothing more than a room with a few ticket machines against peeling paint or flaking plaster, and with one door facing the weedy tracks and another out to the piazza. Given the size of the towns, one can often walk to a hotel or a *pensione*; if the sky threatens or the valise seems too heavy (never in my case), travelers are thrown upon their own resources. In these friendly places this is not much of a problem: there might be a bus on its way, a telephone number for a taxi posted on the wall, or a barista who knows a driver. One might even try asking someone for a lift. The station at San Severino Marche looked like it had been spruced up; low shrubs and trailing flowers brightened the outside walls.

The road curves and dips into an elongated ellipse, the Piazza del Popolo, lined with arcades. Its Renaissance and

---

[1] From "Nostalgia: Wanderings in Italy"

baroque buildings are modest in height, and their colors—faded orange, slate gray, light brown, sulfur-yellow—have weathered together and blend harmoniously. The flat expanse of the piazza, in smooth dark stone, is bare except for the matched fountains in the neoclassical style, neither dull, obtrusive, nor out of scale, at the focal points of the ellipse. The buildings' height in relation to the piazza allows the sky to pour in bounteously on all sides. Towers of the upper town on Monte Nero can be seen from one corner and Monte Acuto rises in the distance. On market days vendors crowd the center of the piazza with their carts and stalls; now it was empty. The late September sun felt more than warm, even hot; towns like this still observe siesta, and only a few people circulated beneath the arcades. Slowly I surveyed the ellipse, which seemed perfectly proportioned, perfect in every way. I drank in its unity of mood, which was dignified and serene. Amid the silence, a deep peace settled around me.

Such moments happen rarely enough and their circumstances have nothing in common. What could have been more unlike the peace of San Severino than one winter evening in Rome, when the city seemed to be rushing faster and faster, and I found myself in the traffic-snarled Piazza Istria beside a flower stand. The fioraia was a stout, old woman bundled up against the cold, so much I could hardly see her face. But our eyes crossed and she smiled as she said brusquely in romanesco, "febbraro corto ma amaro" (February, short but bitter). She had probably been outside most of the day, and she swayed and stomped her feet as she spoke. Other times, it was driving through the shadowy via Aurelia Antica, sunken low, as if weighed down by age, between mossy walls draped with purple and vermillion bougainvillea; or, it was walking on the leafy boulevards of

Cesenatico in autumn, the sea in sight, when the Museo Moretti was inexplicably closed. Though I know that for some people such harmonious moments form a ring in a higher movement of the spirit, I could only vouch for their separate and temporal being.

Not one or two features make the Piazza del Popolo such an astonishing success, it is "the joint force and full result of all." One could point to the silent march of the arcades, some 45 of them, which keep the eye on the move; the human scale of the buildings and their warm coloring; the symphonic agreement of architectural styles; and most formal of all, the gentle swerve of the ellipse. Also, the piazza closes well, which is critical for its geometric beauty. The lane entrances are discrete, and the western end does not expand onto a broad thoroughfare, but to a small street that winds away like an S, continuing the elliptical curve in the contrary direction, a street sufficiently narrow to protect the spatial integrity of the piazza, yet wide enough to be accommodating, until it is lost in the distance turning up to the left. The paradoxical effect of the piazza is one of stillness and motion.

On its northern side is the Teatro Feronia (1823-28), the work of a local architect, Ireneo Aleandri, who built Macerata's Sferisterio stadium. Popular in central Italy, Feronia was a Roman goddess of forests and liberty; slaves were set free beneath trees sacred to her. In Virgil, her incense is the fresh air of the green groves themselves. The theatre curtain, made from sketches by Filippo Bigioli (1798-1878), displays Camurena Celerina, a native priestess of Feronia, and a slave about to be granted his freedom. Who was Camurena? Some wise local woman who joined the rite? some future abbess? Continuing clockwise around the piazza are the beige-brick Palazzo Gentili di Rovellone

(1524), with a bossed portico in a darker shade, and the equally majestic Palazzo Comunale (1764), the seat of town government. A bust of the anatomist Bartolomeo Eustachio, born in San Severino, is placed on a pedestal before it. Across the bottom of the ellipse is the Palazzo Caccialupi with an open loggia on the uppermost floor. At pleasing variance, the church of S. Giuseppe (1765) stands highest and, with the consent of its neighbors, presides over the scene, cheerfully so with its rococo façade and lofty bell tower. It houses three wooden sculptures carved by the local artist Venanzio Bigioli (1771-1854), *Joseph with the Christ Child*, the *Dead Christ*, and the *Risen Christ*, which are lifted and borne through the town on Good Friday and Easter Sunday by the Confraternity of the Corpus Domini. The sculptures survived the disastrous fire on the eve of New Year's 2010 which destroyed a side chapel and did smoke damage to walls, frescoes, and tapestries. Bigioli has a *Crucifixion* in the church of S. Filippo. Lastly, at the eastern end, the Palazzi Luzi and Servanzi-Collio complete the ellipse, without any falling off in architectural interest.

On the eastern edge of the piazza, up the small incline on which I stood, is Aleandri's Torre dell'Orologio: the bells in this "tower" are set behind square holes that puncture a flat wall of cream-colored brick. This forms the outer wall of the small fourteenth-century church of S. Maria della Misericordia, much altered in the late baroque style. Against its delicately pale blue interior hangs Pomarancio's *Madonna of Mercy*, which blazes in reds over the main altar.

In 268 BC a town whose original name is lost was taken over by Rome and renamed Septempeda. Well situated on the east-west route along the Potenza River, it prospered over the succeeding centuries. For a long time it was thought that, when the Goths sacked the city in 545 AD, the people took refuge in the Roman castrum on Monte Nero, bringing with them the remains of their last bishop, Severino. Now it seems more likely that Septempeda was only very gradually abandoned for the safety of the hill-top castrum, which became the nucleus of medieval Castello. Over time the security of the upper town was less necessary or desirable than the economic convenience of living in the valley by the Potenza. People moved down the steep hill, though they did not go as far as Septempeda, which had sunk into ruins (still to be seen across the fields, scarcely a kilometer away, in the direction of Macerata). Instead, they remained just below Castello, on the plain, in what became known as Borgo, and which by 1200 had a thriving market forum, the future Piazza del Popolo. Yet so adhesive is the old to the new that townspeople to this day refer to themselves as settempedani as often as severinati.

In the evening they appeared in force, coming down from the slopes of Castello or across the plain from the river, making for a substantial passeggiata. Some orbited the arcades, most stood and chatted in the piazza, as if the whole town had been invited to the same party in an elegant salotto. I joined in, too, and strolled around the ellipse. Italy must be one of the easiest places on earth to be alone in company. To this day, these towns preserve a communal spirit which Gregory Hanlon depicts in *Human Nature in Rural Tuscany*.

To reach Castello, a couple of hundred meters above Borgo, one may leave by that curving western exit of the Piazza del Popolo and ascend the via Salimbeni. Along the way one passes S. Agostino, which became the town's cathedral in 1827. It is Romanesque in its essential foundation, with a gothic portal and a square, ogival bell tower. In the early nineteenth century, to adorn the altar of his family chapel, the philanthropist Severino Servanzi-Collio had Antonio and Giovanni Gentile d'Alessandro's *Translation of the Holy House and Saints* (1548) repainted by a local artist, Lucio Tognacci, and so transformed into a *Madonna del Carmine.* While the lovely work of the two brothers is still to be appreciated in the four saints and the beggar receiving half of St. Martin's red cloak, the Virgin has been compromised by a ballooning cloak and a large cloud painted over the Holy House where she raised Jesus. This altarpiece was originally in S. Maria della Castreca, Colleluce; two *castreche* (dialect for a shrike or butcher-bird) dart through the air on either side of the Virgin. The sacristy contains Sante Lotti's silver bust of S. Severino (1659), whose grandfatherly image rises above clouds and angels, in low relief. A hexagonal brooch of red garnet over the saint's heart concentrates the only other color.

The Pinacoteca Comunale "P. Tacchi Venturi" honors a native son who was a Jesuit, a jurist, a historian of the order, and a negotiator of the Lateran Pact in 1929. I first had to admire Sano di Pietro's *Madonna and Child*, not unlike the one in the Lowe Art Museum, Miami; the Sienese artist's bottega produced many along the same lines and maintained a high level of quality. Natives of the town, the Salimbeni brothers, Lorenzo (fl. 1400-16) and Jacopo (fl. 1404-27), deserve a room to themselves, as they founded a tradition or at least a style; works have survived by Lorenzo or by both brothers, apparently none by Jacopo alone. Lorenzo's *Mystic Marriage of St. Catherine of Alexandria and Sts. Simon and Thaddeus* (1400), his only known panel painting, shows how he interpreted International Gothic style in his distinctive vernacular. The detached frescoes of the life of St. John the Evangelist once in the duomo vecchio were placed here after the 1997 earthquake.

Lorenzo d'Alessandro, another settempedano and the father of Antonio and Giovanni Gentile, was praised by Berenson as "the best painter in the Marches after Gentile [da Fabriano]" and was celebrated on the 500th anniversary of his death with an exhibition in 2001. While his masterpiece, a polyptych of the Madonna and Child flanked by eight saints, is in the parish church of nearby Serrapetrona, the gallery has an intensely moving *Pietà*, among his last works, blending the Salimbenian influence with Renaissance naturalism. Niccolò di Liberatore, an Umbrian sometimes referred to as Niccolò Alunno or Niccolò da Foligno, spent two years in the town and is respectably represented by a *Virgin Enthroned with Child, Angels, and Saints* (1468); Bishop Severino carries a model of the town in his left hand. Bernardino di Mariotto, another Umbrian, stayed twenty years, and left behind numerous works here and in the vicinity—one cannot effortlessly remove church frescoes. In his *Madonna of Help* (1509) a spiky Prince of Darkness who has flesh of putrid pink, crudely angular features, web feet, and a tail as long as a bull whip, prances in the foreground, as nimble a devil as one is likely to find anywhere in Italy; a terrified child rushes away and into the arms of an angel; eleven watchful putti assure us that the devil does not have a prayer of catching him. Mariotto's *Madonna and Child with Sts. Severino, Catherine of Siena, Dominic, and Ansano* (1513) hangs over the main altar in S. Domenico. Christ wears a coral necklace as a sign of the rosary and touches a pomegranate, associated with the Tree of the Knowledge of Good and Evil, as a sign of redemption. On the left, Bishop Severino holds a more elaborately scaled town model than Niccolò's: the Borgo walled with Guelf-styled crenellation, the campanili, Monte Nero, the duomo of Castello and the tower of the old Palazzo Comunale. On the right, St. Ansano, patron of Siena, carries a plate of inner organs, the iconographical history of which Agnes Kemp-Welch long ago traced through pagan lore to the Etruscan haruspex, Siena being an Etruscan city. Another native son was Ludovico Urbani; but he died young and has no paintings here.

The gem of the gallery is Pinturicchio's *Madonna della Pace* (1489). Of all places for a painting of the Blessed Mother of Peace, none could be more fitting than San Severino whose landscape bears a distant resemblance to the artist's native Umbria and imparts an atmosphere of pastoral antiquity to any soul who lingers long in its midst. Pinturicchio has chosen a soft, diffused twilight for his picture; the seated Madonna holds the Christ Child who stands on a cushion in her lap. His dark blue robe is highlighted and bordered in gold; his right hand is raised to bless, his left carries a transparent globe. On either side, an angel breathes the purest spring air, Feronia's air, while in the background a guard of soldiers and an earthly potentate pass through a triumphal arch of Stonehenge-like boulders, a reference to Herod's Massacre of the Innocents and an analogical reminder of the savagery of the world. Yet predominant is the mood of peace, which Pinturicchio suggests in the long, thin horizontal clouds, the terraced hills, the beech trees and bushes flecked with the gold of the sun's evening rays, the stream winding through a fruitful plain. The Prince of Peace reigns over a world suffused by grace.

Besides the soldiers, another crossing pattern complicates the mood of this painting. The donor Liberato di Sensino Bartelli, robed in scarlet, hands folded in prayer, has a soul of Renaissance self-consciousness, a modern administrator more than a medieval penitent. In profile, he stands below and on a plane in front of the Madonna and

Child, as it were, outside of the icon. His penetrating eyes look up, focused upon the mental image; his mind, which on another occasion might have been bent on practical matters, directs its attention towards the meaning of the icon. A slightly bulging vein throbs in his forehead, a sign of deep emotion not excluding anxiety, so he knows whereof he prays: peace on earth and the difficult art of achieving it. Liberato had gone to Rome, risen in the hierarchy, and was now returning as prior of the collegiate church of S. Severino al Monte. He wanted a precious gift for his church, and his friend Pinturicchio obliged. After the town was raised to a bishopric in 1586, this church would become the duomo and still later the duomo vecchio, when the seat was removed to S. Agostino.

Of Pinturicchio's forty extant panel-paintings, the *Madonna della Pace,* from his middle period, ranks among his finest. Always excelling in technique, he grew detached and withdrawn as he aged and his final period has been criticized for a lack of warmth and feeling. Betrayed by his wife, and neglected on his deathbed (Vasari reports from a woman who was a witness), he had a private life as troubled as his public life was successful. His perplexed, almost numb expression stares out from a corner of his great fresco of the Annunciation in Spello, seemingly cut off from the very miracle that he had painted. His diffidence, which extended to politics, made him easily patronized by warring parties, as if he did not care, or rather cared only for his art, which was what they wanted. Alexander VI employed him to adorn the Vatican apartments; Cesare Borgia mentioned him in a letter of October 1500, "whom we have always loved for his virtues," where *virtù* has its Renaissance meanings of inner strength and specific talents, and not moral quality. But by this time the *Madonna della Pace* had long since adorned

Liberato's church, an outstanding example of the artist's formal excellence, his "diaphanous" and "opaline" color, his rendering of intricate detail (the four haloes, the angel's iridescent wing), and his apprehension of sacred immanence; not yet, observes Corrado Ricci, had he fallen into his "courtly" manner which "conceals little heart under the wealth of the brilliant raiment!" If Pinturicchio had done more panel-paintings of such quality instead of getting caught up in large projects, like the Siena Library, which Ricci finds brittle and over-refined, "he would have been one of our great painters for grace, delicacy, and comeliness, even if not actually in the first rank."

A sound truck wound its way up the street, trumpeting a candidate for office. The echo of the loudspeaker in a narrow street of stone walls drilled into the ear. I saw political advertising like this on my first visit to Italy in 1962—I recall boys throwing stones at a sound truck in Rome—but not recently, as new means of electronic communication have prevailed.

Further along the via Salimbeni is the oldest of the town's churches, S. Lorenzo in Doliolo, which dates from the eighth or ninth century but rests on much earlier structures, even possibly a Roman temple dedicated to Feronia. This is one of those buildings that must have seemed old even to the middle ages, and reminds me of ancient churches off the beaten track in Rome, e.g., S. Pudenziana or Quattro Incoronati. Worn with age but still staying on their feet, they elicit a different response than one, say, to even older churches or classical ruins that have been better cared for. With S. Lorenzo in Doliolo the rough, stubbly courtyard itself makes one think of barnyard animals, mangy dogs, and loud muleteers with their packed carts. The Romanesque campanile is faced by marble half way up, then rough brick—had they run out of money? When Edward Hutton visited the church a hundred years ago, it was under restoration and the masons and bricklayers made him fear the worst: "what it will be like when they have done with it I cannot say." He would be pleased with the results. The extensive crypt, dating from the sixth or seventh century, has a stark monochrome fresco cycle of the life of S. Andrea by the Salimbeni.

In a few steps one is at the Porta Romana, Aleandri's majestic gate in the neoclassical style. Then a short walk brings one to the upper town, with the refreshing Porta delle Sette Cannelle already in view: it dates from the early 1300s and is comprised of seven fountain taps in a row over a large stone basin, once supplying an entire quarter. The narrow lanes, so unfrequented (many houses are now uninhabited), formed the medieval core of Castello. To the left is the via delle Valle that leads to the imposing Porta S. Francesco, showing how these heights could be defended. To the right, one proceeds to the highest point of the town, the wind-swept Piazzale degli Smeducci, the counterpart to the Piazza del Popolo below, one as remote and otherworldly as the other is social and commercial. In its center is the tower (1372) of the old Palazzo Comunale and prison, now destroyed, and opposite it, S. Severino al Monte or duomo vecchio (1061), built on the spot to which the bishop was believed to have been translated by the original inhabitants. Its campanile rises opposite the Palazzo Comunale's tower and balances the square, like the two fountains of the ellipse. The duomo vecchio has lost some of its treasures, like the *Madonna della Pace*; remaining is its eloquent choir carved by Domenico Indivini in the late fifteenth century and completed in the following century by the brothers Acciaccaferri, the third set of artist brothers that the town produced. Liberato's cloisters with their two tiers of arches, said to be among the most beautiful in the Marche, was another of his gifts to the town. On the slopes of Castello are the monastic churches of S. Caterina and S. Maria dei Lumi (Cistercian), S. Teresa (Oblate Convittrici del Bambino Gesù), and S. Chiara (the Poor Clares). On neighboring hills are the monasteries of S. Maria delle Grazie and S. Pacifico (Franciscan) and S. Salvatore in Colpersito (Capuchin).

These religious houses serve as a reminder that while San Severino Marche has many local artists, it also has many local saints; it is called the "city of saints." Besides the patron S. Severino, there is his brother S. Vittorino, a hermit who lived in a mountain fastness beyond Piorarco, where he is buried. S. Filomela lies in S. Lorenzo in Doliolo, which holds the remains of the priest S. Ippolito and the soldier S. Giustino. The local historian Gualberto Piangatelli unrolls a long record of sanctity: from the eleventh-century, the tomb of S. Domenico Loricato is honored in the parish church of S. Anna in Frontale di Apiro; S. Caterina received the relics of S. Illuminato, the twelfth-century Benedictine monk, after the monastery of S. Mariano was destroyed by Frederick II; from the thirteenth-century there is Blessed Pacifico, the poet who inspired some of the Franciscan *Fioretti* and died abroad. Then, from the fourteenth, S. Margherita "La Scalza" is venerated in nearby Cesolo; from the fifteenth, Blessed Camilla Gentili di Rovellone, "murdered by a perverse husband," lies in peace in S. Domenico; from the sixteenth, Blessed Marchesina Luzi, an Augustinian tertiary who met a similar fate at the hands of an "insane brother," awaits sainthood in the family chapel of S. Agostino. In the Servanzi chapel of the same church lies Blessed Marsilia Pupelli, another Augustinian tertiary, who died in 1288. "Nor should one forget the Venerable Francesca Trigli del Serrone (XVI century) whose remains are set within the pilaster to the left of the altar in S. Maria dei Lumi," which also holds the reliquaries of Blessed Bentifoglio de Bonis and Blessed Pellegrino da Falerone. The Franciscan S. Pacifico Divini (1653-1721), a professor of philosophy who suffered lameness, blindness, and deafness, was declared a saint in 1839; his body lies beyond the town in the Sanctuary of S. Maria delle Grazie of which he was guardian. The reputation for sanctity was sustained in recent times by Bishop Mons. Adamo Borchini, buried in the crypt of the duomo vecchio.

The via Eustachio seemed like a relatively new street, though it is centuries old. A plaque commemorates the home of Bartolomeo Eustachio (d. 1574), one of the founders of modern anatomy and histology, most famous for his studies of the ear, teeth, and kidney. He lectured at the University of Rome "La Sapienza" but, fearing prosecution, did not publish some of his more famous engravings in his lifetime (they appeared in 1714). His tomb is in S. Domenico. The name Eustachio is common here; a grotto dedicated to S. Eustachio lies near the road to Castelraimondo. The astronomer Eustachio Divini (1610-1685), born in San Severino, went to Rome where he opened a factory for making optical instruments near the Piazza Navona. He became the most famous maker of telescopes in Europe and published an engraved map of the moon in 1649 based on his precision measurements. One of his telescopes was 52 ft. long.

ORVIETO: SS. SEVERO AND MARTIRIO, S. DOMENICO,
THE DUOMO, S. AGOSTINO

I visited the abbey of SS. Severo and Martirio in 1969, before it had been made into a small luxury hotel. The road wound through the plain of the Paglia river and up a gently rising wooded hill. Shaggy ilex and poplars, olive trees, and unclipped bushes surrounded it, and fireflies drifted among the wildflowers. Unaffected by this profusion of foliage was the soaring, twelve-sided campanile, with its crenellated turret more suited to a fortress than an abbey. Fortress-like too was how the few spare buildings stood close and solid around a courtyard, forming a compact whole collected within itself. These noble walls had aged to diverse colors, from fallow, rose brick, and ash gray to burnt umber, a clay pigment found in Umbrian soil. Yet from a distance the abbey appeared pale golden against the countryside losing its green, turning dry and tawny in the summer heat.

La Badia ("the abbey") traces its origins to the late sixth century, soon after the Lombard invasion, in a time of social upheaval. According to legend, the bier of Severo and his disciple Martirio was being drawn by two untamed bullocks, having come all the way from Interocrea near Rieti. As it approached Orvieto, the Lombard noblewoman Rotruda went down to claim it, but, on touching the bier, her hands became trapped and were only released upon her promise to found an abbey. Pope Gregory the Great tells stories of the two saints in his *Dialogues* of 593. One day the monks were baking bread and forgot to stamp a cross on the unbaked loaves before setting them under the embers. Overhearing their consternation, Martirio turned to the hearth and made the sign of the cross. A piercing noise like the cracking of pottery tore through the room. Later, taken from the ashes, each loaf was found stamped with a cross. In another anecdote, Severo was cutting grapes in his vineyard when messengers arrived asking him to administer the last rites to a dying landowner. Severo replied that he would come as soon as he finished his work. On the road to the man's house he met the same messengers returning to tell him that the man had died. Severo fell to the ground and wept as though he had killed the man. Whereupon the dead man awoke and told of being taken by demons through the darkness and of meeting "a young man with wings" who said, "Lead him back again, because the priest Severo is weeping and through his tears has obtained pardon from God for the soul of this man" (I.12). So Severo performed absolution and the man died in peace.

Gregory writes in the flat, unsentimental, paratactic prose that one finds in good business reports as well as saints' lives. The enigmatic details speak for themselves: the driverless wagon, as if drawn by some mysterious power; the young, untamed bulls, full of energy, in need of guidance like the early Church; Rotruda, so rich that she had only to touch a thing to possess it, desiring the relics for her own soul instead of everyone's benefit; Severo's delay and guilt. The subtler art of this style conveys an embedded mysticism.

The buildings of the abbey belong to the twelfth and thirteenth centuries. Oldest of all, the campanile was the gift of the "Great Countess" Matilde of Tuscany in 1103. There are a Romanesque church with a gothic portal, a single nave, and a well-preserved cosmatesque pavement; a refectory, the hotel's meeting hall, and its fresco of the Crucifixion with Mary, Mary Magdalene, Severo, Martirio, and saints, and the abbey courtyard in the background; and a chapter house in ruins. Nothing remains of the cloister. The gothic arch of the chapter house frames a spectacular view of Orvieto on its escarpment and the duomo's west façade, two miles away across the valley. In 1613 the monks removed the saints' relics for safety to the church of S. Angelo in the town. There they rested undisturbed, until July 2011, when the new sacristy was breached and sacred vessels were stolen. The police recovered the objects by evening in the piazza of the duomo. Built over a Roman shrine (to Diana?), S. Angelo was a Benedictine hospice and has been altered over the centuries, lastly in 1828 with a neoclassic façade. An intricately carved stone from a ninth-century restoration is fixed above the new sacristy lintel behind the church. The old sacristy, to the left the church on the Piazza S. Angelo, is now a restaurant.

Orvieto sits on a stout, oblong butte of ochre colored volcanic rock, rising in isolation over 600 ft. from the valley floor, the final 100 or so ft. being exposed cliff. To get a close look at la rupe ("the cliff"), as it is known locally, one can ride up the funicolare from opposite the train station to the Porta Soliana or walk the trail, the Anello della Rupe ("ring round the cliff"). The rock is tufo or tuff, found everywhere in Italy, hard yet porous and handily cut, so that there are Roman cisterns, Christian tombs, and underground passageways within the cliff. Italy has never lacked for building materials that endure and, for all their terror, it can thank the volcanoes for any number of gifts: "easily workable soils, often of exceptional fertility, defensible sites, structures favorable to a regular supply of ground water, and a wide variety of building stones and minerals" (Walker). Tufo is sometimes confused with tufa; they are, however, completely different because tufo is volcanic and tufa is sedimentary; one forms in rising upward, the other by falling downward. Tufa, of which Italy has abundant stores, is a generic word for various forms of limestone, from travertine, botticino (beige limestone), pietra serena (gray limestone or sandstone), and the inimitable pietra rossa di Verona, to metamorphosed limestones such as Carrara marble. But la rupe is tufo, and so identified is la rupe with the town that the locals have on occasion referred to themselves as *tufacei*, those made of tufo, as if they had emerged autochthonous from the rock itself.

It was not uncommon when I grew up to memorize poems and I never lost the habit. Some verses by Jorie Graham on Orvieto came to mind: "... all round the cathedral / streets hurry to open..." As you gaze down these little streets, they do seem to turn this way and that, rise and fall, split off from one another, with a bounding, tortuous life of their own. In this part of town, tourist shops with doors wide open display all kinds of goods, though the ceramics catch the eye: terra cotta and majolica, glazed and unglazed, monochrome and polychrome; from medallions, cups and saucers, jugs, ashtrays, and picture frames to large vases, garden pots, wide-brimmed urns, and umbrella stands. Inside these cave-like shops the small items line shelves and tables, plates pile up on the floor, and hand-painted chandeliers hang from the ceiling. Egg-yolk colored dragons slither maliciously down the large carafes. Fluted platters are decorated by green-on-white or wine red-on-gray arabesques. The wares spill onto the street where ceramic statues of the saints beseech alms and virtue from passing tourists.

Behind an oaken counter the shopkeeper stood wrapping a plate. She was dressed tastefully in black, with a looping necklace of amber beads. Her manners were at once formal and natural, after the Italian fashion, and she had a pleasantness that had nothing to do with her being a salesperson, because typically Italians are gracious when they don't have to be. Her Italian was so perfect and well-articulated that I could almost visualize her sentences in a grammar book. We talked about language, on which Italians have a never-ending fund of things to say.

"A standard of Italian?" she replied without hesitation. "It is spoken between Siena and Orvieto, pure and simple. Please forgive my local pride in saying so."

"What then of *lingua toscana in bocca romana?*" I asked, at a loss for words, and playing the Roman card.

She smiled, ceding nothing. "I know, it's an old saying. But it really means southern Tuscany, northern Lazio, and western Umbria. And now, who is to say? We are close to southern Tuscany but we lean more towards Rome. We are Etruscan in origin, and only Umbrian by adoption. Our dialect is known for being rather complex and all our own— quite different even from that of Todi or Terni, which aren't far away" (fifteen miles to Todi, twenty-nine to Terni).

Sunlight fell obliquely against the walls in deep golden wedges, never quite touching the pavement. Tufts of grass crop up between the stones in many of the less travelled streets, which refuse to be the platform of a manicured hill-town stage set. We tread in one of D'Annunzio's "cities of silence": "Su le strade ove l'erba assorda i suoni" ("Le città del silenzio: Orvieto I"). "On the streets where grass deafens the sound": the silence "speaks" from the mysterious heart of things. Yet for Charles Eliot Norton the streets were "dark and dirty," the walls "too big" for the population, the palazzi "mostly deserted." John Addington Symonds echoed him: "very dark, and big, and dirty, and deserted, is the judgment we pronounce upon the houses; very filthy and malodorous each passage; very long this central street; very few and sad and sullen the inhabitants." Some quarters must have looked empty, as the urban population had shrunk by two thirds, to about 6000, by the year 1400 and remained at the same level for centuries. Paul Bourget arrived having just traveled through the prosperous Tuscan towns and was appalled: "long, straggling streets of tumbledown old houses take the place of the fine paved passages which led between palaces." Such comments stem partly from a predilection for bourgeois tidiness that captured so many

217

travelers of that era; my favorite example is the New Englanders' preference for neat, "four-square" Florence to baroquely sensational Rome, Florence to anything—except possibly Boston. Yet these remarks had more than a grain of truth. Bourget in particular turned away with exceptional bitterness and blamed the papacy for the economic stagnation and lack of "local spontaneity" in its territories. He focused almost exclusively on the duomo and cast a sternly disapproving glance everywhere else. "Hardly do a few buildings here and there show a trace of feudal grandeur."

A trace? Symonds, Norton, and Bourget were visiting Orvieto at the end of a long twilight of decline and looked back to its zenith in the later middle ages, after which it endured plague, famine, internecine strife, and economic decay. Work on the duomo came to a halt; Lorenzo Maitani's gothic façade, one of the glories of Italian art, was unfinished. "Here once rose splendid houses of citizens and ample palaces," observed Pius II in 1460; "time has destroyed many of them and more still were burned and devastated by civil struggles. What remains now are semi-destroyed towers and collapsed churches." In the sixteenth century, however, Orvieto underwent an urban revival. Its opening act was to bring in Luca Signorelli to paint his frescoes of the Apocalypse in the duomo (1499-1504). Then, gradually, the façade was completed and the interior was richly décorated. Churches and palazzi were built or remodeled after the new classicism. Sangallo the Younger, Michele Sanmicheli, Raffaello da Montelupo who apprenticed with Michelangelo, Davide Ghirlandaio who was Domenico's younger brother, Simone Mosca who studied under Sangallo, and his son Francesco called Il Moschino, all took up residence in the town. Ippolito Scalza, who trained under Montelupo and Mosca, was a native son. Whether they acted independently, or directed the Opera del Duomo (Works Dept.), or contributed to one other's projects, they shared a unified sense of style, a "severe nobility" in Luigi Fumi's description. When it came to the duomo, these artists put aside their own preferences and the taste of the age and adhered to the aesthetic design laid down by Maitani, until Scalza executed the pinnacles of its corner towers, in 1590 and 1605-7, stylistically in keeping with the very bottom of the façade begun three hundred years before.

Even a partial list of palazzi would show that Orvieto had its share of grandeur. Bernardo Rossellino, better known as a sculptor, designed the Palazzo Pietrangeli-Filippeschi that Vasari praised as "a work of great cost and no less magnificence." Its airy, harmonious, internal portico breathes the purity of early Renaissance style. Sangallo's Palazzo Crispo-Marsciano (1543) in Piazza Marconi projects a strength of line and a grace of urbanity for which it became the High Renaissance model for the remainder of the century. Tiberio Crispo, illegitimate son of Paul III, had it built on the eve of becoming a cardinal; he moved across town from Palazzo Aviamonzi-Alberici, abandoning the halls only lately frescoed after the ones in Castel S. Angelo of which the pope made him castellan. Scalza built the Palazzi Buzi, Clementini, Saracinelli, Crespi, and Guidoni, lent his hand to many others, and restored the Palazzo Comunale. Simone Mosca was principal architect of the Palazzi Sforza Monaldeschi and Gualterio, the latter on Sangallo's design); when the Gualterio descendents bought the Buzi, they transferred Scalza's grand portal to the Gualterio in the Piazza Gualterio. This palazzo remained in the family until Filippo Antonio Gualterio, Minister of the Interior, spent his inheritance on the Unification of Italy; in poor mental and physical health, the patriot died in 1874, and the palazzo passed to the Banco di Roma. Nor did Orvieto lack for magnificence in the "forgotten centuries": the Palazzo Febei (1670), the Aureli-Missini (1786), the svelte Faina (1866), which would have been new on Bourget's first visit, and the Bracci Testasecca (1875), which he could have seen on his second.

As for "feudal grandeur," what could surpass the concentrated power and sublimity of the Palazzo [del Capitano] del Popolo? This bastion-more-than-palazzo, completed about 1280, is as solid and rectangular as a strongbox. Blind arches (arches that are "filled in"), three-mullioned windows, and swallow-tailed crenellations lend texture to its broad, bronze-colored walls. As if guarding the town on one of its loftiest ridges, like a crouched lion whose flowing mane is the color of the rock from which it emerges and seems as one, the Palazzo del Popolo is a synecdoche of Orvieto itself.

While the Palazzo Comunale and the Palazzo del Popolo have always been municipal in character, many palazzi that started out as private dwellings have become public institutions. Some are primary or secondary schools, beaten up over the years and looking a trifle worse for wear, yet still imparting their "severe nobility." The Palazzo Sforza Monaldeschi houses the Istituto Statale d'Arte; the Buzi is run by the Mercedari Fathers; the Clementini is the classical high school. Other palazzi are museums (Soliano, Faina, Crispo-Marsciano); still others are (or were) administrative offices (Pandolfi, Ravizza, Alberi), libraries (Febei, Clementini), exhibition centers (Dei Sette, Caravajal-Simoncelli), and hotels (Bracci Testasecca, Piccolomini, Bisenzi, Filippeschi). The lucky ones (Ottaviani, Coelli, Gualterio) have turned into banks, which have the money to restore them to pristine perfection. In a sense they are returned to their original owners, the ones with their hands on the money, such as the Monaldeschi, a banking family.

Early evening in the Piazza della Repubblica. The café occupies nearly the whole ground floor of a palazzo so central and elegant that one might expect it to have a special claim on the past. This is the Palazzo Ravizza which hosted Pius IX in 1857; for the occasion Virginio Vespignani restored the façade in a crisp neo-Palladian style. Today the palazzo effectively anchors the north side of the piazza. People stroll about diverting themselves, half knowing they are a source of other people's diversion, yet hardly enough of them to constitute a passeggiata. The piazza is relatively narrow and cars stream along one side, keeping down the human presence.

Yet the piazza has much to its credit. Filling the short side on the east is the sixth-century church of S. Andrea, which was rebuilt in 1013 (the date is carved in the sacristy), and restored several times. Its bottom third is constructed in white travertine; its middle third, in dusky basalt; and its top third, in a yellowish brown tufo. The mixture of colors and building materials is matched by a variety of styles: Romanesque, gothic, Renaissance, baroque. This church pushes to the limit any notion of architectural coherence, and still manages to hold on to it. When in 1926 its floor collapsed, an unceasing fund of archaeological riches began pouring forth: a paleo-Christian shrine, the ruins of an Etruscan temple, remnants from the Villanovan period (ninth century BC), roads, tombs, a makeshift furnace dug in the floor of the old church to cast bells for the new one. Modeled after the abbey's campanile, the twelve-sided Torre Civica rises in the southeast corner of the piazza, a pivotal position to serve two masters, S. Andrea and the Palazzo Comunale.

Although, even in its truncated form, the Palazzo Comunale proclaims its civic aspiration, one can only imagine the results had Scalza been given his way. In 1573 the city councilors chose him to remodel the town hall in the grand style, adapting Sangallo's ground-floor design. By 1581, whether from lack of funds or local opposition, work stopped and the building remains incomplete. Instead of fronting the entire south side of piazza, as Scalza intended, the Palazzo suddenly ends and a nondescript building half its height opens up a large empty space, so that the piazza loses its ideal of containment along with its sense of balance. Even the well in the classical style that Scalza designed to complement the Palazzo was removed over the objections of the inspector of monuments in 1924 (it is in the nearby Piazza dell'Erbe). The piazza could ill afford to lose anything that lent it lustre.

I walked north along the narrow via della Misericordia, hoping to see the restored Oratorio della Misericordia; it was closed, so I examined its façade. If these *stradette* and *vicoli* prevent extensive views of the churches and palazzi, their narrowness focuses attention on the architectural details—for example, the main portals: columns or pilasters, quoins smooth or rusticated, architrave and keystone, cyma or cavetto moldings depending on the desired shadow pattern, coat of arms, balcony, balustrade, and numerous other parts, the result of architectural design and artisanal execution of a high order. These portals can project well into the street or can penetrate as far as an inner courtyard. No two portals of the finer type are ever quite the same, even by the same artist, who nonetheless will have a distinguishing imprint, just as a lost or forgotten ode, upon its recovery, can often be identified from internal evidence. Superlative examples in Orvieto are Mosca's portal for Palazzo Sforza Monaldeschi and Scalza's Buzi portal transferred to the Gualterio.

My destination, Piazza XXIX Marzo, is large and shapeless and seems filled with cars, though relieved by a small park. On its east side is the gothic church of S. Domenico, founded soon after the saint's death at the time of canonization (1233); it is believed to be the first church dedicated to him. The original structure had three naves extending 300 ft. and capable of accommodating crowds of pilgrims. It was adorned with tomb monuments in the new French style, and it displayed the chair from which Thomas Aquinas lectured in Orvieto (1263-64) and the crucifix believed to have spoken to him upon his writing the office of Corpus Domini: *Bene, Thoma, scripsisti de hoc meo sacramento.* "Thomas, you have written well of my sacrament." With the centuries came impressive additions: Simone Martini's polyptych *Madonna, Child, and Saints;* Scalza's tomb of Girolamo Mangoni, and Sanmicheli's spectacular octagonal chapel for the Sienese banker Girolamo Petrucci under the main altar. In the pavement just before the altar were set sculptured slabs (recently put back in place) and metal gratings through which to view the Petrucci's sarcophagus in the chapel below.

Then S. Domenico suffered an irreversible series of losses. Following the Council of Trent, the choir was altered and the floor sealed, cutting off the main light source for the Petrucci chapel and diminishing its effect. In 1680 half of the nave was removed so that, in conformity with baroque standards, better use could be made of side chapels. The proportions of the church were irreparably damaged and several tomb monuments were destroyed. Alterations and reconstructions continued until, in 1934, the rest of the nave, the façade, and the cloister were demolished to make way for the Casa del Balilla and the Accademia Femminile di Educazione Fisica. Only the apse and transept survive (the transept serving as the nave). The fate of the nave was to end in a gymnastics academy and a parking lot.

Amid these predations Arnolfo di Cambio's tomb of Cardinal Guillaume De Bray (1283-85) survived and is now in the west wall of the transept. The cardinal lies on a sarcophagus decorated in cosmatesque; his hands crossed, he does not appear dead, only sleeping, in expectation of the Last Judgment. Two acolytes draw the curtains as from a simple bed—an original contribution to the genre by Arnolfo. The face of De Bray reveals a tough-minded and plain-spoken man, like the canon from Normandy that he was, someone who could have stepped out of the pages of Bernanos' *Diary of a Country Priest*. Above, on the right, is a second image of the cardinal, kneeling and being presented by S. Marco to the Blessed Virgin at the apex of the monument; S. Domenico is on the left. The tomb is signed by the artist, and likely for that reason the monument was preserved. But, originally placed in the nave, it was dismantled and reassembled several times; many pieces were broken or went missing along the way, while others were put back in the wrong position. At the outset of the twenty-first century the *disiecta membra* were gathered together like the limbs of Osiris and in 2010 the restoration was unveiled. Though the gothic canopy or half-baldacchino that projected from the wall is lost, the restorers chose rightly not to sculpt a substitute but to suggest it, first by showing the ogival outline on the wall; and second, by allowing what was preserved of the twisted gold mosaic columns and railings to establish its perimeter. Statues were repositioned to "communicate" with one another as in the original. The placement of the *turbolanti* or "swirlers" (incense bearers) is yet to be determined; meanwhile, they are on display in the Museo dell'Opera del Duomo.

For a long time it was thought that the small statue of

the Virgin was Arnolfo's imitation of a Roman one. In 1993 the art historian Angiola Maria Romanini identified it as a Roman statue from the second century AD, similar to fertility cult statues of Fortuna, Ceres, Abundantia, and Juno. Arnolfo had brought the *spolium* from Rome, removed any icons identifying it as Roman (a scepter or patera if Juno, a cornucopia if Fortuna or Abundance), and sculpted the Christ Child and the Virgin's left hand to hold him. In an earlier restoration the Virgin's right hand was put back palm downward; the present restorers got it anatomically right and the hand is now turned up, the open hand of the all-giving mother. With his love of the *stile antico*, instilled in him by his teacher Nicola Pisano, Arnolfo brought back other pieces of marble from Rome and fitted them here and there in the monument.

Strange that his half-baldacchino suffered so much from human error and neglect, while his baldacchino in S. Paolo fuori le mura is one of the few works of art to have survived the fire of 1823 that destroyed the 1500-year-old Roman basilica.

In June 1284, while Arnolfo was sculpting the De Bray monument and going back and forth from Rome amid the turmoil of urban politics, the first mention of an agreement over the construction of the duomo appears in a document. Orvieto levied taxes, proprietors deeded lands, neighboring cities and towns paid generous sums, and pilgrims made offerings. Agents were dispatched across Italy to purchase various types of stone and precious materials: black marble from the Sienese quarries, alabaster from S. Antimo, marble form Carrara, the finest used stone from Roman ruins and villas. Some of these marbles decorated with pagan imagery were written over with Christian symbols. On October 15, 1290 Pope Nicholas IV laid the foundation stone. The best

description I have read of events in the early years of construction are by Charles Eliot Norton. Even where people
were driven by mixed motives of private ambition, rivalry,
and local pride, a project of this nature could not have
sustained itself for generations without a higher faith and
the encouragement of seeing the great edifice slowly rising
in their midst. When the wagon-loads of stone arrived in
the valley, the people knew that "the worst part of the way
still lay before them." Then, having confessed their sins,
men and women from all ranks harnessed themselves
alongside the horses and buffaloes and pulled the loads
along "the steep ascent to the uplifted city." Norton draws an
unfor-gettable portrait of the day's end: "as cart after cart
was dragged in by its band of devotees, it was set in its
place in a circle of wagons around the church. Candles
were lighted upon them all, as upon so many altars. At
night the people watched, singing hymns and songs of
praise, or inflicting discipline upon themselves, with
prayers for the forgiveness of their sins." The wagons
become the altars, an image of sacred immanence, and
illustrative too is the "uplifted" city, referring to the faith
that moves mountains and to Orvieto itself, the "city set on
a hill" (Matt. 5:14).

The duomo has the distinction of being "the first case in
the entire history of Italian architecture in which preliminary
designs for the work as a whole have survived" (White): two
detailed drawings of the two gabled levels of the façade.
Arnolfo has been credited as the architect, though not on
solid documentary grounds (one drawing, which is close to
the duomo's final appearance, bears a resemblance to his
Florence cathedral on which he worked in the 1290s). The
duomo has the form of a Romanesque basilica with a nave
and two side aisles. The builders began at the apse and by

1309, proceeding back to front, had completed the choir, transepts, two thirds of the nave in stripes of greenish-black basalt and white travertine, and had set in place the first roof beam. In the midst of construction, the strength of the choir and transepts came under scrutiny and seemed to require intervention. A document of 1310 mentions that the Sienese architect Lorenzo Maitani has been called in as "universalis caputmagister" (*capomaestro*) and granted citizenship: "[he] was and is thorough and experienced in buttresses roof and wall figured with beauty[,] which wall must be made on the front part and with all the other masteries and ornaments appropriate to this same fabric." Buttresses were installed, still visible in the walls, though we now know that they were structurally unnecessary. What Maitani achieved of far greater importance is caught by that remarkably understated phrase, "wall figured with beauty" (*pariete pulchitudine figuratis*), the magnificent façade. The duomo evolves from Romanesque to gothic, and one can see the change in the sculpted nave capitals back to front. "The façade was not simply slapped onto the building, as we had thought; rather, it emerged organically from the ongoing project to complete the nave" (Gillerman). By the time of his death in 1330 Maitani had completed the gound-level of the façade and directed work on the relief sculptures on the pilasters: the human pageant from Genesis and the Messianic prophecies to the New Testament and Last Judgment. The duomo's later history is as illustrious as its beginning, and includes Orcagna's elaborately carved rose-window set in a square frame, and Signorelli.

One walks the entire length of the nave, stripped bare of most of its statues and altars, to reach the S. Brizio chapel. In 1447 Fra Angelico and Benozzo Gozzoli were commissioned to paint frescoes on the theme of the Apocalypse; two years

227

later, with only two sections complete, they were summoned to Rome to work on another project. Over the next fifty years the friars hired artists in vain to finish the chapel, until in 1499 they signed a contract with Signorelli.

In his cycle on the Apocalypse Signorelli makes one of the foremost statements on the High Renaissance attitude towards death and the after-life. Renaissance humanists and artists emphasized so strongly the development of the individual that they refused to accept death as an impediment to further self-realization. So they rejected the anonymousness of medieval death and focused upon the individual's conscious survival in an afterlife. This was not only the popular view of death, but the official version as well. The Fifth Lateran Council (1512-1517), summoned by Pope Julius II, affirmed "the doctrine of individual immortality, which proclaimed personal rather than collective integrity in eternity as well as in history" (Partridge). In one of Signorelli's frescoes, *The Resurrection of the Body*, larger-than-life angels blow their trumpets to wake the dead, and beneath them numerous figures respond by pulling themselves up from the whitish ground, some still skeletal, some in the process of reassuming human flesh, others already standing, walking, conversing, even dancing. They struggle towards being their biographical selves in the next world, putting on their former bodies and minds. One figure offers a friendly hand to help another out of the ground; some who embrace "are readily perceived as old friends from life on earth now reunited," the first appearance of this theme in Western painting (Gilbert). In Jorie Graham's poem, "At Luca Signorelli's Resurrection of the Body," the tourists look up at the fresco and ask why the figures "hurry" to become themselves again: "they hurry to congregate, / they hurry into speech, until / it's a marketplace." Graham rejects Signorelli's version of the Apocalypse because his figures merely recycle their old lives instead of entering a totally new, transcendental space-time. From their happy faces, however, Signorelli makes it clear why he subscribes to the Renaissance survival of identity.

While Signorelli was painting his frescoes, his son was killed in a local brawl. Vasari, who was Signorelli's grand-nephew, might have had privileged knowledge when he wrote his *Lives of the Painters*: the son was "a youth of singular beauty in face and person, whom he had tenderly loved"; Signorelli had the body brought to Orvieto where he stayed by its side for two days, and the "with extraordinary constancy of soul, uttering no complaint and shedding no tear, he painted the portrait of his dead child." Instead of his painting the son, Graham in her poem has Signorelli dissecting him, perhaps to emphasize the violence of the son's death and the use of the palette knife in the making of the frescoes. As she thinks, he was closer to the meaning of the Apocalypse when he was dissecting his son than when he was painting his fresco.

In the northwest corner, almost at the edge of the cliff, is S. Giovenale, the town's oldest church, the one perhaps dearest to Orvietans. Built in honor of St. Juvenal of Narni in the sixth century, it was rebuilt in 1004. Darkened by age, its yellow-brown tufo makes it seem as if it were carved out of the cliff; its campanile might have been one of the medieval tower outposts. The planar Romanesque style with undecorated walls and the geometric façade with a deep-recessed rose-window present an almost Cubist design. How unlike the duomo is it possible to be? the one so humble, the other so lordly. Adjacent is the deconsecrated church of S. Agostino (1264), which displays the Twelve Apostles by Francesco Mochi, Scalza, and others. These once stood before the columns in the nave of the duomo. An enterprising impresario, Scalza opened a national compete- tion that sculptors from all over Italy had entered hoping to be chosen to sculpt one of the apostles. An engraving of 1763 shows the nave of the duomo with Mochi's *S. Taddeo* by the second pillar to the left of the entrance, opposite Bernardino Cametti's *S. Simone.*

When the baroque plummeted in disfavor in the nineteenth century, movements to "purify" the churches (*ripristinare*) sprang up across Italy. In Orvieto the standard was raised by the art historian Luigi Fumi and the architect Paolo Zampi who in 1877 managed to persuade the commission in charge of National Monuments to return the duomo to its "original" interior. The Twelve Apostles (which are in fact late Renaissance in style) were removed, and so too Mochi's *Annunciation* and Nebbia's altarpieces, but at least they sur- vived. Nebbia's frescoes were destroyed, along with chapels and their stucco-work. Even Nebbia's tabernacle panels were discarded (they were only recently discovered and, together with his altarpieces, are on display in the Museo dell'Opera del Duomo). Paul Bourget, who was in Orvieto when the fateful decision was made, attacked the "barbarity of archaeologists" for eradicating the "living" history of the building: "What is called a restoration only introduces the dead coldness of science in place of life—complex, incoherent, teeming—but life." Alberto Sattoli could only find one Italian at the time, Piccolomini Adami, who protested the "shame" of destroying the "communal patrimony." As Sattoli com- ments, "today [1999] the condemnation of art and architec- tural historians is almost unanimous regarding the destruct- tive restoration of the duomo."

While it is unlikely in the near future that the Twelve Apostles and the other statues and altarpieces will be returned to the duomo, at least in S. Agostino they can be viewed in a setting appropriate to them. In the precinct of the former altar, for example, are the two statues of Mochi's masterpiece, the *Annunciation* (1605-1608). Gabriel seems only just to have stopped in flight, the marble of his robe still swirls from his celestial voyage symbolizing his spiritual energy. By contrast, the block-like Madonna is simpler in formal design; she backs off in a state of surprise, clutching her book. She turns to Gabriel in surprise, but also in fear, notes Laura Cretara, as if she were aware of her Child's travail to come. The pair were originally in the tribune of the duomo, placed opposite each other with the main altar, celebrating the Incarnation, between them.

I was leaving Orvieto through the ancient Porta Maggiore. As with most cathedrals, the duomo faces west, so that parishioners face east, towards the altar and the rising sun, the sign of the Son of Man and the Cross, "which announces the return of the Lord." In his *Introduzione allo spirito della liturgia*, from which these words are taken (II.3), Benedict XVI writes that geographical orientation—east or west; facing an altar or away from it—matters less than, and should not distract from, the inward orientation of the spirit.

It is the afternoon and evening sun that dazzles, especially on the road to Bolsena. When the western sun strikes the duomo, light splinters into thousands of glistening rays. The façade has been described as a page of illuminated manuscript. To me, it resembles the canopy of heaven, such as Signorelli depicted in his vision of the Apocalypse.

EVENING IN BEVAGNA

The Valle Umbra begins at Spoleto and stretches forty miles northward, taking in the hill towns of Trevi high up on the east, Montefalco even higher on the west, the Timia river, the Teverone canals, and the springs of the Clitumnus. I saw the springs many years ago: large deep pools beneath tall poplars, water so pure and clear that Pliny compared it to snow. A tempietto rises high above the pools; it appears to have been constructed in the eighth or ninth century from Roman ruins by a Christian people as gripped with nostalgia as the author of *Beowulf.* Swinburne imagines such a monument in "The Last Oracle":

Dark the shrine and dumb the fount of song thence welling.

The melancholy of the line reverses itself at the end with "welling," as if to say, the voice is stilled, the life-giving song endures. According to local legend, the springs account for the spotless skin of the long-horned white oxen. I used to see them, in quiet possession from antiquity, grazing on the lower hills and valleys into the 1970s. One will see them now in Carducci's poetry and Fattori's paintings.

About halfway, at Foligno, the Valle Umbra expands to a broad plain and then curves to the northwest; Monte Subasio dominates the eastern side, with Spello and Assisi lying on its lower flanks. The valley ends at Perugia where the Topino, having collected its many affluents, spills into the Tiber. Up to the curve, the valley never quite loses a sense of enclosed intimacy, and even farther north it is never so extensive as the Val di Chiana in Tuscany. Near the confluence of sluggish, meandering streams, Bevagna lies in the western corner of the curve, at the edge of hills, themselves backed by the Apennines. Propertius, who was probably from ancient Asisium, wrote, "Misty Mevania moistens the low plain with dew." Bevagna has been called a hill town without the hill. The color of the medieval walls and towers that surround about four fifths of the town is a warm limestone in complementary shades of pale honey and creamy yellow. When I first saw it many years ago, Bevagna stood out from the surrounding landscape like daffodils beside a stream.

On the way into town, at the Porta Todi, a short bridge crosses over the slender Clitumnus river that widens into a pond of modest dimensions. The pond is dammed so that the water level just reaches the lip of a marble balustrade. There, sheltered by an arcade, the women of Bevagna had once come to wash clothes and share the town gossip; there is another like it at Piorarco. They can put clothes over the balustrade into the water at waist level without so much as bending forward. Why should they? *la terra è bassa*, the ground is low, as farmers say here. The water exits the pond slowly and evenly in two short drops over a perfectly engineered dam called with a touch of irony, the Cataract on the Clitumnus; the pond maintains the level of the balustrade and is continually refreshed. The women have a constant source of clean water and in summer children jump off the bridge into a makeshift swimming pool. This practical piece of engineering is in tune with the environment, which it heightens, as if it were second nature, the kind of technology that Romano Guardini describes in *Letters from Lake Como*: "the means were always integrated into the interplay of the human unit, and a limit was always set."

The bridge leads into the Piazza Gramsci below the town walls. If you happen to be there on the third Sunday of the month, you will find a market of used books and magazines, pottery, clothes, embroidery, costume jewelry and ornaments, paintings, sculptures, outdated utensils and old appliances—a bargain hunter's or stage-prop mistress's paradise. Though a few vendors make it their living and move about with the seasons, most do it to divert themselves and perhaps pick up some extra money on a weekend. A café is built into the town walls; tables and chairs spread out in the piazza and catch the afternoon sun. To the left, half hidden from view, a narrow lane cuts through the walls like a cleft in a cliff, and broadens into the Piazza Vittorio Silvestri, which has had many names in its history, most recently that of a local son, an early twentieth-century entomologist.

The first glimpse of Piazza Silvestri takes one's breath away, not for its size, nor grandeur, nor particular part, but for a unity of mood that excludes distraction, a quietly intense expression of an age. Its survival is no simple fact; it resulted from hundreds of decisions, major and minor, across the centuries: decisions that might have required imagination, or restraint, or stern resistance. Chance and neglect must have played their roles too. In 1870, with the Unification of Italy and anticlericalism in the air (even Umbrian air, the air of Italia Sacra), they planned to destroy the church of S. Silvestro to enlarge the piazza—this is the church that Giulio Urbini said was among the few twelfth-century Umbrian churches "preserved in its original integrity, not having undergone a single modification on any count." With the nationalist zeal sweeping over the provinces, the little cities and towns wanted to ape the big ones. Some of them razed their walls, much to later regret (though there was no Cluny disaster). In Bevagna, with a population never much above five or six thousand, the piazza was already more than large enough. Wiser heads prevailed, or else not only would the church have been destroyed, but also the piazza itself, which depends on the delicate arrangement of its parts to control its space. The "fourth wall" of a piazza was removed in some cities, so that the space spills out and the piazza loses its closure. The amazing fact is how many smaller cities and towns maintained their "original integrity."

In this compact, yet spacious piazza, paved in black slabs that contribute to its formal dignity, the principal components are the Romanesque churches of S. Silvestro and S. Michele Arcangelo, a Romanesque archway attached to the latter, the mixed Romanesque and gothic SS. Domenico and Giacomo, and the gothic Palazzo dei Consoli. All built within a hundred years of one another, between the end of the twelfth and the end of the thirteenth century, they bear a family resemblance owing to their broad flat surfaces, chaste ornamentation, and appealing stone. However, lest these buildings appear too cozy with one another, the architect ingeniously set the Palazzo at an odd angle, turning away from SS. Domenico and Giacomo and towards S. Silvestro, and he attached a sweeping exterior staircase that puts all the buildings of the piazza into subdued, but palpable tension. The minor roles in this urbanistic drama come from different centuries: a hexagonal fountain in the early Renaissance style, added in 1889 to replace the medieval cistern; a single Roman pillar, half-buried in the pavement and known locally as the Column of S. Rocco, though no one could tell me why. A French saint who made long pilgrimages in Italy, he might have passed through Bevagna combating the plague. He turns up in many Renaissance paintings. One can only marvel how the three churches, palazzo, staircase, archway, fountain, column, and the rest, fell into this asymmetrical, seemingly accidental coherence.

The oldest and smallest of the three churches is S. Silvestro whose architect, Maestro Binello, inscribed his name and the date 1195 on a stone just inside the front entrance.

Almost as wide as it is tall, the church has a façade of dove-gray limestone, punctuated by the single decorated portal in pietra rossa, above which are a central window with three arches, flanked by windows of two arches each. These illuminate, just barely, the austere interior. Gray and beige stone colors predominate, from almost black in the voids to ivory, and many shades between, with travertine on the ground floor, and the faintly pink Monte Subasio limestone above. The columns of the nave and side aisles are thick, unfluted, rough-hewn. There is not a trace of wood. The eye is led up the nave, then up eleven stairs to the raised choir, after the early Christian style; the altar is a slab of gray stone, and in back of it is a single window, and a flood of light pouring in to fill the altar. The transcendent conquers the stone everywhere.

S. Silvestro faces the larger, stylistically more complex S. Michele Arcangelo, built ten or twenty years later, also signed by Maestro Binello together with his assistant, Maestro Rodolfo. The façade is divided horizontally by a line of archetti; in the eighteenth century the line was broken by the addition of a large round window; this aesthetically misplaced window was closed after an earthquake, so it is a window without light in every sense of the word. Rising from the right third of the façade is a square bell tower whose upper section has ogival arches and is capped by a spire: the gothic style had arrived. The tallest structure in Bevagna, it can be seen from afar. The main portal is decorated with a flying angel who seems to sweep by overhead. The interior is richly appointed compared with S. Silvestro. The stone is plastered in pale green; the columns in the nave are fluted and highlighted in gold, lending an elegance for which, however, too great a price is paid. In the eighteenth-century restoration the sculptured carvings on the capitals were cut away to allow for the stucco work; this was only discovered in the twentieth-century restoration when the stucco was removed.

Piazza Silvestri also contains the imposing Palazzo dei Consoli, ca. 1275, which houses the nineteenth-century Teatro Torti; with its two hundred seats, it is almost as small as the Teatro della Concordia in Monte Castello di Vibio, an opera house in miniature. In the church of SS. Domenico and Giacomo (1391) followers of Giotto have painted frescoes of the saints' lives.

Everything is on a human scale in Bevagna. "Una cittadina, non città," a town, not a city, a shopkeeper said proudly. The via Matteotti carves its way through the town with its four and five story houses. It follows the old Via Flaminia, the cardo of the Roman town, and half way along, one can make a turn left up the via Gabriele Crescimbeni, possibly the decumanus.

Streets in this zone follow the pattern of the Roman amphitheater whose ruins lie beneath the houses and, in some cases determine their form. If it is any example, my own hotel is full of angles; no two floors have the same plan, and almost no two rooms, to judge from the schema. A long corridor suddenly turns and stops at a wall within ten feet; the second floor lobby is a square, the third, an isosceles triangle. Floor levels are constantly changing, a few inches up or down, from hallway into rooms, between rooms, even within rooms themselves. I find myself looking down as I walk through these hotels, not to mention the uneven pavements of streets and sidewalks, afraid of tripping, slipping, sliding, stubbing a toe in the middle of the night. Hotels are often assemblages of houses that have gone back two or three centuries, and in some cases much longer, quintessentially Italian in their organic development, tasteful adaptation, complexification, and individuation. Nor have the Italians seemed to notice. It is like their lack of gadgetry, serviceable faucets, shower heads, electrical outlets, air conditioning, simple conveniences—they seem almost unaware of what many foreign tourists, particularly *gli americani*, have come to expect. Or take the absence of signage: how often, on opening a door, have I plunged down a step or two before finding my feet. In a restaurant no less, not only was there no sign of an immediate step downward beyond the door, but the stairwell was curved. I almost landed in an abyss. Why do Italians ignore such discomforts when they are generally such a pleasure-loving people, as Barzini says, masters of *the art of living*? George Stillman Hillard, the Boston attorney who wrote the classic *Six Months in Italy* (1853), remarked, "in handiness and management, in labor-saving contrivances, in the adaptation of means to ends, in economy of time and labor, these people are lamentably, ludicrously deficient. The philosopher who defined man to be a tool-making animal did not make his observations upon the Alban or Sabine hills." Is it a survival of the old hierarchies, when the nobility had the comforts and everyone else did not and simply put up with it?

As one approaches the Piazza Garibaldi, sections of a Roman temple with brick columns projects into the street; its columns were incorporated into the church of the Madonna della Neve, which itself lies in ruins, one ruin in the arms of another. Piazza Garibaldi is on high ground; with no tall buildings it is sunny through the afternoon and evening. Here spreads out the activity of sidewalk cafes, shops, and restaurants, for the strange thing about Piazza Silvestri at the other end of town was the absence of people, no outdoor cafes, just two or three shops and a few chairs in a corner. It is as if, with its dramatic shadows and silence, Piazza Silvestri reserved itself for formal occasions; in Piazza Garibaldi the town let go. It ends in the Porta Perugina, which has Roman stonework in its lower wall. Left off the piazza is the via Porta di Guelfa, down which one can find the recently restored ruins of the Roman baths. The frigidarium has a black-and-white mosaic floor with dolphins, crabs, squid, seahorses and other marine creatures, real and mythological. The sea at last found its way to Umbria.

I mentioned the "old" Via Flaminia not to emphasize its age. The road, which went from Rome to Ariminium (Rimini), was built ca. 220 BC by the censor Gaius Flaminius whose engineers rebuilt rugged local tracks and integrated them into the new and (as often as possible) straight-as-a-dye road: it was even called Via Recta, "straight way" (Livy 32.29.6). As the main road north from Rome, it was hardly less important than the Via Appia Antica (320 BC), "queen of roads," leading south. Mevania initially prospered as a road station. However, it lay at the foot of the Monti Martani and travelers came to prefer a less arduous, if more roundabout, way of crossing the mountains. At some point it was decided to split Via Flaminia into two branches for a 35-mile stretch, the only such branching along its 217 miles. Coming up from Rome, the main road forked at Narni, with the "old" Via Flaminia serving as the western branch, passing north over the mountains through Carsulae, Acquas Partas, Vicus Martis and down to Mevania, and a new eastern branch connecting Interamna Nahars (Terni), Spoletium (Spoleto), Trebiae (Trevi), and Fuliginiae (Foligno), rejoining the main line at Forum Flaminii, and thence as one proceeding majestically across the Apennines. Though the eastern or Spoletium branch was roughly six miles longer than the western one, its terrain was easier, it became the route of choice, and its towns grew robust. Western-branch towns like Carsulae and Mevania fell into decline.

To the right off the Piazza Garibaldi, one walks up a short esplanade to the highest elevation in Bevagna, crowned by the church of S. Francesco with its thirteenth-century façade. The interior was renovated in 1756, though in a plain style befitting the saint. In the Chapel of the Sacrament is an impressive *Pietà* by the local artist Ascensidonio or Ascensionio Spacca known as il Fantino di Bevagna. I had never come across that first name. Before Ascensidonio, the prize went to Igina, from Hygeia, Greek goddess of health, daughter of Aesclapius; and Egisto, the English Aegisthus, Thyestes' son, Agamemnon's cousin, Clytemnestra's lover, bully tyrant. Aeschylus has absolutely nothing good to say about Aegisthus and Orestes assassinates him in *The Libation Bearers*, eliciting neither pity nor fear. Why would one want to name a child after him? Perhaps to be unique? A member of my family born in 1827 was named Stellario, from the Italian *stellare*, to cover with stars, after the model of rosario, from the Latin *rosarium*, a rose-garden. Rosario means a rosary, the beads of which are "roses"; a stellario is a set of litanies and, like Rosario, a first name (much rarer than Rosario).

The church of S. Francesco contains, in the wall on the left, the sacred stone upon which the saint stood and preached to the birds. The story runs that, having announced the idea of a Dominican lay order in Cannara, Francis took the road to Bevagna about five miles away, uncertain whether to devote himself henceforth to private meditation or to preaching. In a meadow called Pian d'Arca he paused for a moment and some birds flew down to him. Then he began to preach to "my little sister birds." As more and more birds alighted on the branches and the grass,

Francis found the answer to his dilemma. Afterwards the birds flew off to the four corners of the sky, proclaiming the extent of his mission. This is told in the sixteenth chapter of the *Fioretti*, one of the most charming books in Italian literature. Francis's preaching to the birds characterized a fundamental shift in the Western attitude towards the natural world, hitherto a den of demons or a vale of tears, now the site of God's immanental presence. Iacopone da Todi, the mystical poet who wrote his *laude* in the Umbrian vernacular, was a Franciscan lay brother.

The next day, which was cool and sunny, I visited the shrine a few miles beyond the walls where Francis had preached. It was surrounded by olive groves with grape vines and a few ilex trees. The song of birds filled the air. Across the plain one could see Spello and farther off Assisi against the slopes.

Bevagna never had a rail station. Was it the curse of the old Flaminia? Unless one has a car, one has to take a bus or taxi the five miles from Foligno. As usual Hutton went on foot. Yet if the town is harder to reach, it is less touristed as a result.

Serene, honey-colored Bevagna, where I once spent a few idyllic evenings.

WORKS CITED

Bourget, Paul. *The Glamour of Italy (Sensations d'Italie)*. Trans. Lauretta Maitland. 1891; London: E. Matthews, 1923.

Fumi, Luigi. *Orvieto*. Bergamo: Istituto Italiano d'Arti Grafiche, 1910.

Gilbert, Creighton E. *How Fra Angelico and Signorelli Saw the End of the World*. University Park: Pennsylvania State UP, 2003.

Gillerman, David M. "The Evolution of the Design of Orvieto Cathedral, ca. 1290-1310," *Journal of the Society of Architectural Historians* 53 (Sept. 1994): 300-321.

Graham, Jorie. "At Luca Signorelli's Resurrection of the Body." *Erosion*. Princeton: Princeton UP, 1983.

Guardini, Romano. *Letters from Lake Como: Explorations in Technology and the Human Race*. Trans. Geoffrey W. Bromiley. 1923-25; Grand Rapids: William B. Eerdmans, 1990.

Hutton, Edward. *Cities of the Romagna and the Marches*. New York: Macmillan, 1913.

Norton, Charles Eliot. *Notes of Travel and Study in Italy*. Boston: Houghton, Mifflin, 1859.

Paciaroni, Raoul. *Bernardino di Mariotto da Perugia: Il ventennio sanseverinate (1502-1521)*. Milan: Federico Motta Editore, 2005.

_____, ed. *Lorenzo d'Alessandro detto il Severinate. Memorie e documenti*. Milan: Federico Motta Editore, 2001.

Partridge, Loren. *Michelangelo: The Sistine Ceiling*. New York: George Braziller, 1996.

Piangatelli, Gualberto. *San Severino Marche*. 3rd. ed. San Severino Marche: Bellabarba Editore, 2007.

Platt, Dan Fellows. *Through Italy with Car and Camera*. New York: G.P. Putnam's, 1908.

Ricci, Corrado. *Pintoricchio*. Perugia: Vincenzo Bartelli, 1915.

_____. *Umbria Santa*. Trans. H.C. Stewart. New York: Oxford UP, 1927.

Romanini, Angiola Maria. "La sconfitta della morte: Arnolfo e l'antico in una nuova lettura del monumento De Braye," in *Bollettino d'Arte*, volume speciale—2009: *"Arnolfo di Cambio: Il monumento del Cardinale Guillaume de Bray dopo il restauro"*: xi-xxvii.

Satolli, Alberto. *Orvieto. Nuova guida illustrata*. Città di Castello: Edimond, 1999.

Symonds, John Addington. *Sketches in Italy and Greece*. London: Smith, Elder, 1874.

Urbini, Giulio. *Spello, Bevagna, Montefalco*. 2nd ed. Bergamo: Istituto Italiano d'Arti Grafiche, 1929.

Vasari, Giorgio. *Lives of the Painters, Sculptors, Architects*. Trans. Mrs. Jonathan Foster. Vol. 3. Bohn's Standard Library. London: George Bell, 1882.

Walker, D.S. *A Geography of Italy*. London: Methuen, 1967.

White, John. *Studies in Late Medieval Italian Art*. London: Pindar Press, 1984.

INDEX

Agnew, Spiro, 89
Ajani, Filomena, 155
Albano, Angelo, 59, 61, 63, 73, 75, 76
Alighieri, Dante, 21, 22
Arata, Daniel, 65
Arbuckle, Fatty, 189

Bair, Deirdre, 173, 198
Bakhtin, Mikhail, 169-170, 176, 182, 185-186, 198
Barolini, Helen, 170, 198
Barreca, Regina, 170
Becnel, Harry, 99, 100n
Benny, Jack, 189
Bertoli, Carolina, 148, 149
Bianchi, Domenica, 133, 134, 158
Bigioli, Filippo, 203
Bigioli, Venanzio, 204
Binelli, Mark, 4,189-198
Boito, Arrigo, 165
Bona, Mary Jo, 170
Bourget, Paul, 218, 219, 221, 242
Brahm, John, 169
Brown, Sterling, 1, 5, 5n, 7, 13-19, 23, 25
Bruno, Anthony, 171, 189, 199
Bruno, Giordano, 21

Cabrini, Frances Xavier, 3, 123, 125, 125n, 126, 126-139, 141-145, 148-164
Cahan, Abraham, 171, 184

Canfield, James Lewis, 84, 86
Cannon, Anthony, 167
Capietti, Umilia, 162
Cappello, Mary, 170
Carlson, Jody, 90, 91
Carnera, Primo, 190, 196
Carrari, Louis, 61, 62, 63
Carter, Dan, 90, 93, 96
Cavallo, Diana, 170
Chaplin, Charlie, 189
Ciardi, John, 22, 22n
Coen, Cheré, 121, 122
Connolly, Mary Lorini, 118
Correnti, Mike, 104, 106
Cunningham, George, 67, 67n, 117, 122
Cutler, James Elbert, 64

Davies, Christine, 171, 178, 179, 199
De Certeau, Michel, 126n, 129, 157, 157n, 159, 163
De Planches, Edmondo, 64, 64n
De Pretis, Agostino, 12
De Voto, Bernard, 170
Debray, Régis, 127, 163
DeLillo, Don, 191
Di Cambio, Arnolfo, 225
Di Donato, Pietro, 4, 170, 176, 182
Di Prima, Diane, 1, 5, 5n, 7, 13, 19-25
Di Rosa, Tina, 170, 171
Diotti, Gesuina, 136, 151

Dormon, James, 109, 118, 122, 168, 195, 196, 199
Drexel, Katharine, 38-40, 43

Eliot, T. S. 22
Eustachio, Bartolomeo, 204, 113

Ferlinghetti, Lawrence, 170
Ficarotta, Costanzo, 59, 63, 65, 73, 75, 76
Fumi, Luigi, 220, 231, 242

Galilea, Segundo, 125, 139, 139n, 140, 144n, 146, 164
Gallico, Paul, 170, 192
Gallo, Patrick, 90, 91
Gambino, Richard, 59n, 72, 92, 123, 124, 164
Gardaphé, Fred, 21, 25, 44, 58n, 92n, 171, 182, 189, 199
Gates, Henry Louis, 18n
Giunta, Edvige, 170
Glazer, Nathan, 127, 164
Gordon, Mel, 193, 199
Green, Rose Basile, 170

Haas, Edward, 46, 48, 58, 66n, 69n, 73n
Hamill, Pete, 82, 85-86
Hansberry, Lorraine, 183-184, 199
Hardy, Oliver, 189
Harrigan, Edward, 3, 167-169, 184, 194, 198-199
Hart, Tony, 167, 168, 199

Hendin, Josephine Gattuso, 19, 25, 170
Hennessy, David, 3, 71n, 123-126, 128, 134, 149, 160
Herman, Joanna Clapps, 34, 36, 44
Higgins, Earl, 116, 122
Higham, John, 67, 67n
Hofstadter, Richard, 67, 67n
Howe, Louise Kapp, 95
Howells, William Dean, 171
Hutton, Edward, 211, 242, 243

Jacobson, Matthew Frye, 93, 94
James, Henry, 169
Johnson, James Weldon, 171

Keaton, Buster, 189
Keller, Hellen, 189
Kendricks, Ty, 16-17
Kennedy, Robert, 83, 87

Lapolla, Garibaldi, 170
Laurel, Stanley, 189
Laveau, Marie, 98
Lee, Johnny, 102, 102n
Lee, Rosemary, 102, 102n
Lloyd, Harold, 189
Lodge, Harry Cabot, 71, 71n
Lyotard, Jean-François, 197, 198

Macheca, Joseph, 72, 72n

Mangione, Jerre, 4, 9, 10, 12, 28, 59n, 170-181, 187, 189, 194, 198-200
Marcello, Leo Luke, 1, 26-44.
Marchesi, Rosario, 137, 157
Marciano, Carmella, 101-106
Margavio, Anthony, 78n, 110, 125, 164
Marks, Sonny, 26, 29, 44
Marx Brothers, 192, 193, 196
Mascheroni, Edoardo, 165-166
Mauss, Mercel, 127, 128, 161, 164
McCaffety, Kerri, 116, 117, 122
McCullough, Kate, 70, 70n
Mike, Ditta Lucy, 120, 122
Moroni, Gerolamo, 76
Morreale, Ben 2, 9-10, 59n
Morrison, Toni, 6, 25.
Moynihan, Daniel, 127, 164
Mussolini, Benito, 18n, 178, 179, 196

Napoli, Donna-Jo, 2, 46-51, 54, 56, 57
Nixon, Richard, 83, 86-89
Nolen, Claude 10, 19, 25
Norton, Charles Eliot, 218, 219, 227, 243

O'Connor, Flannery, 189
Olney, James, 173, 200

Perise, Janet, 102, 102n
Pinturicchio, 208-210

Pizzati, Salvatore, 154, 156
Progresso Italo-Americano, Il 60, 62-63
Pulera, Dominic, 68, 68n
Puzo, Mario, 4, 170-171, 181, 183-184, 186

Regan, Ronald, 171

Sacco, Nicola, 3, 22, 182, 189, 190-194, 198
Salomone, 78n, 110, 125, 164
Salvetti, Patrizia 59-63, 66n
Savaré, Maddalena, 137, 159
Schaffer, Pamela 39, 40, 45
Sciascia, Leonardo, 166, 200
Serrati, Antonio, 132, 132n
Signorelli, Luca, 219, 228-230
Skinner, Beverly Lanier, 16, 25
Speranza, Joseph, 61, 65, 68, 77
Steiner, Edward, 172, 200
Symonds, John Addington, 218, 219, 243

Tallulah, 2, 46-51, 53, 54, 56, 66, 66n, 69
Tangipahoa Parish, 3, 97n, 99, 107, 109-12, 117-118, 120, 122n
Thompson-Anderson, Terry, 118, 122
Tusa, Marie Lupo, 113, 114, 122

Valeri, Diego, 4
Valery, Paul, 128
Vallisneri, Bernardina, 133,
   151, 156
Vanzetti, Bartolomeo, 3, 22,
   182, 189, 190-194, 198
Verdi, Giuseppe, 165, 166,
   200
Visconti, Luchino, 201
Viscusi, Robert, 18, 25, 27,
   31, 45, 183, 200

Wade, Leslie 32, 45
Walker, George, 195
Wallace, George, 2, 79-91,
   92n, 93-95
Webb, Clive, 47, 49, 50, 76,
   61n
Williams, Bert, 195

Zanoncelli, Teresa, 133